500MM
I0796152
SEAT UNDERSIDE
SIDE
LEG
45mm
cut line
ROUGH ARMBOW
CENTRE

ARMCHAIR
FORMS & PLANS

12MM - 2 MORTISES
20MM
76MM
435MM
CUT @ 500 MM
ARMBOW
100MM
250MM
625MM
ARMBOW BENDING FORM
(BOW @ 138 CM x 28 MM x 32MM)
54"L x 1 1/8"W x 1 1/4"H
350MM

52MM
5MM CHAMFER
'TOPSIDE' SPINDLE LAYOUT
1"
1"
16.5°
24°
'UNDERSIDE' LEG DRILL LAYOUT
20MM Ø
14 MM Ø
5MM

THE ART OF CHAIRMAKING

A GUIDE TO MAKING BEAUTIFUL CHAIRS

THE ART OF CHAIRMAKING

A GUIDE TO MAKING BEAUTIFUL CHAIRS

JASON MOSSERI

CONTENTS

INTRODUCTION

I've always made stuff; I can't help it. As a boy I would make wooden boats, bows and arrows, dens and treehouses. I was encouraged to explore my artistic side as a teenager, which led me to art college first at Kingston, near London, and then in Brighton. In 1990, fairly disillusioned with art college, I left Brighton to spend a few years immersed in the acid party scene, first in India and later back in the UK. It was in Goa that I discovered my true expression, and where I had my first formative experiences with a subculture. I painted huge eye-popping backdrops, screen-printed fabrics, and made many unusual costumes. I found the fun in creativity.

During these years of travel, I also became intensely curious about the art of tattooing, and in 1997 I returned to Brighton to start learning the craft. After some lucky breaks, I tattooed full-time for the next twenty years, and eventually, I co-founded a studio with my friend and mentor, Alex Binnie. We had some great years, in what I now see was the peak period of tattooing in the UK.

But by 2012, I felt I needed a fresh experience in my life. I didn't quite know what I was after, but I knew I wanted to make something wooden, and preferably outdoors, and I saw a six-day 'log to leg' Windsor chairmaking course which sounded perfect to me. Little did I know that it would be the first tentative step on a new creative path.

I felt a profound sense of satisfaction on that course, making such a beautiful and characterful chair using hand tools. A chair can have a peculiar amount of personality: this could be due to the fact that it is creature-like, having legs, arms, a bottom and a back. Or perhaps it is because it exists to hold the human form, making it a nurturing and comforting object. Perhaps it's because that although chairs are functional everyday objects, beautiful examples of chairs can step beyond functionality into sculptural elegance. Whatever the reason, I find chairs fascinating.

The chairmaking course I went on was taught by a lovely man, Paul Hayden, who teaches at the arboretum Westonbirt, and the course was a revelation – particularly the pole lathe, which is still my favourite 'machine'. We made English-pattern side chairs without arms, so they can tuck under a table, and I still treasure my chair. I attended Paul's courses each year for the next three years, built myself the basic tools for chairmaking – a shave horse and a pole lathe – and started exploring chairmaking. In 2016, and inspired by Paul, I took the plunge and became a full-time professional chairmaker.

Curtis Buchanan is a master chairmaker in the American Windsor tradition. His work style is very zen-like in a small one-man workshop, with everything made by hand. He is also very generous with his wisdom and knowledge, and has hundreds of hours of free informative videos online. His chairs embody craftsmanship, and his work encompasses both traditional and contemporary designs while remaining very true to tradition. I am just one of his many grateful students.

My first act in my new trade was to arrange a visit to his workshop in Tennessee and spend a week with him, learning to make one of his 'Birdcage' armchairs. I applied for some funding and booked a flight. To make this chair, Curtis requires that students arrive with their own parts and steam bends made to his exact patterns. He was delighted when I turned up with a load of chair parts made from English ash turned on a pole lathe. (Much more delighted than the slightly bemused customs officials.) Arriving at his workshop was an experience akin to visiting a holy site, and I almost prostrated myself!

I had a fantastic time learning with him. He has a great relaxed teaching style, lots of stories and, obviously, a very high level of skill. It was a great foundation in American chairmaking. I travelled home elated, with my chair in pieces, again in my luggage, to be glued up at home. It is lush. My wife, Abby, sits in that chair every morning to drink her coffee, and I'm sitting in it now as I write this.

So, my chairmaking is still fairly influenced by these formative experiences, and is a blend of both the English and American traditions. I like the 'stance' of American chairs and their strong painted silhouettes. And I like the more primitive examples of West Country English chairs, with their pared-back simplicity.

Being pure to the art, and to nature

When I took the plunge and started my chairmaking business, I decided that I would stick to using as many traditional methods as possible. I do all of my turning on a pole lathe, I draw all my spindles using a drawknife, and as long as my elbows are working, I carve my seats with an adze.

The pole lathe is a wonderful tool and a real pleasure to use. Its design is rudimentary, but it is easy to build and to transport. It enables the user to 'turn' shapes to a very fine degree, and it was a bodger's primary tool (see page 11). Being portable, it can be set up outdoors, in a sunny spot, and there is no need for a power supply, except a strong pair of legs. When the treadle is pushed firmly to the ground, the workpiece spins and the turner makes a cut. A rhythm is established. Once you have mastered the knack of it, the combination of the rhythm, the exercise and the cut can become very trance-like – and it keeps you warm in winter.

I have never graduated to an electric lathe. I don't have the extra indoor space, and I'm not a big fan of machine noise and protective face shields. I'm happy with the work that I can produce on a pole lathe, and I really enjoy the process. A pole lathe doesn't produce dust, it stops and starts instantly, and it is relatively safe for the turner.

I hope that my work embodies and reflects the many hours of care that I invest. I want my chairs to ooze character and charm, to be strong and sculptural. The structure and elegance are of as much importance as the comfort, form and function.

It's very important for me to make a living using my artistic sensibility, and to do so by treading lightly in the world, and chairmaking has offered me the perfect medium. I am able to produce useful and beautiful objects that are made using materials that are part of my immediate landscape. It has brought me closer to nature.

We live in an age of huge technical advances and comprehension, but in many ways, we are becoming distanced from our environment and our own nature. Many people feel disturbed. By connecting with nature, using time-honoured methods and natural materials as we work with our hands, we can bring huge satisfaction and an abiding sense of accomplishment. It can deeply ground and connect us.

Sharing the art

I now teach six-day 'log to leg' Windsor chair- and stool-making courses at my woodland workshop. This allows me to share the joys of chairmaking with others who also have a love of traditional crafts and working outdoors.

The ethos is based around using traditional tools – in particular, the pole lathe and shave horse – to create authentic and characterful furniture in the green woodworking tradition. It's very satisfying to see the happiness and fulfilment that the course offers to people. The courses are also a great getaway for people wanting a break from the hustle of modern life, with the lack of phone reception or wifi a blessing rather than a curse.

CHAIRMAKING TRADITIONS

From milking stools to thrones, the existence of chairs stretches back to early human history and pictorial evidence of them can be found in many different cultures around the world. And more often than not, they are made of wood.

The history of British chairs is reasonably old and peculiarly regional. There are distinct traditions throughout the British Isles, with Orkney chairs, Welsh 'stick' chairs, Northern 'ladder back' chairs and Windsor chairs being the main examples. Often the style or method of making is dictated by the materials to hand in that particular region.

Windsor chairs, or Windsor construction, is nowadays a generic term that refers to being made of parts socketed into a solid seat or slab. The Windsor tradition has humble origins, being from English country furniture that was made by village carpenters and wheelwrights for local people. These chairs are functional and basic, nothing fancy. Many of the tools and objects needed for rural life would have been made locally, using a combination of time-honoured traditions of craftsmanship. Greenwood crafts were widespread and in common use, and many of these crafts existed harmoniously within the landscape. There would surely have been stools and chairs made with socketed parts long before 'Windsor' became a description.

Welsh chairs are constructed similarly and have comparable rural origins, but because they have developed in Wales, the tradition has become proudly and distinctively Welsh.

Small workshops flourished, and they started to develop their own nuances. The humble country chair became quite grand – an object of status that was produced on scale – and some makers became widely known. In the 1700s, rapid population growth led to the establishment of furniture-making factories in and around the Thames Valley, mass-producing basic furniture for the expanding city population. Windsor would become the main centre for the trading and export of factory-made wooden chairs during this period, and this is the most probable explanation for the term 'Windsor' chair.

A highly skilled, almost itinerant worker, the 'chair-bodger' (or simply 'bodger') would have worked in the beech woods in the Chilterns (Thames Valley), renting acreage to fell, cut, split and turn the wood into thousands of legs, stretchers, arm posts and other parts for chairs. These would be carefully stacked or pushed into hedges by the hundreds to dry. The parts were sold to the chairmaking factories down the river and assembled into chairs. The bodgers then moved on with their pole lathes and shave horses to the next area to be felled, building temporary shelters to stay in. In the winter months, I expect they returned to their villages to take up other tasks and seasonal work, returning to the woods in the spring.

By the 19th century, the factories in the Thames Valley were producing hundreds of thousands of chairs each year. These are easily recognizable as being mass-produced and – in my opinion – they lost some of their rustic charm. One of the most popular of these chairs is the hoop back with a back slat carved with a wheel.

Eventually, the Thames Valley chairmaking centre went into decline, due to the development of laminated timbers and the use of plastics and metals in mass-produced furniture, though some factories and workshops were operating until the Second World War. However, the Windsor tradition was carried into the modern era by designers such as Lucian Ercolani, whose designs became popular around the middle of the 20th century. Ercol still manufactures Windsor-style seats to this day.

THE WINDSOR CHAIR IN OTHER COUNTRIES

Throughout the 18th and 19th centuries, the Windsor chair developed in its character and its reputation, and some examples became quite sophisticated. The tradition spread around the globe, travelling to North America as well as to Australia. Sweden also has a similar chairmaking tradition. And as the tradition spread, it developed its own distinctive styles. American Windsor chairs are distinctly different from English Windsor chairs. American makers took the form and ran with it, developing unique turning styles and pushing the boundaries of the tradition, making it their own. Many of the chairs have widely splayed legs, lots of decorative carving and accentuated seat shapes.

A REVIVAL OF THE GREENWOOD CRAFT

Since the 1980s, traditional craft has undergone a revival, and greenwood crafts such as spoon-making, basketry and chairmaking have all seen a huge surge in popularity. There is a growing appreciation for handmade products and a recognition of their artisanal qualities and their uniqueness. The membership of groups such as the Association of Pole-Lathe Turners and Green Woodworkers (APTGW) has multiplied, and experienced pioneer teachers such as Mike Abbott have produced great books detailing the world of green woodwork and have taught the craft to thousands of people.

Today, there are many good makers and suppliers of the tools needed for the work. This has enabled many craftspeople and toolmakers to flourish, and there is a whole host of smaller businesses that have benefitted from this popularity. Platforms such as Instagram have provided a further boost to the profiles of these crafts, and now there is a global community of folk who enjoy the simple pleasures of making objects in the greenwood way.

There also seems to be a growing awareness of the sustainability of historic crafts. Many of the greenwood crafts exist within a deeply rooted connection to nature and the countryside and are deeply connected to natural materials. Some craftspeople are involved in the harvesting and sometimes even the growing of the materials they use. I have experienced a much keener awareness of the woodlands that provide me with the timber that I use for chairmaking, and I rely on close relationships with the men and women who are the custodians and stewards of these environments – it is a fascinating and unexpected learning experience.

ABOUT THIS BOOK

This book is divided into three parts. The first part covers setting up your own workshop and choosing your tools.

The second part takes you through the steps you'll need to go through in order to make a Windsor chair, whether you're trying one of the projects in this book or creating your own from scratch.

The final part of the book is made up of the projects. If you're unsure of your own skills, try the three-legged stool first. But a more experienced woodworker may want to dive into the deep end with the lobster pot chair.

Regardless of which project you choose, always pay attention to the measurements in the project's plan and jigs. Those given with the materials are for the blanks, while the measurements in the plans are the final ones after cutting and shaping. Take care as these final dimensions are not always the same. For example, the swell at the thickest point on a piece is sometimes in the centre but sometimes it's off-centre, and they may vary in diameter from piece to piece. For this reason, it's always wise to double-check your measurements: in fact, remember to check twice (or thrice) and cut once.

I hope that this book will excite and inspire you to make something by hand, or to at least try some of the techniques within these pages. Maybe you will make all the projects, or maybe join one of my courses in the woods – whatever way it inspires you, it's all good!

SETTING UP

Before you get started on the projects in this book, you'll need to set up an appropriate workshop space and ensure you have the correct tools. You may already have many of them, and may be able to find others second-hand. There's no need to have absolutely everything – just start with what you need for the projects you intend to work on first.

THE WORKSHOP

I am fortunate to have a garden that is large enough to accommodate a decent-sized workshop, but before that, I made chairs in a potting shed. There was no room to swing a cat, but it was big enough to make things on a small scale and you shouldn't need anything larger than that if you have access to some outdoor space.

WORKSHOP EQUIPMENT

The major pieces of equipment you'll need are a workbench; a kiln or some kind of rack in an airing cupboard for drying green wood; a steam box and a water trough for preparing wood for steam bending; and ideally a treadle pole lathe for woodturning and a shave horse. If you don't have a lathe, you can make square or octagonal parts for chairs using a drawknife. If you don't have a shave horse, you could use a vice on your workbench and shave the wood with a bench plane. Aside from your workbench, most other chairmaking equipment can be stored and used outdoors and won't take up too much space.

A bandsaw is useful, but it is also large and expensive. Many of the operations that it is used for, such as seat blank cutting or cutting lengths of timber for steam bending, can be covered with a good large circular saw with a 9¼in (235mm) blade and a powerful jigsaw.

WORKBENCHES

A solid workbench – even a small one – is a very useful surface to have in a workspace. You can mount a vice on it and attach it firmly to a wall. You can spend a lot of money buying a workbench, or you could build one yourself using two sheets of 1in (24mm) plywood sandwiched together for the surface on a simple, robust frame. If you have limited space, a folding workbench is a very useful alternative. Like many types of older equipment, the older folding workbenches were built to be robust – I have a Workmate from the 1990s that is terrific. There are also interesting trestle table options available nowadays that pack and fold up easily.

Japanese-style low workbenches are great, and there are many patterns out there for making your own. They can be fitted with a vice, and some designs allow you to pack them up for easy storage. Being quite low, they are at a useful height for drilling and are a good alternative to having a full-height bench that is fixed in place.

Vices

If you have room for a bench vice, that's great; I like the older quick-release Record vices. A large engineer's vice is almost more useful than a bench vice, with the added advantage that you can remove it from the bench easily if you need the space. A Record no. 4 or 5 is robust and a good size.

If you can, get both vices. If you only have space for one, I would slightly favour getting a good-sized engineer's vice over a bench vice because it is versatile and a better height for chairmaking, but either will do. Do also bear in mind your worktop: an engineer's vice will interfere with the top surface as it bolts on top, whereas a bench vice is fitted to the side and is flush with the top surface.

Engineer's vice

Bench vice

MY WORKSHOP

Throughout this book you'll see photos taken in the workshop in my leafy garden, so I'll describe here what it's like and how it is kitted out. It is timber framed and about 20 × 16ft (6 × 5m) in area and 13ft (4m) high, with lots of glazing, particularly on the north-facing side. It is big enough for me to be working on up to six chairs at a time, but it is also small enough that I must keep it pretty tidy, which in any case is good practice.

There is a long workbench fitted with both an engineer's vice and a bench vice. The main piece of machinery is a powerful bandsaw, but otherwise it's mostly hand tools. I also have a drying kiln, a further work surface and a small area with a half-speed grinding wheel for sharpening my blades.

The bandsaw is a powerful model that has a ¾in (19mm) blade with 3TPI (3 teeth per inch). It will cut shallow curves, but it is mainly good for re-sawing heavy timbers. I can cut seat shapes and circles down to 11¾in (300mm). I process a lot of timber for the courses I teach, so the bandsaw takes a lot of strain. While you could get away with a smaller model, most of the tabletop models don't have the power to cut through hardwood of a substantial size. You would be better off investing in a circular saw and jigsaw.

There is room for a shave horse in the winter, but at other times of the year, I try to work outdoors if possible, moving my shave horse to a sunny spot, or working in my outdoor workshop. This is a simple shelter with my pole lathe and a workbench to hand and is a nice place to work in the summer.

I also have a storeroom, where I store timber, and an animal water trough that is used as a soaking tank for timber. My steam box is affixed to the side of the workshop. This may seem like a lot, but I make chairs to order all year round, and I have a busy teaching schedule in the warmer months, so it's a very busy workshop! However, especially if you are just starting out, all the processes and equipment can be more basic for your own needs.

DRYING KILN

This book shows you how to make Windsor chairs following the traditional greenwood method, but certain components made of green wood – particularly tenons – have to be thoroughly dried before assembly. There are several ways to do this. I have a kiln, which is just a cupboard with holes of specific diameters (to match the tenons I make) drilled in the top and some wire racks in it. At the bottom of the cupboard are two small plug-in oil radiators to provide a constant and safe heat source. The warm air rises through the kiln, slowly drying everything within. The tenon end of the legs can be stuck through the holes in the top, which dries the tenons while keeping the legs themselves from drying out too much. There is enough room inside the kiln to fit in the arm bows and tall spindles.

Alternatively, you could make a kiln quickly from sheets of insulation taped together, with an oil radiator at the bottom. Other possible methods of drying parts include using a rack next to your wood burner, in an airing cupboard or above a radiator; a shelf high up in a greenhouse or placing the wood in the oven with the door ajar.

In the woods where I teach, I have a barrel kiln, where a low fire burns below, with the chair components stacked above it. It is very efficient, but only because it is drying so much material – and is heated by burning the wood shavings produced by my chairmaking students.

Workshop kiln

Outdoor kiln

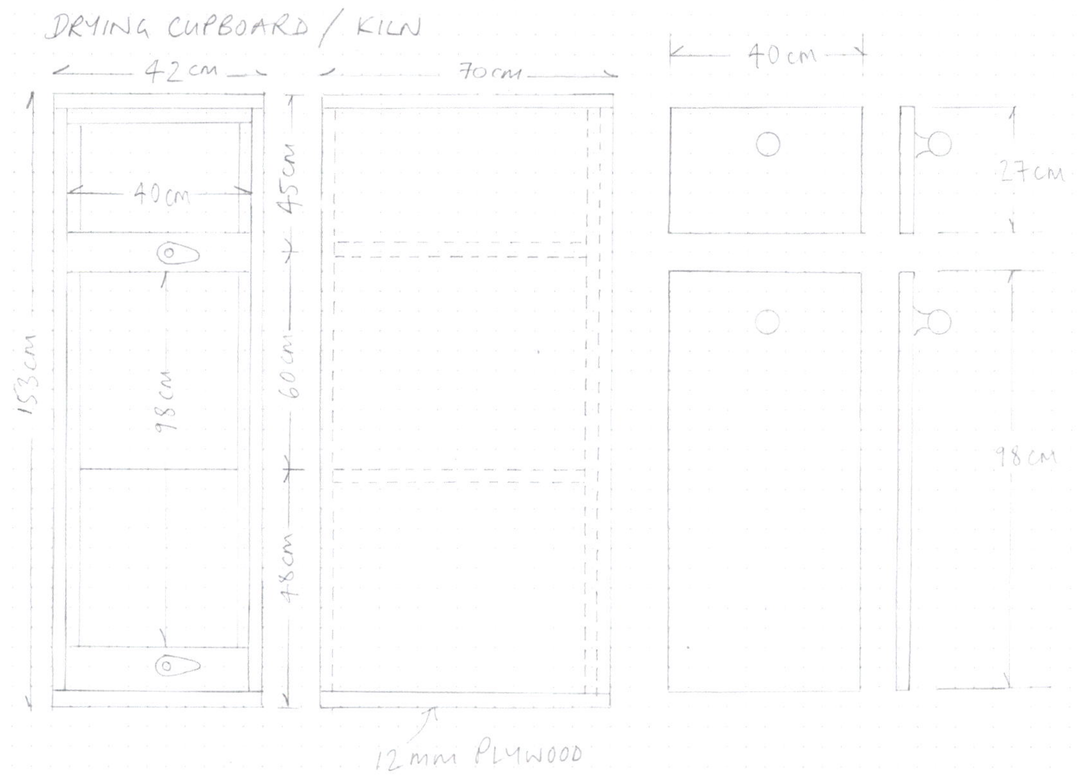

Kiln plans

STEAM BENDING EQUIPMENT

To make the bows for the armchairs or other parts that require steam bending, you'll need two pieces of kit: one to get the wood nice and wet before steaming it and the other for actually steaming the wood. All the blanks for steam bending need to go into a soaking trough for a week or so before being steamed, particularly if you are bending kiln-dried material. I use an animal water trough, but you could use a length of capped guttering for longer lengths, and a water butt for smaller bits. This is, of course, better set up outside, not inside a workshop.

Soaking tank

Steam box

There are many ways to make a steam box, and here are a few suggestions. I use mine frequently, so I have invested some time into making it well.

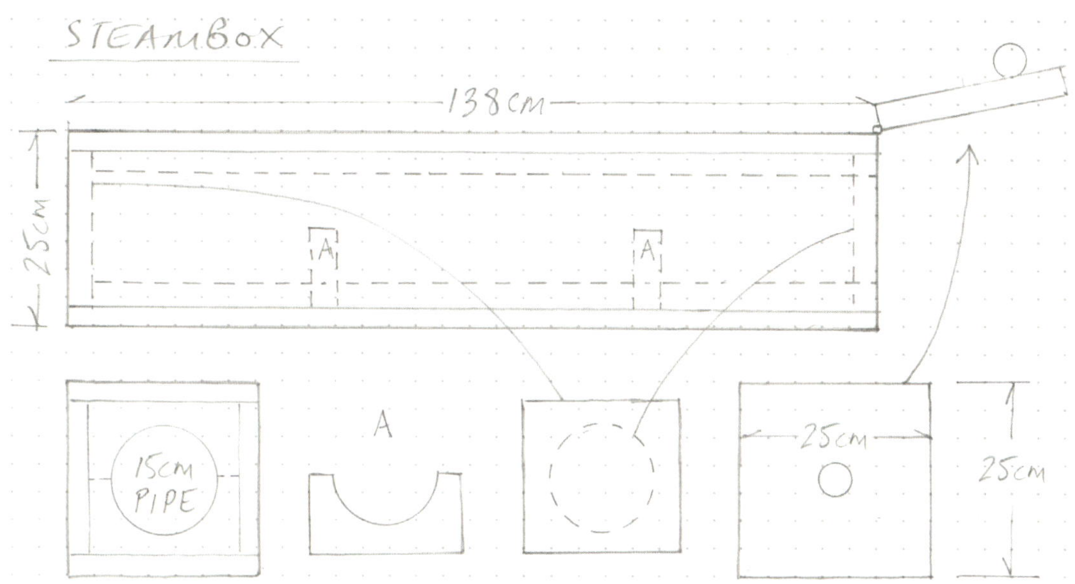

Steam box plans

To make one, suspend a 4½–8ft (1.5–2.5m)-long section of 6–8in (150–200mm)-diameter gas pipe suspended inside a box made from marine plywood. The space between the pipe and the box is filled with expanded foam to support the pipe. Construct the box so it's a few inches larger all around the pipe but the same length, but don't add the top yet. Cut out a circle to match the exterior diameter of the pipe in one end. Place the pipe in the box, fill the box with the foam and then add the top. Make sure the lid is a little loose, so pressure doesn't build up.

Add a hinged lid to cover the open end, plus a wire rack that you can pull out so you don't have to plunge your arm into the steam. Plumb the hoses of a pair of wallpaper strippers into the middle of the pipe through one side of the box. As one runs dry, the other can be turned on. Always wear heat-proof gloves when using the steam box.

An easier option would be to use a 6½ft (2m) length of 4in (100mm) downpipe, with a roofing batten strapped along the top to stop it sagging.

Insert the end of a hose from a wallpaper stripper into a hole cut into the middle of the pipe, then wrap the pipe in an old blanket for insulation and stuff sponges in the end to seal it. Tie pieces of string to the wood lengths being steamed before inserting them, so that you can pull them out without burning yourself.

Steam box

SHAVE HORSES

For me, the most important green woodworking tool is a shave horse. It is a simple clamping device which allows you to work on pieces with both hands, and it has been used for many hundreds of years. Drawknives are used in conjunction with shave horses, and the two tools are symbiotic. Over the years, I have made many different shave horses, but the first one I built is still my favourite.

You can buy shave horses online, or you download plans to make your own.

TREADLE LATHES

The treadle lathe is an ancient tool, with the earliest pictorial evidence of one dating back to the third century BCE, and there are objects that have potentially be turned on a lathe dating back to as long ago as 1300 BCE. The treadle lathe can be referred to as a 'pole lathe' if it relies on a pole for its action or a 'bungee lathe' if it depends on a bungee. Both versions need a leg-powered treadle. Although it's a relatively primitive contraption, the pole lathe version is one of my favourite machines. I use it to do all my turning, and I also teach how to use a treadle lathe in my chairmaking courses.

The workpiece is fixed between two centres on the lathe bed, and a cord runs around the workpiece to a treadle below. Some kind of spring, either a long pole or a bungee, is attached to the other end of the cord. When the treadle is pushed firmly to the ground, the cord spins the workpiece towards the turner.

Like shave horses, you can buy treadle lathes online or you can download plans to make your own.

Shave horse

Treadle lathe

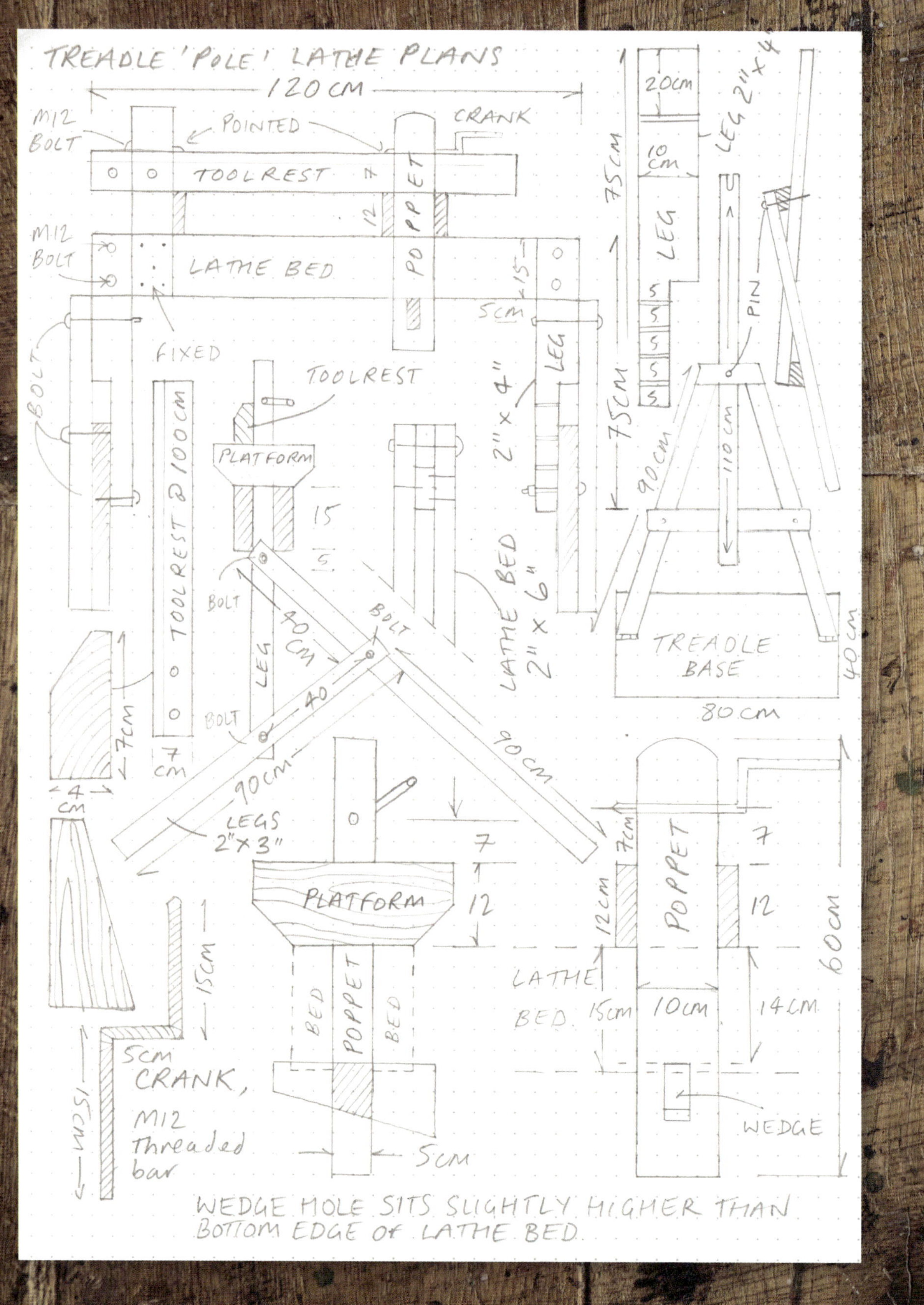

TREADLE 'POLE' LATHE PLANS
120 CM
M12 BOLT
POINTED
CRANK
TOOLREST
POPPET
12
M12 BOLT
LATHE BED
POPPET
15
5CM
FIXED
BOLT
TOOLREST
TOOLREST Ø 100CM
PLATFORM
15
5
2" x 4"
LEG
LATHE BED 2" x 6"
BOLT
40CM
BOLT
LEG
40
BOLT
7CM
4 CM
7 CM
90CM
90CM
LEGS 2"x3"
20CM
10 CM
LEG 2" x 4"
75CM
LEG
5
5
5
5
5
75CM
PIN
90CM
110CM
TREADLE BASE
40CM
80CM
7
PLATFORM
12
15CM
5CM
CRANK,
M12 Threaded bar
15CM
BED
POPPET
BED
5CM
7CM
POPPET
7
12CM
12
60CM
LATHE BED
15CM
10CM
14CM
WEDGE
WEDGE HOLE SITS SLIGHTLY HIGHER THAN BOTTOM EDGE OF LATHE BED.

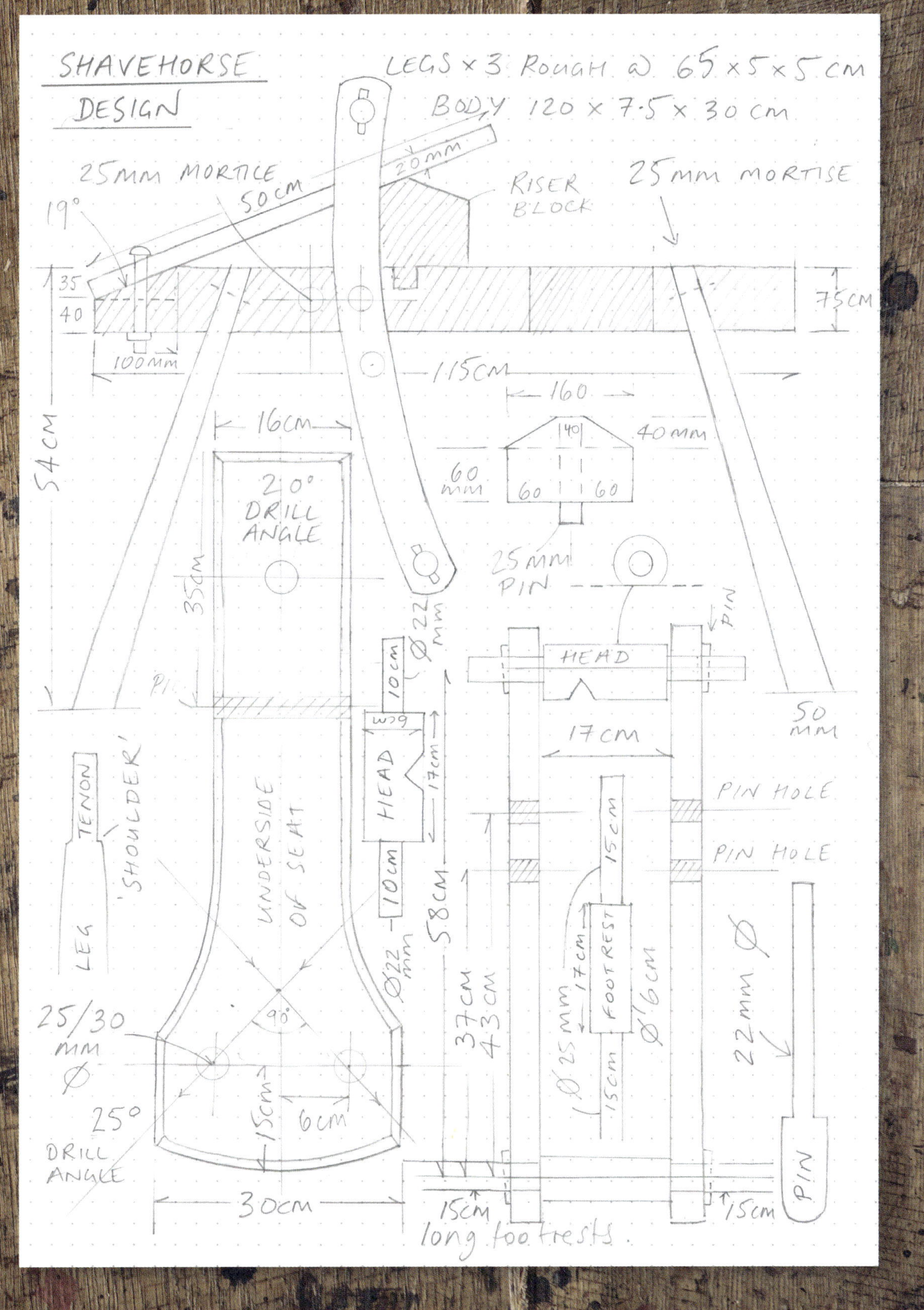
SHAVEHORSE
DESIGN
LEGS × 3 ROUGH @ 65 × 5 × 5 CM
BODY 120 × 7.5 × 30 CM
25MM MORTICE
20MM
50CM
RISER BLOCK
25MM MORTISE
19°
35
40
100MM
7.5CM
115CM
160
40
40MM
60 MM
60
60
25MM PIN
16CM
20° DRILL ANGLE
35CM
54CM
PIN
HEAD
PIN
Ø 22 MM
10CM
6CM
HEAD
17CM
10CM
Ø22 MM
58CM
17CM
50 MM
TENON
'SHOULDER'
LEG
UNDERSIDE OF SEAT
PIN HOLE
PIN HOLE
15CM
17CM
FOOTREST
Ø 6CM
Ø 25MM
15CM
37CM
43CM
90°
25/30 MM Ø
25°
DRILL ANGLE
15CM
6CM
Ø
22MM
PIN
30CM
15CM
15CM
long footrests.

TOOLS

Most of the tools that I use for chairmaking are traditional hand tools used for many types of carpentry, but I also use a few specialist tools such as travishers. If you wish to explore green woodwork and chairmaking, it's definitely worth investing in good-quality tools, especially if you will be spending a lot of time using them. There are some great suppliers of new tools, but another option is to buy older, used tools, provided they are in good condition. If you are purchasing older tools, look for particularly well-made ones made from the 1940s to the 1960s. Don't buy tools that have excessively worn-out blades.

MAKING A SKEWED CUT

Any tool with a blade, particularly drawknives, planes and travishers, can be used to make a skewed cut. To do this, the blade is held at an angle between 20 and 45 degrees, but it is still used to make a slicing cut in a backwards and forwards direction. Working with the blade at an angle eases the pressure on the cut by reducing the area of the edge that is cutting. It can be used whenever you are struggling with a tool or when you need more control of the cut.

JAPANESE SAWS

Unlike traditional European hand saws, Japanese saws cut by being pulled towards the user rather than pushed away. These are very fine saws that are particularly good at making a nice, controllable cut. They are affordable, have easy-to-replace blades and have become increasingly popular with Western makers. However, they are also the easiest tool to have an accident with, usually by cutting into a hand on the through stroke.

Japanese saws come with a long handle that sits nicely down the inside of the forearm when cutting small pieces of wood, or it can be held with both hands for larger pieces. To use the saw, hold it with the part of the blade nearest the handle at the cutting mark or in the kerf. Pull the saw towards your body, but don't use too much force or you may kink the blade. Make even, easy strokes, letting the blade do the cutting. Work slowly and carefully as you exit the cut to avoid travelling through into other parts of your work – and your hand.

DRILL BITS

It's really important to have a good selection of drill bits, and when appropriate, the corresponding tenon cutter. I recommend buying new ones as many older bits are blunt or the lead screws are sheared. Drill bits are a little confusing: if you are mainly using a cordless electric drill, you will easily find drill bits in metric measurements and with hex shanks to fit your drill. However, if you prefer to use a hand brace, the brace will commonly be an old traditional model suited to older bits that come in imperial measurements. These traditionally have a square shank to fit the square jaws in a drill brace.

GAUGE

LOG SPLITTING AND ROUGH SIZING TOOLS

The following tools will enable you to split logs into the rough sizes of timber blanks you'll need for your projects.

Steel wedge

You'll need two or three steel wedges for splitting logs. They should be 8–10in (200–255mm) long with an even taper, with each one weighing 2lb 3¼oz–3lb 5oz (1–1.5kg).

Sledgehammer

To strike steel wedges when splitting logs, you'll need a steel-headed sledgehammer in a decent size. Depending on your strength, it should weigh 6lb 10oz–11lb (3–5kg) and have a 3ft (915mm) long handle. Always use protective eye goggles when striking steel with steel, because there is a risk of steel splinters getting into your eyes.

Splitting axe

Choose a standard hatchet-shaped axe for splitting logs. A 2lb 3¼oz (1kg) head is about average for a hand axe. If you're buying an older, used axe, it should weigh 1lb 8oz–2lb 8oz (680g–1.13kg). You can also use the head of an axe as a splitting wedge; if you do, make sure the handle doesn't travel into the split of the log as it could become jammed or damaged.

Copper hammer

You could use a copper hammer rather than a steel hammer for striking the splitting axe. Not only should it minimize the chance of damaging the axe, but it should also avoid the issue of the flying steel splinters that can result from striking steel with steel. Thor is the brand of hammer I use, and ideally you want a no. 3. This type of hammer might have one face in copper and the other in rawhide, which can be useful.

Side axe

Ideal for shaping rough timber, a side axe has a blade with a completely flat face on one side and comes in right- or left-handed varieties. It could be replaced with a more conventional small carving axe. Note that neither of these axes are suitable for being struck with a hammer.

Froe

With its handle set at the end of a long blade, a froe can be used for cleaving and riving in conjunction with a cleaving brake (see page 60). There is a limited range of froes produced nowadays and they are generally very similar to each other.

1 Sledgehammer
2 Splitting axe
3 Side axe
4 Copper hammer
5 Froe
6 Wedges

1
5
4
THOR
2
3
6

ROUGH SHAPING TOOLS

The tools in this category can be used for shaping timber blanks, but some are also suitable for adding finer details when shaping or carving wood.

Drawknife

A drawknife is the quintessential woodworking tool for green wood. It must always be held in both hands, usually with the bevel facing downwards. The drawknife gets its name from the fact that it is drawn towards you when working – unlike most bladed tools, which are usually pushed away from the body. I prefer to use a 14in (355mm) drawknife when working at a shave horse and an 8in (200mm) drawknife for smaller work. As you should be using them often, it's worth paying for quality. Look for nice, older examples made by Brades or Marples. Make sure the handles have small metal washers on the ends, which prevent the handles coming loose.

Carving knife

Small carving knives are readily available and have many uses, such as making details, trimming small pieces and carving. Look for ones with 2in (50mm) long blades, which are nice and controllable. There are many good brands, particularly Mora.

Spokeshave

When used on dried timber, a spokeshave can shape curves, add detail or flatten smaller surfaces. The bottom surface of the spokeshave is known as the sole, and it comes in different shapes depending on the use. Spokeshaves with curved, convex soles are used for inside curves, while spokeshaves with flat soles are used for outside curves and flat surfaces.

Straight chisel

There are many uses for a chisel with a straight-edged blade: for cutting details, splitting and making wedges, and splitting the ends of spindles. It's a good idea to have both a 1in (25mm) chisel and a ½in (12mm) chisel.

Shallow curved chisel

You'll need a shallow curved chisel for taking the tops off leg tenons after they've been glued. I use a ¾in (19mm) wide carving chisel. It is also suitable for gouge carving.

1 Large drawknife
2 Small drawknife
3 Spokeshave
4 Shallow curved chisel
5 Straight chisel
6 Carving knife

1
2
3
4
5
6
SWISS MADE 4/25

POLE LATHE CHISELS

Differing slightly from machine lathe tools, pole lathe chisels are typically wider so they can make the most of your leg power. Pole lathe chisels are limited in availability, with only a couple of manufacturers making them, so there's not much choice. I recommend buying a set that includes a 1¼–1½in (32–38mm) wide roughing gouge, a 1–1½in (25–38mm) planing chisel and a standard skew chisel, plus ¼–¾in (6–20mm) detail gouges.

Roughing gouge
The roughing gouge is the most useful and easiest to use of the chisels. It's used for the initial shaping of billets. It will not produce a nicely finished surface. It's used with the bevel facing downwards. They commonly come in widths ranging from 1¼ to 2in (32–50mm), and you'll find them with curves which vary from gentle to quite deep.

Skew chisel
Skew chisels are used to create shapes, particularly convex or round. It has a slanted blade; the point is called the toe, and the back edge is the heel. The toe is used to cut V-shaped details, and the heel is used to turn over corners into smooth curved shapes.

Planing chisel
The planing chisel is used with the bevel facing downwards, and it creates clean, flat finished surfaces. They come in widths from 1 to 2½in (25–63mm) wide.

Detail gouge
Also known as finger gouges, these smaller gouges can be used to create concave shapes on turned workpieces. They're used with the bevel facing downwards.

1 Large detail gouge
2 Roughing gouge
3 Skew chisel
4 Planing chisel
5 Small detail gouge

1
2
3
4
5

SEAT CARVING AND PLANING TOOLS

Travisher

It's hard for me to imagine carving seats without using a travisher – a carving tool that is particular to chairmaking for both smoothing rough surfaces and giving it a fine finish. Antique travishers are particularly rare beasts, but there are a handful of contemporary toolmakers who make good modern versions, and kits are available to make one yourself. The travisher is a costly tool, but it will be a sound investment for making Windsor chairs. You will only need one, of whatever size you can find. You can use a travisher by either pushing it away from your body or pulling it towards yourself. To smooth a rough surface, use it straight across or diagonally across the grain. Use it with the grain to achieve a finely finished surface. Always cut downwards from a high point to a low point.

Block planes

The small size of block planes makes them very useful for detail work, and I particularly like the older Stanley no. 9½ model. Apron planes, which are small enough to pop into your apron pocket, are really nice and worth investing in.

Smoothing and bench planes

The larger size of these planes makes them suitable for flattening seats and larger rough areas. I recommend buying an older plane that has a blade made from good-quality steel. Don't buy cheap and new. Look for a plane, such as a Stanley or Record no. 4 or 5, from a reputable second-hand tool dealer.

1 Contemporary travishers (made by James Murcell)
2 Antique travisher
3 Homemade travisher
4 Small block plane
5 Block plane
6 Large smoothing plane
7 Bench plane

1
2
3
4
5
6
7
MARPLES
SHEFFIELD
ENGLAND

OTHER SHAPING AND CARVING TOOLS

Carving adze

An adze, sometimes referred to as a bowl adze, is similar in appearance to an axe, but it has a shallow, curved cutting edge that is perpendicular to its handle.

Carving chisel

If you don't have a travisher, a carving chisel could be used for seat carving. A 1³⁄₁₆in (30mm) or 1½in (38mm) bent gouge chisel would be perfect.

Rasp

You can make a rasp simply by adding a handle to an old farrier's file, or you could just buy a new one. Rasps are very useful for shaping seats.

Cabinet scraper

Also referred to as card scrapers, cabinet scrapers are invaluable tools for achieving a nice smooth surface on chair parts, particularly the seat. You can buy them in sets that include a shallow curve, straight neck and goose neck. I typically use a scraper after getting as smooth a surface as possible with a travisher. You can use the tool pulling it towards you or pushing it away from you in the direction of the grain. It's easier to take a cut away from you, using both hands to flex the blade slightly. The scraper is held almost upright and should cut a clean shaving.

1 Rough rasp
2 Carving chisel
3 Carving adze
4 Cabinet scrapers

1
2
3
4
SWISS MADE 8L/30

SAWS AND HAMMERS

The type of cut you need to make will determine the type of saw you should use. Saws are designed with teeth in different directions for either cutting across the grain or with the grain. Having a few different hand saws available will be invaluable for cutting wood, whether to reduce the length of a blank or to cut down a protruding tenon when assembling a chair. Hammers will also come into their own during assembling, as you fit pieces together and knock them apart to make adjustments.

Japanese crosscut pull saw
This is an essential saw for making cuts cleanly across the grain, best used with two hands holding the long handle.

Japanese rip-cut pull saw
The teeth are arranged on this saw for making rip cuts along the grain, such as down the length of a plank.

Small Japanese flush-cut pull saw
Although this saw is not essential, it's useful for trimming spindle ends and cutting in hard-to-reach areas.

Panel saw
Also known as a joiner's saw, this is a multi-purpose, general use saw that will come in handy in the workshop for numerous different tasks, from cutting plywood when making jigs to trimming blanks to size.

Ball pein hammer
I particularly like the shape of this hammer head, with one flat face and one rounded (pein or peen) end. A good selection of hammers in various weights, such as 8oz (225g), 16oz (450g) and 32oz (900g) – or small, medium and large – is essential. They can be used for a variety of tasks: sometimes when you'll need a light touch, but other times something heavier will be more appropriate.

Dead blow hammer
Really more of a mallet with a lead shot-filled hollow head, it's designed to keep damage to a minimum and is great for knocking things together – or apart! A 32oz (900g) hammer is suitable for chairmaking projects.

Carving mallet
Made from a dense wood, such as cherry or beech, a carving mallet is designed for striking any chisel with a wooden handle. You could make one yourself on a pole lathe or by using a carving axe.

1 Panel saw
2 Japanese crosscut pull saw
3 Japanese rip-cut pull saw
4 Small Japanese flush-cut pull saw
5 Large ball pein hammer
6 Medium ball pein hammer
7 Dead blow hammer
8 Carving mallet

8
7
2
3
6
1
5
4

CLAMPS

When it comes to holding your project steady, whether for cutting, drilling, carving or marking, there's no such thing as owning too many clamps. Having a variety to hand will give you the most flexible options.

F clamp
I favour the large F clamps for their extreme grip and strength. They have loads of uses, from steam bending to seat carving and holding jigs to chairs. I recommend a variety of sizes, up to 8in (200mm) or 10in (255mm) jaws. You can buy good new ones or look for them second hand. They will be a worthwhile investment.

G clamp
These G-shaped clamps have an adjustable screw that offers good amounts of clamping strength. They are readily available second hand.

Spring clamps
These are really useful for grabbing and gripping thin pieces. While they don't offer much clamping strength, they will hold something in place when you need a spare hand. They are usually best to buy new and they easily wear out.

Quick grip clamps
Also called 'squeezy' clamps, these can be used one handed, and they are very useful for holding things in place with medium strength. They have soft jaws, and they come in a variety of different sizes and lengths.

1 Large F clamp
2 Small F clamp
3 G clamps
4 Squeeze clamp
5 Quick grip clamps

1
SANDVIK
5
BESSEY
4
2
3
5
3

TENON CUTTERS AND DRILLS

Cylindrical parts that need to fit in holes can be fine-tuned by using tenon cutters, and the holes themselves can be made with a drill bit, either by using it in conjunction with a cordless electric drill or a hand-operated brace.

Veritas cutters and most wooden cutters are made to imperial measurements, but they can be adjusted slightly to cut to rounded metric measurements. The cutter sizes you'll need and what they should be adjusted to if you're using metric measurements are: ¾in (20mm), 11⁄16in (18mm), ⅝in (16mm), 9⁄16in (14mm) and ½in (12mm).

Tenon cutters

The most accurate way to make tenons is on a pole lathe (see pages 65–67), but I still find tenon cutters to be really useful for longer or thinner parts such as spindles, and you can also use them if you don't have a pole lathe. Tenon cutters will make your life a lot easier – as long as you have drill bits to match their size. If using traditional wooden cutters, it's best to mount the workpiece in a vice and turn the cutter down the workpiece.

Veritas cutter

Veritas produce tenon cutters with spirit levels set into them. When you grip the workpiece in a vice, use the spirit level to get it flat, then aim the cutter straight down the workpiece, looking at the spirit level to align the cutter with the workpiece before advancing the cutter.

Auger drill bits

I favour the auger bits designed for drilling into wood. They have a lead screw that pulls the drill cutter through the wood. Keep a selection of drill bits to match the sizes of the tenon cutters you'll be using. You'll also need a 5⁄32in (4mm) bit to drill the mortice for the plug in the crest of the lobster pot armchair.

Square jaw drill brace

The old fashioned way of drilling is to use a drill brace, with one hand turning the handle while the drill is braced with your body. As these traditionally have square jaws, you will need to use either older bits or use it with a hex shank adapter.

Hex shank adapter

Almost all new drill bits, whether imperial or metric sizes, will have hexagonal shanks. If you have a drill brace with square jaws, you may need an adapter to fit into its jaws to accept hexagonal drill bits. They are difficult to find, but it will save on mashing up your hex shafts using a brace.

1 Auger drill bits with hex shanks
2 Square-jaw drill brace
3 Hex shank adapters
4 Veritas tenon cutters
5 Wooden tenon cutters

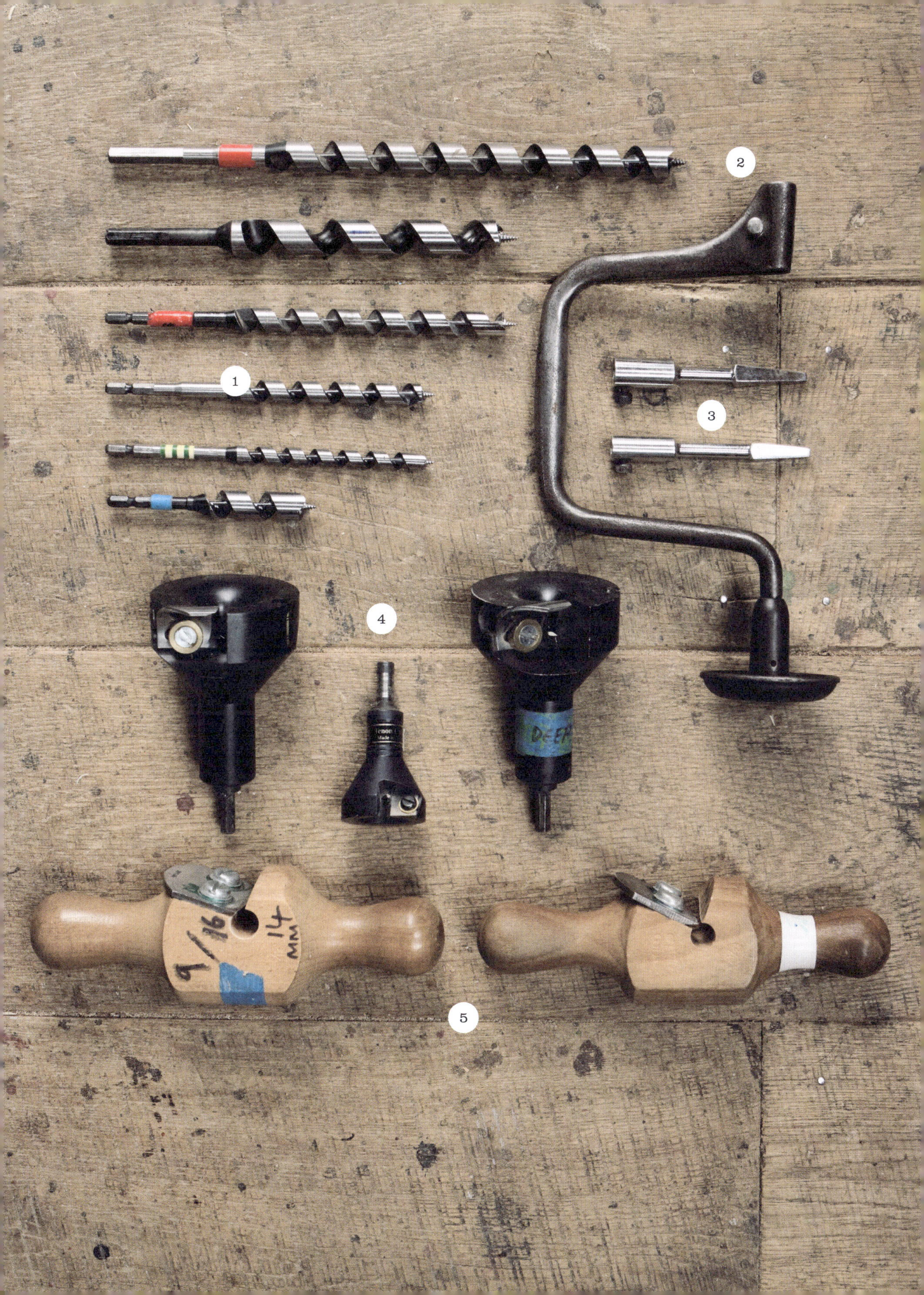
2
1
3
4
9/16
14 MM
5

POWER TOOLS

You can make a chair solely using hand tools and without electricity. However, an electric drill, a circular saw and a jigsaw will greatly speed up and ease some chairmaking processes. If you have space and you are doing a lot of carpentry in general, a bandsaw is hugely versatile and useful, but it's certainly not necessary.

Cordless electric drill
A decent cordless electric drill that is run by battery power will serve you well. Choose one made by a reliable brand, with as high a torque as possible, and that comes with a spare battery that charges rapidly.

Circular saw
A good-quality saw with a 7½–10½in (190–265mm) or larger blade is useful for sawing boards into the smaller sizes needed for steam bending, and for cutting up boards to make seat blanks with straight edges.

Jigsaw
A jigsaw with a sufficiently long blade can cut 2⅛–2⅜in (55–60mm) boards if you work slowly and carefully. It is useful for cutting out seat blanks with a curved shape.

1 Circular saw
2 Cordless electric drill
3 Jigsaw

1
2
3
HITACHI
HiKOKI
HiKOKI
3.0
Li-ion
HITACHI
HITACHI

MARKING AND MEASURING TOOLS

There is a huge variety of tools available to help measure distances and transfer marks onto workpieces. Some of these are useful for making straight lines, others are designed for creating curves. I use both imperial and metric measurements in my chairmaking, but I am of a particular generation that was raised to be comfortable with both. Choose whichever one you're most comfortable with and stick to it throughout a project.

Rulers and tape measures
At a minimum, you'll need a 12in (305mm) and a 24in (610mm) steel ruler with metric and imperial measurements as well as a tape measure that is at least 10ft (3m) long. As well as measuring small distances, the steel ruler will be essential for marking straight lines.

Dowel plate
Very useful for sizing tenons, a dowel plate has a series of holes drilled out of a small steel plate. I made my own, drilling holes for ⅜in, ½in, 9⁄16in and ⅝in (10mm, 12mm, 14mm and 16mm) dowels. To make your own, use pieces of ⅛in (3–4mm) thick steel for the plates, and drill the holes with the drill on a slow setting. Use metal drilling bits and a little motor oil as a lubrication.

Bevel gauge setter or protractor
Angles are marked on this rectangular sheet of steel for setting your bevel gauge angles from 0 to 60 degrees in half degree increments. Alternatively, you can use a standard semicircular-shaped protractor to mark out angles.

30/60 degree set square
This right-angled, triangular-shaped tool is very useful for marking and checking angles and for dividing into sixths. You should get a large one.

Circle template
Holes of various diameters are made into a thin sheet of plastic or metal to create a circle template. To use one, simply position the desired size where you want to draw a circle, then run a pencil or pen around the inside edge. These can be bought from stationer's shops; look for one with circles from 5⁄32 to 1in or more (4–25mm).

French curve
This thin sheet of plastic is configured with a variety of curves that you trace around to replicate them on your work. They are very useful for laying out seat shapes. These can be found as standard online from stationer's suppliers.

Marking gauge
This is an adjustable gauge with a sharp point that is used for making marks on wood. It is probably one of the most useful tools ever: I drill mine to fit a pencil or pen, for marking out seats, blanks for steaming, final thicknesses of elements, etc.

1 Ruler
2 Dowel plate
3 Circle template
4 Bevel gauge setter
5 French curve
6 30/60 degree set square
7 Tape measure
8 Marking gauge

1
2
3
4
5
6
7
8
BEVEL GAUGE
iGAGING
Helix
OXFORD

Bevel gauge

This adjustable tool has two legs that can be set at any desired angle, which is held in place by tightening the wing nut. It is super useful and essential in a woodworking workshop. You can set it at an angle for drilling, or use it for marking for cuts on handholds, etc. when used in conjunction with a protractor to set the angle.

Bradawl

A tool that goes by many names, including awl, gimlet and hand auger, it is basically a handle with a metal shaft that ends in a point. This point is used for making small indentations in wood to mark a measurement. It is super useful and essential for marking drill points, where it also helps to centre the drill bit as it goes into the wood.

Spring callipers

A spring and pivot hold together a pair of legs, which can be adjusted to measure the thickness of an object, such as a spindle or leg being turned on a lathe. These range from small to large, but a couple of medium-sized 3in (75mm) callipers will do for making chairs. Good second-hand ones are easy to find.

Vernier callipers

Looking like a small F clamp, these are engineer's callipers, but they are also useful in woodworking, such as when turning pieces on a lathe. It's worth investing in a nice set as the cheap ones are rubbish! Some have a digital monitor, but the batteries can run out at the worst time – which is why I prefer the analogue variety.

Dividers

Similar in appearance to spring callipers but with straight legs, dividers are ideal for making a series of marks at equal distances. They are indispensable for marking out evenly spaced drilling points. They are fairly generic and can often be found second hand.

Try square

A try square usually consists of a steel blade, often with measurements on the outer straight edge, and a wooden stock that are held together at a perfect 90-degree angle ('try' is a reference to this angle). Both edges of the two pieces are perfectly straight. You can use a try square to ensure lines are perpendicular, to check edges and ends of boards are square with adjacent boards, to check the flatness and the width or thickness of boards and to measure small distances.

Framing square

Similar to a carpenter's square but larger in size, this right-angle L-shaped tool is useful for finding the centres on bows fitted to seats. You'll find a 12 × 24in (305 × 610mm) framing square useful for the projects in this book.

Small spirit level

A bubble floating in liquid enclosed in a capsule set on a flat bed, a spirit level can tell you if a surface is level. They come in various sizes, and a small one is crucial for levelling the height of the finished chair.

1 Framing square
2 Bradawl
3 Small spirit level
4 Bevel gauge
5 Try square
6 Vernier callipers
7 Spring callipers
8 Dividers

1
2
3
4
5
6
7
8

HOW TO MAKE A CHAIR

Part of the appeal of chairmaking using traditional tools and techniques is that every chair, stool or table you make will have its own character – the grain of the wood, the marks from the tools, the choice of facets and other finishing touches and so on will mean you'll instantly be able to tell one chair from another even when they're made to the same plan. However, the basic techniques and the stages you'll work through are broadly very similar, whatever project you're making. In this part of the book, I'll take you through all the stages of chairmaking, from choosing and cutting your logs to painting and waxing your final chair.

When you come to making the chairs themselves, don't be intimidated by the number of steps involved: the projects may seem complicated at first, but they follow the same stages covered in this section of the book. The projects are ordered in difficulty, so if you're new to chairmaking, start with the basic three-legged stool and then work through the others at your leisure, building up your skills, knowledge and confidence.

When I make chairs, I often act on inspiration, intuition or simply from playing with shapes. There can be loads of creativity in chairmaking, so if you have your own ideas, I'd encourage you to try them. You can use the plans and jig patterns to simply give you a sense of where to start and how to proceed.

SOURCING, STORING AND PREPARING TIMBER

Whether green, air-dried or kiln-dried, sourcing and storing timber can be a complex, but also quite fascinating, subject. It can bring you into contact with the wider world of sawyers and woodland managers and owners, and it can help you form a connection with the landscape and to the trees themselves.

SOURCING TIMBER

Trying to locate a source for timber can be a really enjoyable and interesting experience, but it can also be challenging. It has brought me into contact with the widest variety of folks – particularly people who work locally in forestry and woodland management or conservation. It provides me with an ongoing learning process that I had not foreseen when I started out on this path.

I always look forward to wandering through the woodland, discovering new species and watching the wildlife and the flowers that change with the season. I feel, increasingly, the value of being in the woods, just walking, sitting and observing. If I can sit still and tune in to the environment, I can often feel the vast ambient energy of the woodland, with all the life rising up and humming.

It's no wonder that people who work in the woods tend to have extensive knowledge and wisdom on trees and their environment. It is a joy for me to learn from these people about the complex life and intelligence of trees and not to see them just as a material resource. I would always prefer to source material from organisations who are doing their best to conserve the forest environment, promoting growth and diversity.

Where I live in the south of England, there is an abundance of woodland habitat and, consequently, some great sawmills. They often deal with timbers sourced from the local area, and will usually be able to suppy all types of hardwood, whether in the green, air-dried or, more usually, kiln-dried. They will also often have a selection of imported timber.

It's best to buy kiln-dried boards for seats and larger parts that don't need steam bending. For turning parts on a pole lathe or for making octagonal parts, you should use straight green logs that are split and shaved down to size. If you are using an electric lathe, you can use air-dried or kiln-dried material, sawn into blanks. For steam bending, green boards are best, but air-dried are fine. You can use kiln-dried boards, but they will need a thorough soaking.

Timber becomes more expensive as it goes through each process, so buying freshly cut green timber is the most economical way to purchase it, while kiln-dried and machine-thicknessed timber is more costly. Kiln-dried material will blunt your tools faster than green material, while traditional joiners' tools such as planes and spokeshaves can get caught up or jammed in green materials.

Sourcing green wood

If I am looking for green logs, my preference is for recently felled ash, which is widely available in the round. Cherry, chestnut, beech or occasionally oak are also nice timbers in my area that are suitable for chairmaking.

You could try asking your local tree surgeons if they have a load of cut timber in their yards. Another good source is community woodland projects, which will often need to have trees felled to create space or remove dangerous material. Over the years, I have nurtured various working relationships with foresters and estate managers. Although these people are often too busy to be able to help small-scale buyers, there's no harm in asking. I usually buy around 65ft (20m) at a time, which I go through quickly when teaching.

Sourcing kiln-dried boards

Sawmills are where I look for wide boards. I usually look for nice, interesting boards. I avoid boards cut from the centre of a log because they tend to crack centrally; the boards taken from either side of the centre are more stable, and they don't cup or 'crown' as much as the outer boards. Boards should cut to size after being marked up, so make sure they're about ¼in (6mm) longer, wider and thicker than the final part. For seats, I normally buy 2⅛–2½in (55–63mm) thick boards, with 1½in (40mm) being the absolute thinnest that I could use – and that's after planing it flat.

I only look for trunk material and I choose sections that are straight, knot free and 10–24in (255–610mm) in diameter. I'm also prepared to pay a premium for this timber: if you spend a little more at this stage, it will ensure you will get good-quality timber that will make working with the blanks and workpieces so much easier.

Choosing wood for steam bending

When deciding on which wood to use for steam bending, I mainly use species of timber that are commonly found in the UK, with the exception of walnut, of which I use American walnut as well as European. Choose straight-grained timber without any knots or blemishes. Ash is the best material for steam bending as it remains strong when bent; however, its fibrous nature can make it trickier to work than other woods. Green wood is ideal, but it can be difficult to source freshly cut boards, so you will probably need to use air-dried boards. You can use kiln-dried boards, but it's harder to steam bend. Whatever wood you use, it will need to be soaked for a while before it is ready for steam bending (see pages 82–91).

Cutting logs

Oak is also great for steam bending. It's best if you can find straight-grained offcuts from a yard that is sawing for timber framing – it is more difficult to find a suitable green log in the round. British oaks are wonderful trees – they're very characterful and huge, but they are seldom straight! They are very heavy to move and have a high moisture content. Only the heartwood is useful for bending. Oak is in high demand and so it can be a little expensive.

Yew doesn't need to be so straight grained, and it bends easily and is resistant to splitting. It's available green from tree surgeons and in board lengths from yards. It's quite hard to work, but it's very characterful and colourful.

Cherry bends well and is a nice, characterful timber, but it is less common in the round or at sawmills.

Walnut is a favourite of mine, particularly when matching it to seats, and it bends very cleanly. However, it's relatively rare in the UK, and although it is easy to source from abroad, it's also quite expensive. It's often super straight and clean and is usually kiln-dried.

Moisture content

Knowing the moisture content of your timber is important. Freshly cut timber can have up to an 80 per cent moisture content, depending on the species, and will shrink over time as it loses moisture. After proper air drying, that level of moisture is reduced to as low as 15 per cent. Ideally, for making contemporary furniture, that level needs to be lower still, as low as 8 per cent. If you are unsure of the moisture content in your timber, moisture content meters are available online.

Air-dried boards

When I refer to 'super-dry', I'm usually referring to the tenons on workpieces, such as stretchers, legs or spindles, that are almost without any moisture at all. You can achieve this level of dryness by using a homemade kiln or drying cupboard (see pages 18–19).

Ideally, the moisture content of a workpiece with a mortice should have a higher moisture content than the super-dried tenon. Then, when the furniture sits in a heated home, the mortice will shrink around the tenon and all the tenon can do is expand – if it changes at all – creating an even tighter join.

Wood	Properties	Ideal for	Moisture content
Ash	straight, strong, flexible; turns easily; a good all-round chair timber	great for turned parts; good for seats and steam bending	low
Oak	strong	seats and steam bending	high
Sycamore	nice to carve and turn	seats and chair parts, but not spindles	medium
Beech	turns well; splits nicely	turned parts	high
Cherry	turns well; steam bends well	great for seats; good for steam bending and turned parts	high
Elm	difficult to work	great for seats; good for steam bending	medium
Sweet chestnut	splits and turns well; light when dry	turned parts	high
Walnut	visual appeal and it's nice to work with	seats, backs, steam bending and turned parts	medium
Field maple	very hard	turned parts	high
Service	good for turning	turned parts	high
American white oak	great for riving and steam bending	steam bending	high
American red oak	great for riving and steam bending	steam bending and turned parts	high
American white pine	softish	seats	medium
Birch	nice and light	turned parts	medium
Tulip poplar	paints well	seats	medium
Alder	soft but easy to work	turned parts	high
Australian blackwood	attractive and easy to work	seats, backs, steam bending and turned parts	medium

Ash

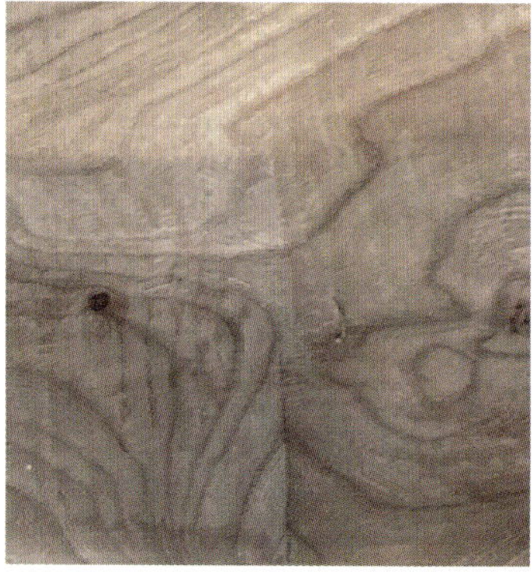

Elm

Oak

MOVING LOGS

Foresters will usually prefer to cut the material for you, but sometimes you will need to do the cutting yourself – green logs hold lots of water and are heavy! Try not to lift them completely; roll them if possible or slide them on their length. They can be split in half using a sledgehammer with a long handle and two or three steel wedges (see pages 28–29). When using the wedges, try to use them in a crack that has already developed in one end of the log. Once a crack has begun to open up, drop the wedges into the split along the side of the log and tap them in with the sledgehammer, which will release the wedge closest to the opening of the split. Follow the crack until the log pops open. You may have to cut wood fibres that are still connected inside the split with a small axe in order to separate the pieces completely.

You can use a large bowsaw to cut up larger lengths, but you will find it easier to split the wider diameter sections into quarters, and then cut these to length. This is a method that I used for years until I started teaching and I needed a larger supply of lumber, which is when I bought my first chainsaw. If you are confident with a chainsaw, you can cut logs into smaller sections before splitting.

However, you'll need to undertake an appropriate course before using a chainsaw. In the UK, it's the Certificate of Competence in Chainsaw Maintenance and Cross-cutting, which will give you the knowledge and confidence to use a chainsaw safely. You'll also need the basic protective gear of a helmet with ear defenders, chainsaw gloves, trousers or overtrousers, and protective boots.

Tools and safety equipment

Shortened logs for transporting

STORING TIMBER

How you store your timber will depend on whether you've sourced it as logs or boards, as well as how green or dry you want the material to be, which in turn will depend on where it will be used in the chair and at what stage in the project.

Storing logs

Once you have bought some timber, you should prepare it as soon as possible, before the logs dry out and become tricky to work with when using hand tools. If you do need to store it for a while, pile it in a shady spot and wrap a tarp completely over the pile to protect it from the weather. You can also help to slow down the drying process by painting the ends of the logs; any paint will do, but gloss or bitumen are good choices.

If any of the logs are particularly wide – say more than 12in (305mm) in diameter, or if they're too heavy for you to move comfortably – then I would recommend splitting them in half to release any tension and reduce cracks or 'checking' in the ends. You can stack the two halves back together again in the pile.

Storing boards

If you want to keep a stock of boards or you have green boards that need to air dry, they can be stacked in a pile with 1 × 1in (25 × 25mm) sticks in between them, placed at 12in (305mm) intervals. Again, cover the stack so it remains dry, but this time you want to encourage airflow, so don't cover the sides.

The general rule of thumb is that timber needs one year per 1in (25mm) thickness to dry, plus one year for good luck! The boards will then need to be stored in a warmer environment before use. I tend to cut boards to shorter lengths and allow them to sit in my workshop for a few months for further drying before use.

PREPARING AIR-DRIED AND KILN-DRIED BOARDS

Air-dried boards are planks that were cut when green and then have been stacked for some time and allowed to dry. If they are then put through a kiln, they will have a more reduced moisture content. During the drying process, boards shrink and move, sometimes twisting, sometimes bending. So, when using kiln-dried or air-dried boards, they will become distorted and need to be flattened. They can be passed through a thickness planer if you have access to one. I know a couple of workshops that have larger models big enough for 24in (610mm) wide boards. Smaller seat-sized boards can be flattened using an electric hand-held planer and then a hand plane. This is the process that timber always undergoes before you buy it at a timber merchant.

Boards separated by sticks

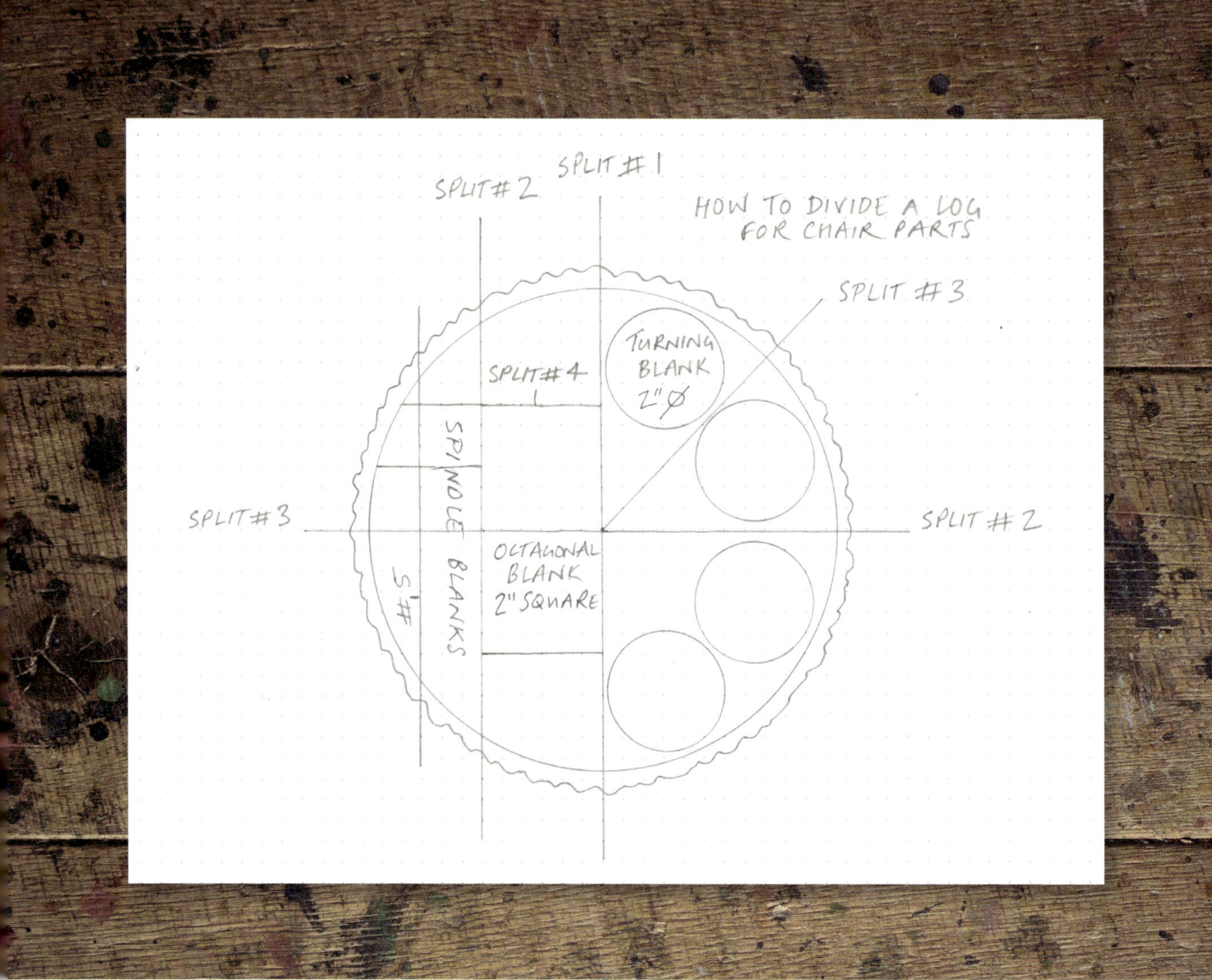

SPLITTING LOGS TO SIZE

I use two methods for splitting logs to sizes that are suitable for making parts. The first method is done with an axe, which I tend to use for shorter lengths. The second method, known as riving, involves using a froe and a brake, which is what I do for longer, thinner lengths, particularly long spindles. Shorter logs will generally split straight when struck in half with an axe, but over longer lengths, the split can tend to wander. Using a froe and a cleaving brake will control the split.

Whichever method you use, first consider what parts you'll want to get out of the log and make a plan to work out the best way to split it. Mark the order of the splits; for example, split 1 is for splitting the whole log in half, split 2, for splitting each half into halves again, and so on. Consider whether the parts will be for legs, stretchers or spindles and plan accordingly.

Splitting logs with an axe

The general guidance for splitting material is to split it in half, particularly as the size of the material gets smaller. This is because the split should run straight down the log if the mass of the material is roughly equal on either side of the split. Having the grain run straight down the length of any component, turned or shaved, provides strength and makes it easier to work. It is this

strength that allows Windsor chair parts to be both fine and flexible. Larger logs can be split into thirds or halves, then these smaller pieces can be split in half again.

Choose a log that has a straight grain with no significant knots and make sure it's only the trunk section. In the example here, I've selected a sweet chestnut log. Saw a length of the timber long enough for the parts you are making using a bowsaw, coarse crosscut panel saw or a chainsaw.

1 Mark out with a pen or pencil the width and thickness of the pieces that you want to take out of it.

2 If there is an existing natural crack in the timber, place your axe blade on it; otherwise, choose the halfway point. Strike the back of the axe head with either a copper or a steel mallet until it splits the log in two.

3 Check your pen or pencil marks and adjust them if necessary, then split the piece again.

4 Keep splitting in half until you have all the sections you need.

5 If the split starts to run out to the side, turn the log over and split from the other end to save the section.

Brake

Splitting a log with wedges

Riving

Riving – also known as cleaving – is the technique of splitting down the grain of a green log using a froe while controlling the direction of the split by levering the froe against one of the sides of the log being split. Traditionally, this method was used by coppicers to split long lengths of chestnut to make post and rail fencing and cleft timber gates. I use this method when I want to divide a longer, straight-grained log into lots of even lengths for spindles. My brake is an old gate post with a pair of notches cut into it, one 2in (50mm) wide and one 4in (100mm) wide.

It's essential to use clean, straight-grained timber for good, even riving. Dividing the log mass in half will give the best chance of splitting the log straight. As the sections become smaller, the splits are more likely to stray, but they will also be easier to direct. If you do lose control of the split, you can always turn the section upside down and try to meet the existing strayed split with a new split. In the example here, I'm splitting an ash log, using a froe and the rawhide end of a copper mallet, but you could also use a leather mallet. If the log is more than 12in (305mm) diameter, use wedges and a sledgehammer for the first division.

1 In this example for making spindles, start by marking a 1 × 1in (25 × 25mm) grid on the end of the log with the froe. To do this, simply lay the blade of the froe on the log and give it a light tap – it will leave a nice, clean marking line.

2 Now, using the froe and mallet, divide the log into half: place the part of the froe that is nearest to the handle on the log, then strike the back of the blade with a mallet.

3 Keep splitting the log by pushing down on and levering the froe, always trying to split the mass of the log in half.

4 As you drive the froe into the log, keep an eye on the split, and if it starts to run out to one side of the log, drop the log into one of the slots in your brake. As you push on the froe, lean your weight onto the handle, pushing against the stronger section of timber, which should steer the split back towards the centre of the log.

5 You can divide a section into halves to create two 'sheets' of timber, which you can then divide into four or five spindle roughs, again by splitting in half. As the 'sheets' of wood are thinner, just tap the froe in gently and watch as the split develops.

1
2a
2b
3a
3b
3c
4
5a
5b

MAKING LEGS AND STRETCHERS

If you're using green wood, there are two methods to choose from to make the legs and stretchers for the chairs. Octagonal parts can be made using a drawknife while sitting at your shave horse, while round parts are easiest to make with a lathe. If you prefer not to use green wood and instead you will be sourcing wood from a timber merchant, then you can use a bench plane and vice instead.

The legs and stretchers in my chairs have a swell at the widest point of their diameter that tapers down to the ends, adding visual appeal. For the stretchers the swell is at the centre of the part, but for legs I like to make them off-centre, normally with 12in (305mm) above the swell and 8in (200mm) below.

A lot of my work features octagonal parts shaped with a drawknife. They look great – they're very characterful, and the facets catch the light nicely. If you prefer the smoothness of rounded parts, you could use a spokeshave or block plane to refine their shape after kiln drying. However, this is a very labour-intensive and time-consuming method, and it's much easier to create rounded parts by turning billets on a lathe.

The final stage before you can use the parts is to super-dry them in a drying kiln for around a week.

ESTABLISHING AN OCTAGONAL PROFILE

To get eight equal-sized sides to an octagon, use a circle template to draw a circle that touches the four sides of the square on the end of the billet, then repeat this on the other end. Next, draw an octagon inside the circle. The octagonal faces that you will be creating will also touch the circle when you remove the corners from the square section.

Lathe tools

2a

2b

4

USING A LATHE TO MAKE LEGS AND STRETCHERS

Although you can create very detailed turnings using a lathe, you only need to create quite simple turnings for the projects in this book. They can be faceted lightly using a spokeshave once the turning has dried thoroughly.

To use a lathe, you need to create a steady rhythm by pressing the treadle to the ground, and then letting the bungee or pole return it to a raised position. Each time you press, you make a cut.

The steps below are for making legs; the process is the same for stretchers, but you will shave the billet into a 1½in (38mm) blank in step 1, the swell in step 8 will remain 1½ (38mm) in diameter and halfway along the piece, and both ends will be ⅞in (22mm) in diameter.

1 First, split a 20in (505mm) long log into rough 2in (50mm) square billets (see pages 60–61). Now, sitting at your shave horse, shave the billet into a 1¾in (45mm) square blank with a drawknife. Next, give the blank an octagonal shape by shaving the corners off, then continue shaving it until you have a roughly round, straight blank.

2 You'll need to make a centre in the middle of both ends of the blank. To do this, clamp one end of the blank on the ground between your feet then push the point of a bradawl into the wood and move it around to create a dimple. Repeat this on the other end, then put a little oil or wax on these two points – any oil you happen to have around will do, whether it's motor oil or olive oil!

3 Remove the tool rest from the lathe and knock the wedge loose on the movable poppet. Adjust the position of the lathe centres to match the length of the blank, then drive the wedge back in to secure the poppet and lathe centre crank.

4 To mount the blank, wind the cord once or twice around it, then align the lathe centres with the centred dimples on either end of the blank. If you are right handed, you'll need the cord to run on the left of the workpiece, and vice versa if you are left handed. Tighten the crank to secure the workpiece and replace the tool rest.

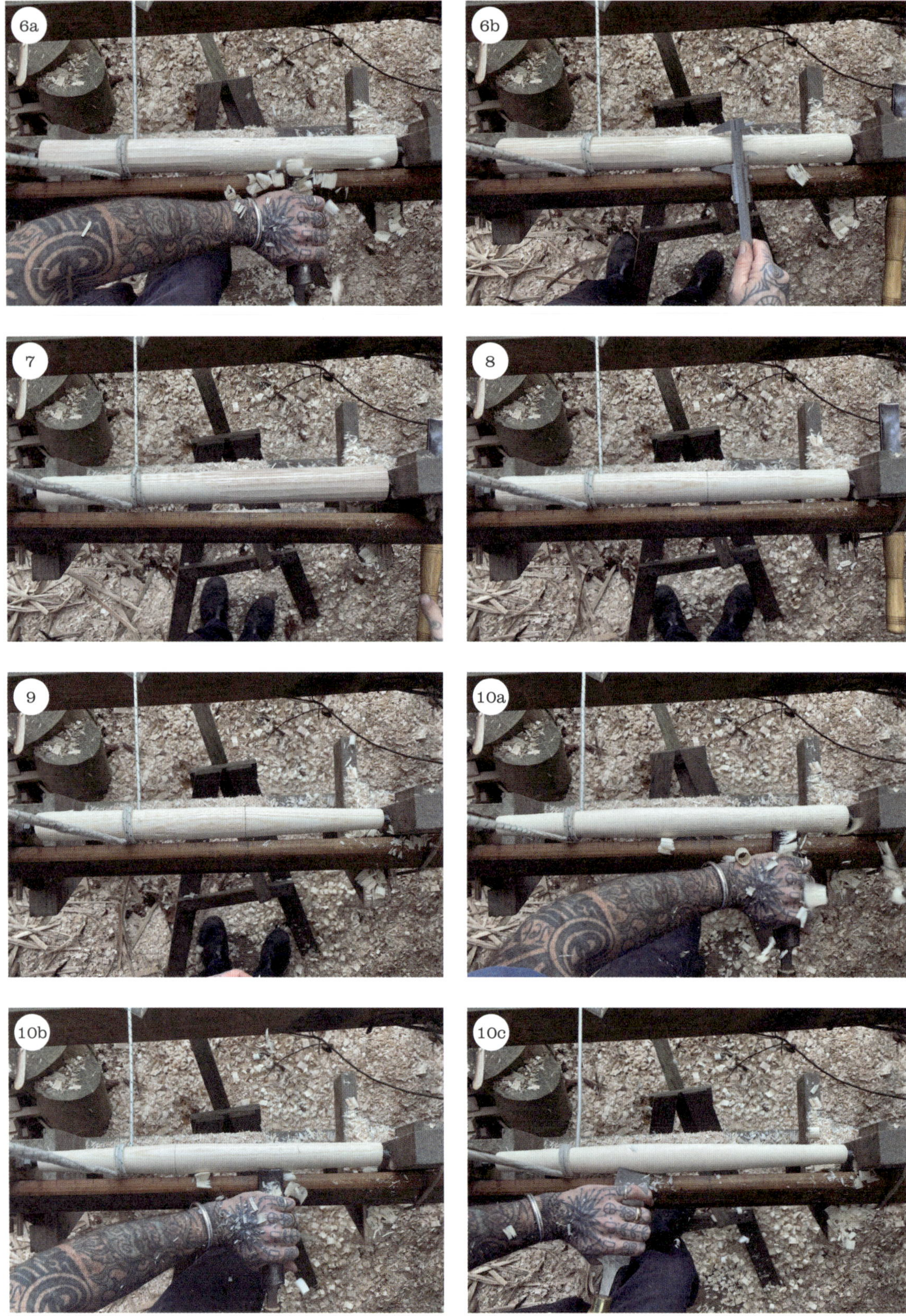
6a
6b
7
8
9
10a
10b
10c

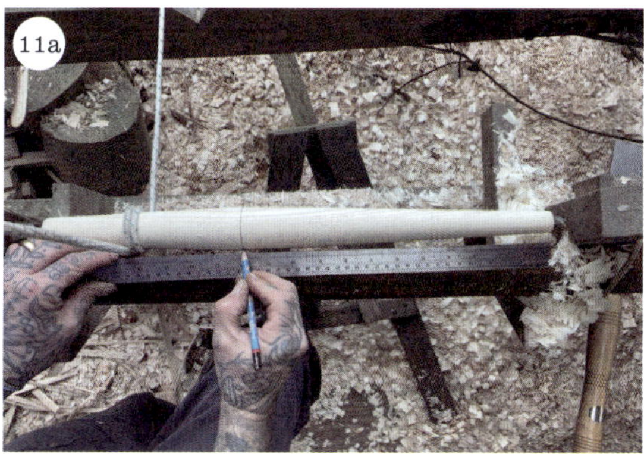
11a

11b

5 At this point, the treadle will be raised. When you press it to the ground, the blank will spin towards you from the top – if it spins in reverse, you have the cord wound backwards.

6 Start by using the roughing gouge, making light cuts working from the centre. If you're right handed, work towards the right-hand side and if you're left handed, work towards the left. Your goal is to make a rough, round cylinder that is 1¾in (45mm) in diameter. Use callipers or a vernier gauge to check the size.

7 When you have finished that half, loosen the crank, release the workpiece, unwind the cord and turn the workpiece over; then rewind the cord, remount your workpiece and work the other half.

8 When you have made the cylinder, make a mark 8in (200mm) from one end, leaving 12in (305mm) from the mark to the opposite end. This is where the swell of the leg will be. Set your gauge or callipers to 1¾in (45mm) and check this is the diameter at the dividing line on the leg. If it's larger, use a flat planing chisel to cut lightly until it's the right size, then re-mark the dividing line.

9 The next stage is to use the roughing gouge to taper the 8in (200mm) length to a diameter of 1½in (38mm) at the end. This will be the foot of the leg.

10 Repeat step 7 to turn the workpiece back over, then use the roughing gouge to taper the 12in (305mm) length, this time to about 1⅛in (28mm). Use a planing chisel along the length of the taper so that the final diameter of the top end is 1in (25mm). Always use the planing chisel 'downhill', that is, from the larger diameter to the smaller. Make a mark 2in (50mm) from the end.

11 Re-mark the line at the swell on the newly planed surface, then turn the workpiece around again. Use the planing chisel to plane the taper on the 8in (200mm) length flat until the end is 1⅜in (35mm) diameter.

12 The moisture content of the turned parts will be too high at this point, so they will need to be dried before they are used, particularly the ends which need to be super-dried for a week before any tenons are cut.

USING A DRAWKNIFE TO MAKE LEGS AND STRETCHERS

1 First, split a 20in (505mm) long log into rough 2in (50mm) square billets (see pages 60–61). Next, supporting one end of a billet in the shave horse, use a drawknife to shave one side flat, then turn the piece through 90 degrees and shave that second side flat.

2 Using one flat, clean surface as a guide, use a marking gauge to mark 1¾in (45mm) along the length of the second clean surface if you are making a leg, or 1½in (38mm) if you are making a stretcher. Then use the second clean surface to mark 1¾in (45mm) for a leg or 1½in (38mm) for a stretcher along the length of the first clean surface.

3 Shave along one of the lines to create another flat surface, and repeat on the second line to form a square profile.

4 Now you can shave the corners off the square down the whole length of the part, creating a uniform octagonal piece.

5 Use a ruler and pencil to make a mark all around the piece where the swell is. For a leg it will be 8in (200mm) from one end and for a stretcher it will be halfway along the length.

6 If you are working on a leg, first work on the shorter 8in (200mm) section, which ends at the foot. For a stretcher you can start on either end. Place the drawknife on the pencil line, and as you cut towards yourself, increase the downward pressure to remove more material, thereby creating a taper. The final diameter of the foot of the leg should be no smaller than ¾in (20mm), while both ends of the stretcher should be no smaller than ⅞in (22mm) in diameter.

7 Turn the part through 90 degrees and repeat. You will end up with a square section at the end and an octagonal section in the middle.

8 Re-establish the octagonal facets, working again from the pencil line at the swell and taking a tapering cut towards the foot.

9 Turn the leg or stretcher around in the vice. If you are shaping a leg, you'll now be working on the longer 12in (305mm) section that is the top part of the leg. Repeat steps 6 to 8, though this time the end should be 1in (25mm) in diameter for the top of the leg, while the end of the stretcher is ⅞in (22mm) to match the opposite end.

A blank at the end of steps 3, 4, 7 and 9.

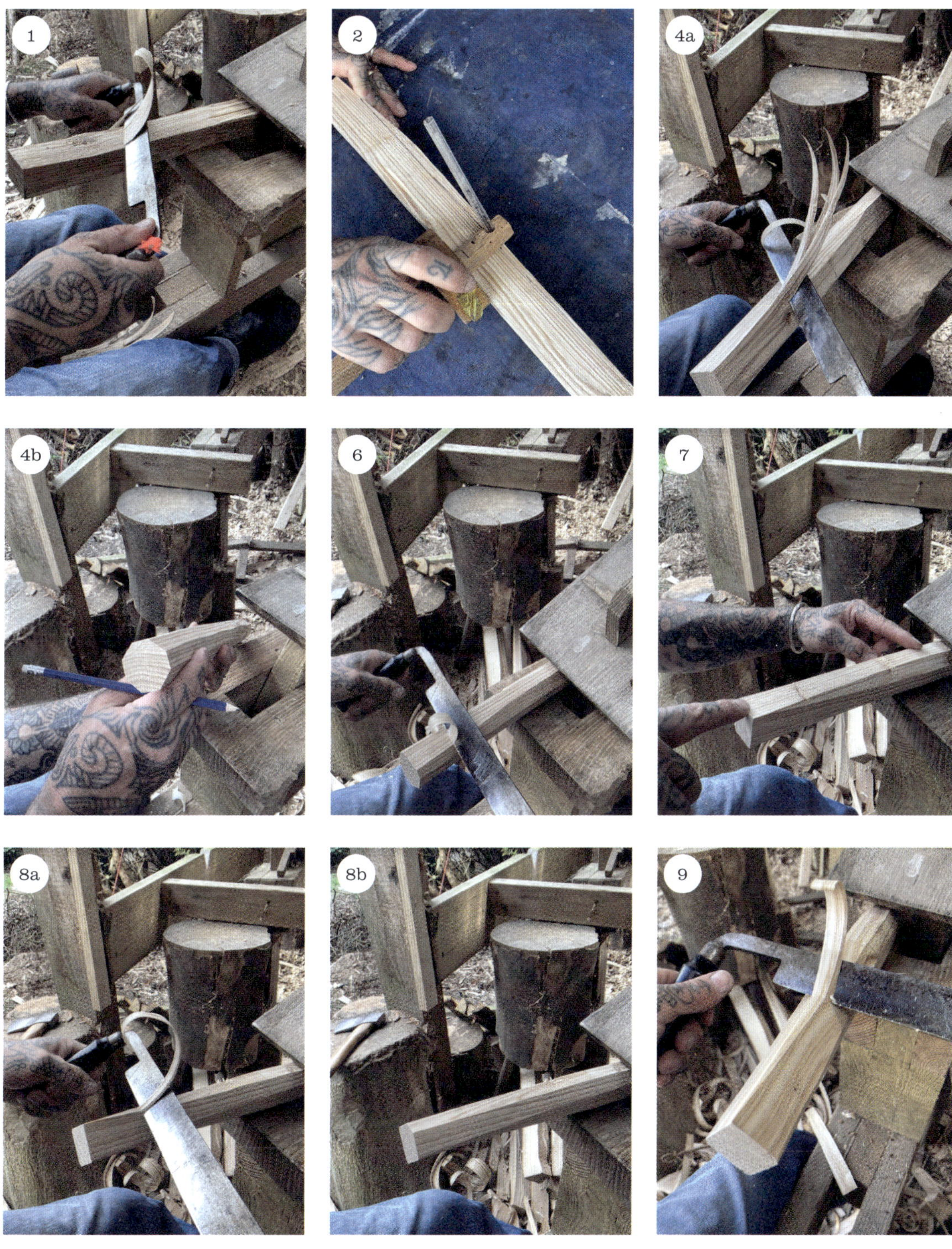
1
2
4a
4b
6
7
8a
8b
9

USING A BENCH PLANE TO MAKE PARTS

If you're using kiln-dried boards rather than green wood, you can make nice, elegant legs, spindles and stretchers using a bench plane with a bench vice. This method is more suited to octagonal or square parts that are either straight or tapered from one end to the other, rather than in both directions from a swell in the part. You'll first need to make a jig following the details in the diagram (see below). Choose a piece of kiln-dried timber with a straight grain – most hardwoods are suitable. I am using a piece of 2in (50mm) thick oak.

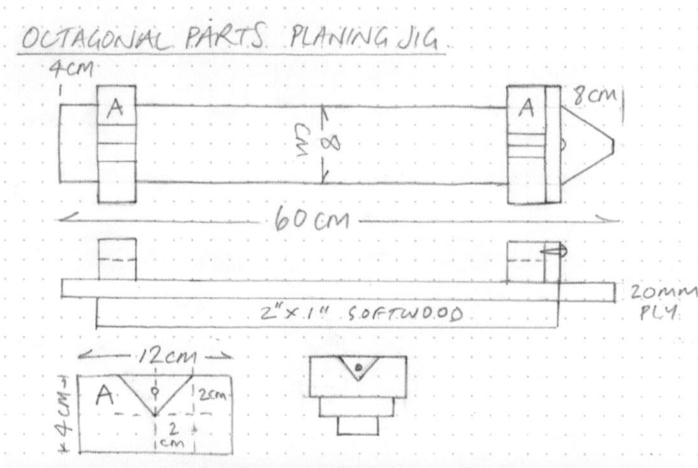

The jig to the left is for making 20in (505mm) parts; for shorter parts, make a second jig with an overall length of about 16in (405mm).

The following method is for making tapered legs. For stretchers, use straight 1½in (38mm) sections in steps 1, 2 and 3, and for spindles, use ¾in (20mm) sections. Don't taper the shape.

1 Mark a 20in (505mm) section from the timber across the grain, keeping the lines parallel. Draw tapered sections between these marks, making them 1¾in (45mm) wide at one end and 1in (25mm) at the other. Alternate the pattern to get the most parts cut from the board. Cut across the board with a crosscut panel saw or a circular saw to remove the entire 20in (505mm) section with the layout drawn on.

2 Cut out blanks along the tapered lines so they are 1¾in (45mm) wide at the bottom and 1in (25mm) wide at the top.

3 These pieces now taper on opposite sides, but they are still 2in (50mm) thick on the cut sides (the board's thickness). Draw the same pattern on one of the sawn sides. Make sure that the pattern is the right way up, with the 1in (25mm) width at the top of the leg. Cut them out using a bandsaw.

4 Place the blank in the jig with the fatter end towards you, and use a bench plane to remove the corners of the square section, creating a taper.

5 Rotate the piece in the jig and plane another corner, then repeat for the remaining two corners. Once you have planed all the corners of the square taper, rotate the part in the jig and plane the remaining saw-cut surfaces flat.

1
2
3a
3b
4a
4b
5a
5b
5c

MAKING SPINDLES AND DOWELS

There are a few different ways to make spindles, but I have settled on a technique that I find both satisfying and creative. It was taught to me by my teacher in America, Curtis Buchanan. Spindles are created in several stages, with the aim being to create nice, regular shapes that can go into a kiln to be super-dried before they are refined and fitted. Dowels are made in a similar way, but from kiln-dried boards and without being tapered.

I have a fondness for the facets on octagonal spindles and have chosen them for my chairs. However, if you prefer a round shape, you can easily turn these spindles into the round by removing the corners of the octagons with a sharp spokeshave or block plane, but do this after they have been dried and sized to the chair.

The initial spindle sizes are oversized, which allows for shrinkage in the kiln. The swell of the spindle will be the ¾in (20mm) size they're first shaved to. Once shaved to these proportions, the spindles should go into your kiln to be dried, after which they'll be ready for cutting the tenons (see pages 92–93). The spindles need to match in shape, so it's worth making a few extra spindle blanks to allow for errors made when shaping and cutting the blanks or the tenons and spindles bending randomly during drying.

SPINDLE BLANKS

I mainly use ash because I can source it locally, and occasionally chestnut or oak that is also local to me. You will need to find out what timber you can source in your area. Start with the cleanest, straightest log from the trunk of a tree that doesn't have any knots – it makes a huge difference to the finished work and the process is so much easier and more satisfying.

Make sure you have the right length log. For most of the projects in this book, you'll need logs that are 20in (505mm) in length to make the spindles, but for the lobster pot chair, you'll need a log 28in (710mm) in length to make the longer spindles at the back of the chair. See pages 62–63.

SHAPING SPINDLES

When you are ready to begin shaping the spindle blanks, find a calm space to set up and sit on your shave horse. It is useful to have a ⁹⁄₁₆in (14mm) hole and a ⅝in (16mm) hole drilled into your shave horse's clamp, so you can test the spindles' size as you make them. When you're shaving the octagons, remember to avoid shaving off too much – if ends are made too small, you won't be able to use a tenon cutter when it comes to fitting the spindles into the seat of the chair.

MAKING DOWELS

Use kiln-dried boards at least 20in (505mm) long and 1in (25mm) wide and thick to make dowels. Follow the steps overleaf, but don't make a mark for a swell or taper the dowel; simply shave it into an octagonal shape ¾in (20mm) in diameter along its whole length. When you finish making the octagonal shape, round off the corners to make a more circular shape.

Spindle blanks

Shaping the spindle

Spindle carving

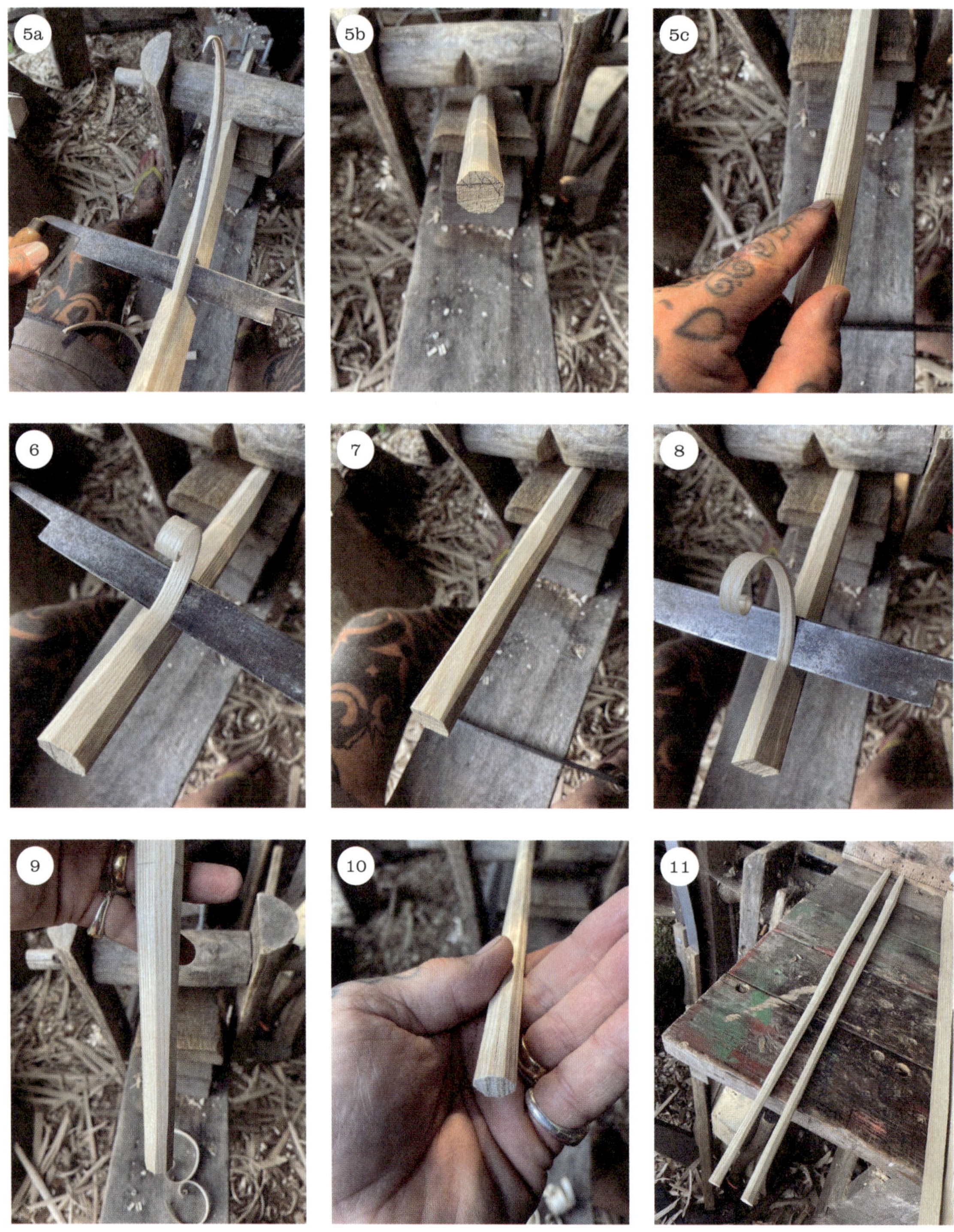
5a
5b
5c
6
7
8
9
10
11

USING A DRAWKNIFE TO MAKE SPINDLES

1 Use a drawknife to shave flat one side of the rough 1in (25mm) blanks into ¾in (20mm) square blanks. Then turn the blank through 90 degrees and shave that side flat.

2 Next, use the straight corner where the two flat sides meet to register a marking gauge and mark ¾in (20mm) widths on the flat surfaces. The two remaining rough sides should now be shaved to these marks.

3 Mark the swell of the spindle. For the low back and lobster pot chairs, the swell is 6in (150mm) from the bottom end, aside from the front spindles of the latter where the swell is 8in (200mm) from the bottom. For the Shaker bench, the swell is 7in (180mm) from the bottom end.

4 The square blanks are now ready to be shaped into octagons. Shave the ends to a diameter of no less than 9⁄16in (14mm) for the top ends and ⅝in (16mm) for the bottom ends, with the exception of the front and side spindles of the lobster pot chair, which should be shaved to ⅝in (16mm) at both ends. It is useful to have a pair of holes of these sizes drilled into your shave horse's clamp, so you can test the spindles' size as you make them.

5 Use the drawknife to shave off the corners of the square stock to create long octagonal lengths. You can do this by eye; remember that you are aiming for eight facets of the same size.

6 Work on the shorter section of the spindle first, which will taper to a diameter of ⅝in (16mm) at the bottom end. Place the blade on the pencil line, then draw the blade towards you to take a heavy cut, shaving evenly from very thin to fat.

7 Turn the spindle through 90 degrees and repeat the shave, then repeat this twice more until you have made tapering cuts on four sides of the octagon. You should have an octagon at the swell and a square at the bottom end.

8 Now re-establish the octagonal shape by placing the blade at the pencil line on one of the four remaining original octagonal facets and drawing the blade towards you, cutting carefully as the blade comes towards you to create even octagonal facets. Repeat for the other three original facets of the octagon.

9 You should now have the original large octagon at the swell where the pencil line is and a small octagon at the bottom end of the spindle, which should just squeeze into a ⅝in (16mm) hole.

10 Turn the spindle round and repeat these steps on the longer 20in (505mm) length, but this time tapering down to an octagon that will squeeze into a 9⁄16in (14mm) hole.

11 These spindles are ready to be super-dried in a kiln for a week before being fitted and refined.

MAKING SEAT BLANKS

Whether you're making a seat for one of the stools or for a chair project, the techniques for preparing the seat blank are much the same, just with different dimensions for the finished seat. They all start with cutting out a seat blank and then planing it to an even thickness with a nice flat surface.

PREPARING A SEAT BLANK

Select a hardwood board for making the seat that is at least ¼in (6mm) longer and wider than the intended final length and width of the seat – enough space to mark the shape of the seat – and cut it out without too much wastage. I like the board to be 2¼–2½in (55–63mm) thick, with the final ideal size being 2in (50mm) thick. It's possible to use a 2in (50mm) thick board and work with a final thickness of 1½in (38mm), but anything thinner won't have enough depth for the seat to be carved. Regardless, you need to allow for flattening the board with a hand plane. This means losing a little thickness, which is why you should start with a thicker blank as indicated. I normally cut out the seat shape from the board before I flatten it.

Shaped seat blank

Cut out the section from the board for your seat blank using a bandsaw or a circular saw. Choose the side that you would like as the topside of the seat. This might depend on factors like whether the timber has interesting features or its 'cleanness'. Base your choice on the quality or features of the timber, and hide defects beneath the seat (or if you think they add character, you may wish them to be on the top).

USING TEMPLATES TO CUT THE SEAT SHAPE

The two stools don't require templates – the correct shape can be made by following the instructions and measurements in the projects. For the two chairs and the bench, you'll need to create a template from the plans provided, and you'll also need to create templates for the steam bending forms (see page 82).

In my workshop, templates are very precious. Not only do they show me the drilling points and angles of the chair, but I also keep notes about the chair on the reverse side. These, combined

Marking the positions of the leg mortices

The marked-up seat blank

with my plans, help me to make chairs accurately and consistently.

You can transfer the plans to make your templates by making a ½in (12.5mm) grid on some card or a piece of plywood or hardboard – or even newspaper if you're not intending to use the template again – and then scaling the drawing up by hand. Alternatively, you could go to a print shop and have the plan drawing enlarged until it is the correct size; you could then use this to transfer the plan to the card, hardboard or plywood.

The templates for the chairs and the bending forms are of half the overall shape, to be mirrored on a centre line. Trace around the template, then flip it on the centre line and trace around it again to complete the template (it doesn't matter if the grain of the wood runs side to side or back to front of the seat). The plan for the bench is for the ends of the bench; after using the template to draw the outline of one end, you'll need to add a straight section of the required length before using the template to draw the opposite end. Now cut it to shape with a bandsaw or jigsaw, following the template marks.

The templates also include the points where the leg mortices will be drilled and sight lines so you can angle the mortices correctly. Make marks on the template where the sight lines cross the edges of the template, then draw diagonal lines between them using a ruler and pencil. Measure and mark where the centres of the leg mortices are on the lines, then drill holes through these marks using a drill with a bit that is slightly larger than your bradawl. When you've flattened your seat (overleaf), you can transfer the sight lines to the underside of the seat in exactly the same way you transferred them to the template, then you use a bradawl to make marks for the leg mortices on to the seat blank through the holes in the template.

FLATTENING THE SEAT

Once you've cut out the shape from the blank, you'll need to make both the top and the underside flat. If you have access to a large thickness planer, you can run the board for the seat blank through it at 2in (50mm), but otherwise you'll need to flatten it by hand.

1 Start with the underside, removing as little wood as possible but ensuring you get it completely flat – you'll be using it as a gauge to level the topside. Using a large smoothing plane or a scrub plane, make long strokes in a diagonal direction across the grain until the blank is flat.

2 If you view the blank from the side, you may be able to gauge whether there is any twist, or wind, in the seat blank. If you're unsure, you can use a pair of straightedges (often called winding sticks) to assess whether the planed surface is flat. Lay them parallel to each other on the planed surface.

3 Then, ducking down, look across the straightedges to see if they line up with each other. If one 'corner' is high, you will need to plane that area a bit more.

4 Using a marking gauge set to the thickness you want for the seat against the now flat underside of the seat blank as a reference, draw a line around the side of the blank. You want the blank to be as thick as possible. If you have started the process with a 2¼–2½in (55–63mm) thick board, you want to end up with a 2in (50mm) thick finished blank.

5 Now plane the topside of the seat blank down to the marked line that you've just made.

Once you've achieved a flat seat, it's normally best to drill mortices for the legs (see pages 94–95). If you are following a chair project, it is only after these holes are drilled and you have done a dry fitting of the undercarriage that you should proceed to carving the seat (overleaf).

Either a metal or a wooden plane can be used

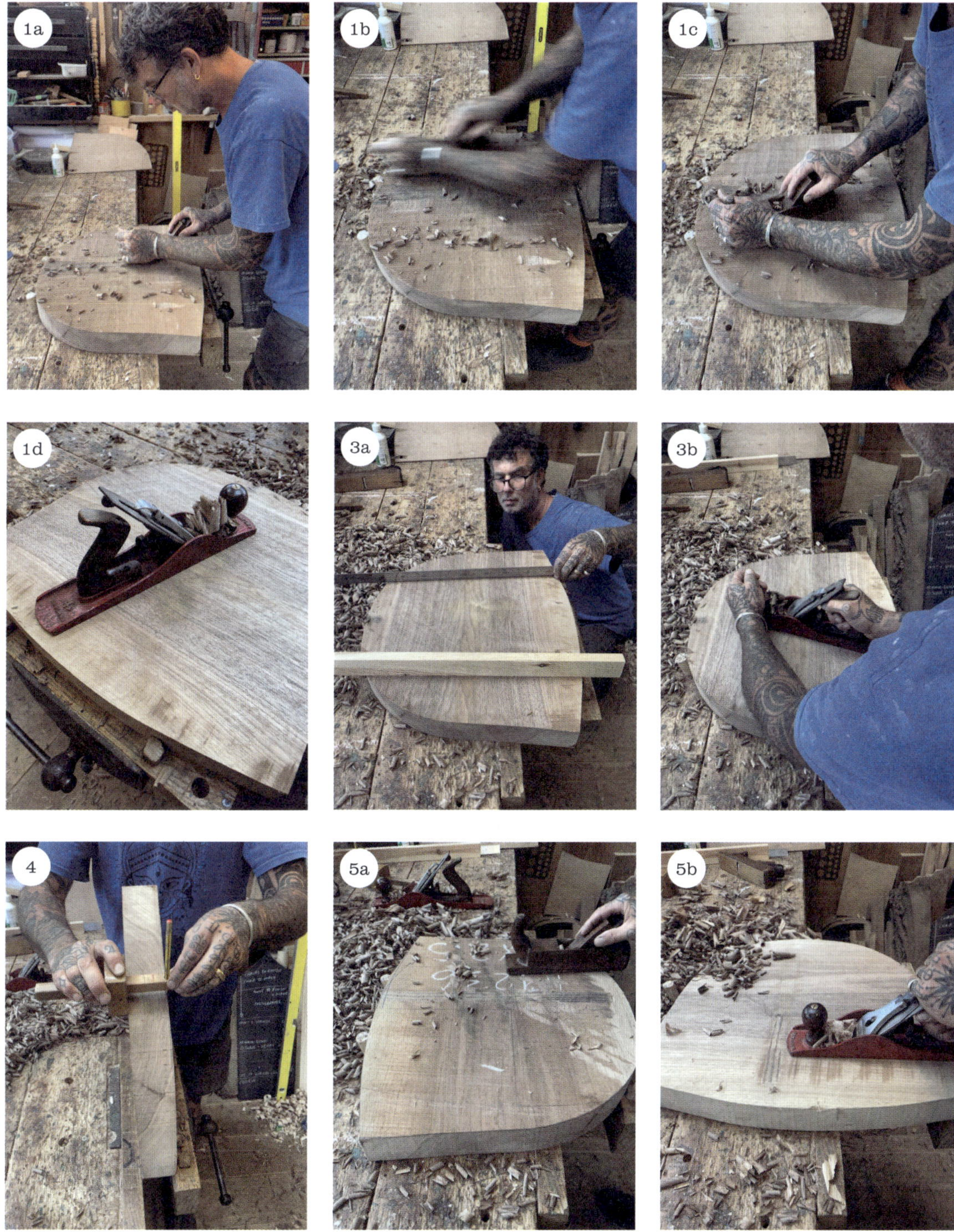
1a
1b
1c
1d
3a
3b
4
5a
5b

MAKING ARM BOW AND CREST BLANKS

For making arm bows and curved crests which you will be steam bending, you'll need a green or air-dried hardwood board; for a straight crest, it should be kiln-dried. For steam bending, choose a board with fairly uniform and straight grain. For a straight crest, you could choose a kiln-dried board with an interesting, funky grain because it won't be subject to the strains of steam bending. When ripping with a saw, make sure you follow the grain as much as possible, particularly in the middle section that will be the most curved.

The 54¼in (1380mm) long blank that is bent to make the arm bows for the low back and lobster pot chairs has a 4-degree angled cut made at each end.

The reason for this is that the arm bow will sit in between the handle blocks of a bending strap that you will use during steam bending. The strap handles will fit the blank snugly, and these blocks prevent the outside of the bend from stretching when the blank is bent. The inside of the bend is forced into compression, which is much more tolerable for the wood fibres than being stretched. The angled cuts allow for a small gap between the strap handle blocks and the inside face of the bow blank.

The angled cut allowing the arm bow to bend correctly

2

3

5

MAKING THE BLANKS

1 For an arm bow, choose a board that's at least 54¼in (1380mm) long and 1½in (38mm) wide and thick. For the lobster pot chair's crest, the board should be at least 26¼in (665mm) long, 2¼in (55mm) wide and 1¼in (32mm) thick, while the Shaker bench's crest should be at least 47½in (1205mm) long, 4¼in (110mm) wide and 1¼in (32mm) thick.

2 If you are making an arm bow, use a marking gauge to mark a 1¼in (32mm) wide strip. Ideally, this strip will contain the straight grain all down its length. If you are making a crest, the strip should be 2in (50mm) wide for the lobster pot armchair and 4in (100mm) wide for the Shaker bench. Use a bandsaw or a circular saw to cut off the strip.

3 For an arm bow, turn the blank on its sawn side, set the guide on the saw to 1¼in (32mm) for the lobster pot chair and 1⅛in (28mm) for the low back chair, then reduce the width of the sawn side to this width. If you don't have a guide on your saw, use a marking gauge to mark a strip, then cut by eye. For crests, reduce the width to 1in (25mm).

4 The whole blank should be reduced to 54in (1370mm) in length for the arm bows, 26in (660mm) for the lobster pot's crest and 47¼in (1200mm) for the Shaker bench's crest.

5 If you are making an arm bow, use a bevel gauge and a saw to cut a 4-degree angle off each end of the 1⅛in (28mm) side of the board for the low back chair or one of the 1¼in (32mm) sides of the lobster pot chair. The cuts should be in opposite directions to make a trapezoid shape.

STEAM BENDING ARMS AND CRESTS

Steam bending is a somewhat dark art: even after years of practice, failures still often occur. However, its miraculous nature when it works is never lost on me, and if you stick to the guidelines below, you will increase your chances of achieving successful steam bends. You'll need to steam bend the arm bows for the low back and lobster pot chairs, and you'll also need to steam bend the crest for the latter.

You should be very well prepared before starting a steam-bending session. Make sure the forms are lined up and have any tools to hand. Always set aside plenty of time for steam bending – it never goes well when rushed – and put on a pair of leather gloves before you start.

Despite following every detail in these instructions, a bend may fail. There are many possible reasons such as the timber used for the blank not being suitable or having an unknown weakness. Try not to be disheartened; check that all the working methods have been followed and try a different stock of timber. It is a process that initially requires a lot of trial and error, and you will need to accumulate some knowledge in order to be more successful, but persevere – it will be worth it!

Before you start, you'll need to make a form for bending the blank, and a base that you can attach to the form to allow you to clamp both to your bench. You will also need to make a bending strap that holds the work to the piece until it dries.

MAKING A FORM

To make a steam-bending form, you will need some sort of thick sheet material. I look out for old sections of kitchen work surfaces in skips, which are perfect as they are strong (and free). Enlarge the plan for the form to create a template of the correct size (see pages 76–77). Trace around this template onto your section of kitchen surface, mirrored on a centre line, then cut the shape out. The notches indicated on the plan are to enable you to use clamps during steam bending.

MAKING THE BASE

The form will need to sit on top of a base, which could simply be a double thickness of plywood, or in my case a section of hardwood kitchen work surface. I fit bolts to the base and then screw the base to my workbench. The form is drilled with the same pair of holes on the centre line, so it can be bolted onto the base. The advantage of this system is that if you are doing a lot of steam bending, you can swap forms as you go along, removing a form with a bend strapped to it and replacing it with a new form for the next bend.

The base should be about 26 × 20 × 2in (660 × 505 × 50mm). The template is on page 220. Decide which is the top surface of the board, then turn the board over to mark it for drilling. Measure the centre point along the longer side and divide the board in half with a pencil line, then draw a line parallel to the longer

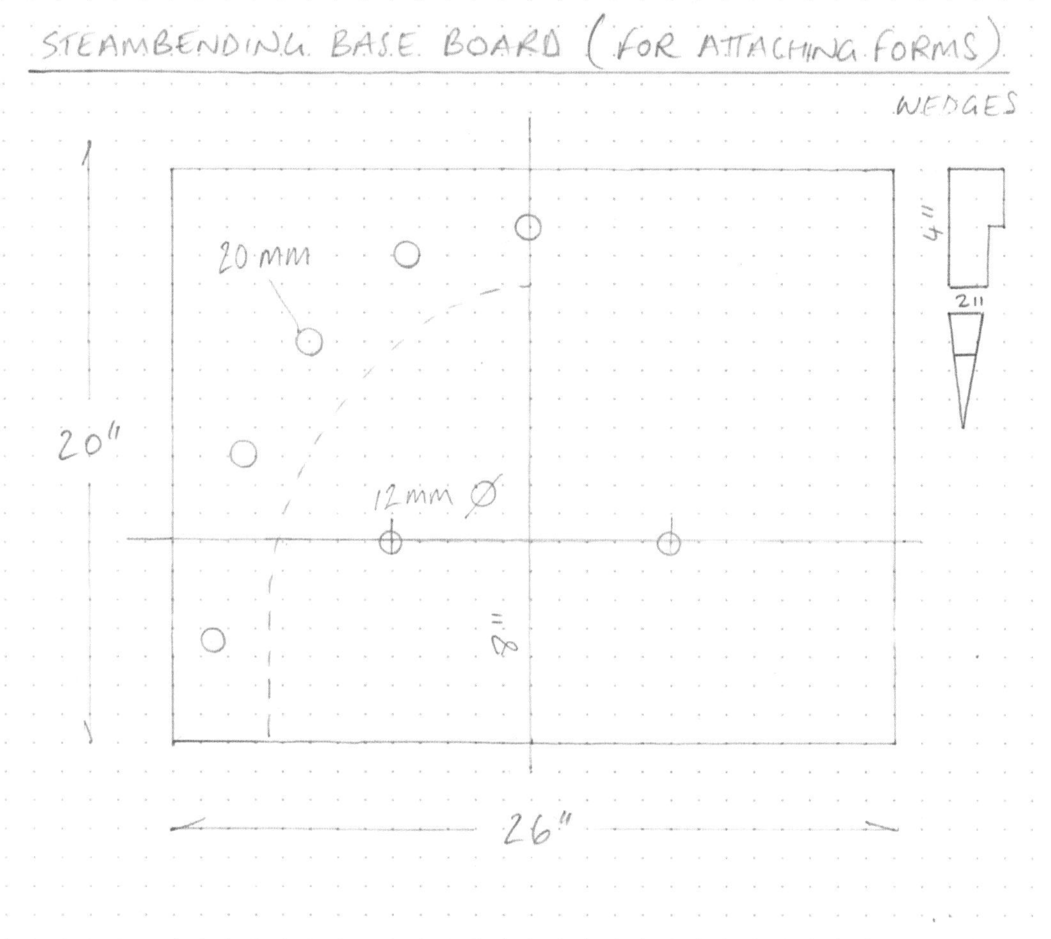

front edge, 4in (100mm) from the edge. Measure along this line from the centre line 7in (180mm) in either direction. This will be the drilling points for the bolt holes.

You will be drilling two holes to take ⅜in (10mm) bolts. First drill ⅜in (10mm) deep with the biggest drill bit you have, at least 1in (25mm), to house the top of the bolt so that the base can sit flush on your work surface. Now drill through to the other side with a ½in (12mm) auger bit to make holes for the bolts.

You will notice that in the diagram of my base there are a number of holes marked on it. These are ¾in (20mm) holes to take pegs, so that as you pull the bend you can peg and wedge it in place. To mark these out, place the bending form in position and bolt it loosely to the base. The material for steam bending will be 1¼in (32mm) wide, so draw a line that is 1¾in (45mm) from the edge of the form (you can cut a small block that is 1¾in/45mm thick, and tape your pencil to it). Then, starting at the centre point, mark for a drill hole at 4in (100mm) intervals.

MAKING A STEAM BENDING STRAP

You will need to make a bending strap to hold the wood in place. You can purchase a sheet of stainless steel online: 5⁄64in (2mm) is the thickness needed because 3⁄64in (1mm) will stretch and 1⁄8in (3mm) won't be flexible enough. Stainless steel is the best choice as it won't leave stains on the timber. If you are steaming a lot of material, and fairly often, it is helpful to have at least a couple of these bending straps to allow for a little cooling between uses.

MATERIALS

- 2 wooden blocks: 15¾ × 2 × 2in (400 × 50 × 50mm) in ash or oak
- 1 stainless steel strap: 64 × 1 × 5⁄64in (1640 × 25 × 2mm)
- 4 M4 coach bolts, with nuts and washers: 2½in (60mm) long
- 5⁄32in (4mm) wood drill bit
- 5⁄32in (4mm) metal drill bit

Cut out the handles from the wooden blocks following the provided plans, making the slot in them 5⁄64in (2mm) thick and 5in (125mm) long.

Slot the steel strap into the handle slots, then hold it in place to the handles with squeeze clamps. Measure the length of the strap between the angle block ends to ensure it is 54in (1370mm), which is the length of the bow blank to be bent. If the strap is oversized, cut the 5⁄64in (2mm) slot so it's a little longer.

You should then drill a pair of holes through the whole of each handle and the metal strap. Make sure the handles are firmly clamped to the steel strap. Mark for drilling according to the plan, marking the drilling point with a bradawl. Drill through the first side of the handle with the wood bit until it hits the strap, then swap to the metal drill bit, and drill slowly through the steel and the rest of the wood. Tap the bolts through, and then add the washers and tighten the nuts.

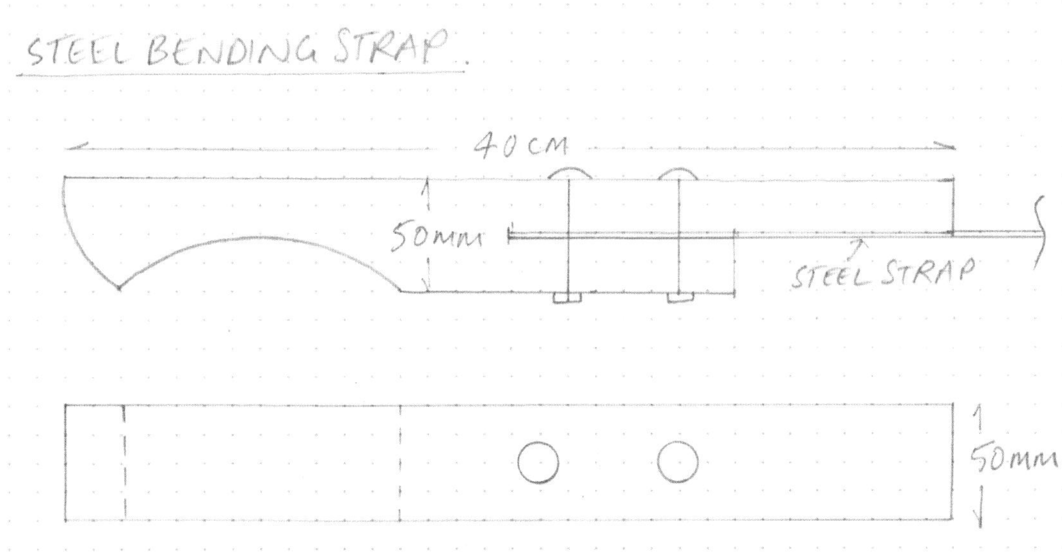

OCTAGONAL TABLE
18" LEGS.

SOAKING AND STEAMING THE WOOD

At this point, the blank is ready to soak for a few days before steam bending. Whatever you use, soak the pieces for a week or so in a trough or a pipe filled with water so that they are sopping wet (see page 19). This might seem counter-intuitive since steaming will dry the wood out, but the reality is the wetter the better.

The piece will then need to be steamed in a very steamy container (see pages 19–20) for one hour per square inch (6.25cm^2), but make it a bit longer if the wood is ash or it has been kiln-dried. An hour and a half should normally suffice. If you have placed a few pieces in the steamer to bend, you could bend the smaller pieces first while allowing a bit more steaming time for the larger pieces.

While the wood is inside the billowing steamer, make sure you have everything ready and in place for bending. For an arm bow, the bending form should be bolted to its base, which in turn should be clamped to the bench. For a crest, secure the bending form in a vice. Have the bending strap, clamps, ratchet straps, a hammer, pegs, wedges and any other needed tools standing by, ready to be used, and ensure you put your leather gloves on.

If you are bending a crest, have some plywood blocks to hand, so that when affixing a clamp, you can place them between the clamp head and the steamed wood to avoid damaging and discolouring the wood.

UNDERSTANDING THE NATURE OF WOOD

Live trees need to be flexible and be able to bend in the wind, particularly at the base of the tree, where it enters the earth. This part of the tree is often very fibrous and intrinsically strong. Wood will therefore bend, too, especially in heat. There are some basic principles involved that are useful to understand. In simple terms, as you bend a length of wood, the outer side stretches while the inner side compresses and the middle remains the same length.

You can render the wood more pliable by steaming it in a box or tube, or if small enough, by boiling. This will loosen the lignin and cellulose in the wood so that, for a short time, its fibres can slide against each other before resetting when the wood cools down.

Timber tends to compress more easily than it stretches, so with northern European timber species, it is best to use a steel strap on the outside of the bend. The blocks of the strap limit the outside stretch and force the inside edge into more compression. Compression can cause a rippling effect through the timber, which is the distortion caused by the compression. This is easily cleaned up with sharp tools.

I have seen chairmakers in the USA easily bend white oak without straps. In the UK, freshly riven ash will also bend without straps, but these are exceptions, not the rule. I find it difficult to find young fast-grown ash in my locality, so I tend to buy air-dried or green rough-sawn boards.

Note that kiln-dried boards are trickier to bend because the cellulose sets during the kiln-drying process, but it is still possible, often very successfully.

2a

2b

3a

3b

4a

4b

4c

5a

5b

BENDING AN ARM BOW

1 Remove the 54in (1370mm) long arm piece from the steam box, use quick grip clamps to secure it to the steel strap and handles, and if there is a gap at one end, use a thin layer of plywood to fill it. The longer edge of the bow which was cut at a 4-degree angle should be at the top against the steel strap.

2 Place the whole piece, with the steel strap on the outside, on top of the bending form. Put a centre peg into the base, tap it in and drive a wedge hard into the gap between the strap and the peg. Drive the wedge in from right to left. This will clamp the wood to the form.

3 Now bend one side against the form, pulling against the top wedge. Make sure not to twist the strap, and be mindful to pull the 'corner' of the wood into the 'corner' of the form. Bend halfway, and add a peg to the form to stop the bend opening. Repeat for the other side of the bend, again to about halfway, adding a peg to secure it.

4 Next, go back to the first side and pull the remainder of the bend tight to the form. Add a peg and wedge. Repeat for the second side.

5 Pass a ratchet strap around the ends of the wood and the handles of the strap and ratchet the two ends tightly to the form. The form with the arm bow strapped to it can now be unbolted from the base and they can be put somewhere dry and relatively warm for two or three days.

6 The bow needs to be removed from the form before the final kiln-drying stage so that the inner curve dries properly. However, if the arm bow is released, the bend will open up almost fully, but after a few days of drying, the tendency of the bend is to do the opposite and close up. Adding a batten and strap will prevent this from happening. First measure the distance between the widest point of the bend and cut a piece of batten to that length. The batten should have a profile of roughly ¾ × 1½in (20 × 38mm).

7 Loosen the ratchet around the arm bow by a notch and remove the form. Place the batten between the bend ends and re-tighten the ratchet. The bend can then be left to kiln dry for a couple of days. It is then ready to use, but keep the batten in place until you need to use the bow in your project.

BENDING A CREST

1 Using a strong F or G clamp, clamp one end of the steaming hot crest blank tight to the form.

2 Apply your body weight to the other end and add a large F or G clamp close to the midpoint, tightening it as far as you can.

3 Position another F or G clamp towards the bending end and tighten. Tighten this and the midpoint clamp alternatively until you have achieved the bend.

4 Once cooled, the crest clamped to the form can be air dried for two or three days.

5 Since the crest has a much shallower bend than the arm bow, there's much less risk of it losing its shape when the form is removed. Unclamp it from the form and clamp it to a board so the inner curve is clear. Put it in a kiln for another couple of days to dry out, then it's ready for use.

2a

2b

2c

3

2a

2b

3a

3b

4a

4b

REUSING THE STEEL STRAP

If you wish to reuse the steel strap, you'll need to remove it from the form and the arm bow.

1 To release the steel strap, ratchet a second ratchet strap around the form above the first ratchet strap, high enough to avoid trapping the handles of the bending strap. Ratchet it tight.

2 Undo and remove the original ratchet strap and then, with a hammer, knock the steel strap's handles outwards from the ends of the bent wood.

3 This will leave a gap underneath the steel strap that you can pass the original ratchet strap through, then tighten the ratchet to secure the wooden bend to the form.

4 You can now release the second ratchet strap, and that will free the steel strap for use again.

TENONS AND MORTICES

Cutting accurate tenons that fit snugly in mortices is important to getting nice tight joints, and you can make them on a lathe, with a tenon cutter or with a spokeshave. Regardless of how you make them, you will need a drill bit in the same diameter as the tenons to drill their mortices.

MAKING TENONS

However you choose to make your tenons, they should only be cut on parts after they have been super-dried (see pages 18–19). If there is still moisture in the part, the tenon will continue to shrink after fitting and will likely become loose. Super-drying ensures that the tenon has no moisture in it and therefore cannot shrink. It can only expand with humidity, which renders the joint tighter.

After cutting a tenon, you can remove any shoulder with a block plane for a nice smooth profile and tight fit. For more on fitting tenons and making adjustments, see page 110.

Making tenons with a lathe

I usually turn my tenons for legs and stretchers on my pole lathe. It is the most accurate way to make them because it ensures the tenon remains in line with the axis of the whole piece, helping these parts to remain straight when fitted. Turning tenons on a pole lathe can be performed on both turned parts and octagon parts. For the latter, you will have to find the centres of each end and add lathe centres with a bradawl.

When turning the tenons on a lathe for stretchers, you need to make sure that you keep the final length marks before turning the tenons. To do this, mark these lines with a skew chisel. Turn the tenons on the stretcher, check the measurements and then trim the length with a Japanese saw.

Making tenons with tenon cutters

If you don't have a lathe, you'll need a tenon cutter to cut tenons on legs and stretchers, along with a drill bit in a matching diameter. Tenon cutters come in a variety of sizes, and the ones you'll need for the projects in this book are ¾in (20mm), $^{11}/_{16}$in (18mm), ⅝in (16mm), $^{9}/_{16}$in (14mm) and ½in (12mm). Veritas also make lovely tenon cutters that fit into a drill chuck, but they involve making an investment.

Using a tenon cutter

Measuring sticks and a stretcher

Making a mark aligned to the tape

If you are cutting the tenons on a stretcher with a tenon cutter, trim the stretcher to its final length in the project before cutting the tenons. Remove any shoulder so that the stretcher will have a nice smooth fit.

Making tenons with a spokeshave

You could also carefully make an octagonal tenon with a spokeshave, then take off its corners. If you make it slightly oversized, it will twist nicely into a round mortice.

Making tenons on spindles

Longer or thinner parts such as spindles do not turn well on a lathe due to their flexibility, so it's easier and more accurate to use a round tenon cutter. The tenon cutter has to be aimed straight on the end of the spindle. For most projects, the tenon at the top of a spindle will be thinner than the tenon at the bottom. Ideally, the long tapered top part will have a slight concavity.

Measuring for stretchers

A pair of sticks is a great tool for measuring the distance between two opposing mortices when fitting a stretcher. Simply place a stick in each mortice and hold the sticks together where they meet. Make sure they are pushed into the holes before making a mark across the sticks with a pen, then, while keeping an eye on the marks, remove the sticks and place them on a ruler, lining the marks up with each other. Measure the distance on the ruler. Simple.

On all stretcher measurements, I add $\frac{3}{16}$in (5mm). This ensures that the whole structure is stretched ever so slightly upon assembly, creating a little tension. I usually write these measurements on the component in between the parts measured, neatly and small.

MAKING MORTICES

The appropriate stage for making the mortices in which the tenons fit will depend on both what part is being worked on and what type of project you are making. For example, leg mortices should always be made after preparing a seat blank (see pages 76–79), but before the seat is carved, because the process of drilling the mortices can cause wear and tear. By drilling these holes while the seat has a flat surface, the measuring tools needed to guide the drill will be sitting level to allow you to get the angle of the drill correctly. If you are making a chair with a carved seat, it is only after these holes are drilled and you have done a dry fitting of the undercarriage that you should proceed to carving the seat (see pages 102–8).

To make the mortices for the spindles and arm posts, you can choose to drill their mortices before or after carving the seat, but you'll need to do so using the jig specified in the project, which will ensure the holes in the bows or crests align with the holes in the seat.

When drilling a mortice to a specific depth, you can mark the drill bit with a piece of tape at the required length.

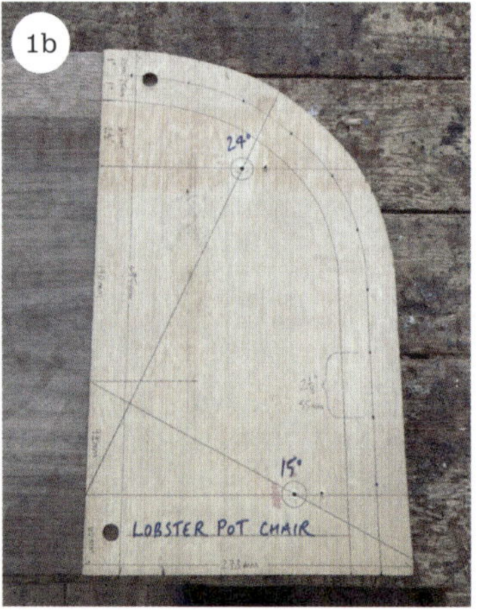

DRILLING LEG MORTICES

Having accurate leg mortices is a crucial part of the chairmaking process. You want the front pair of legs to be well balanced with each other, and the same goes for the rear pair. There is a little tolerance to the drilling – a degree or so won't necessarily be noticeable to the eye – but if your drilling is very wayward, the end result may look like your chair is going for a walk rather than sitting steadily!

For the purposes of this book, and to make this process as accessible as possible, the leg mortices for all the projects are drilled with a ¾in (20mm) auger bit and are kept as straight mortices, though you could use a tapered reamer if you wish.

There are lots of different angles of legs in chairmaking and the patterns vary. For this example, we will look at the back leg mortices being drilled at 24 degrees, with the front legs set at 15 degrees. However, when working on a specific project always check the plans and follow the degrees recommended for drilling.

When drilling mortices for legs through a seat it is important that you have the underside of the seat planed nicely flat. If you have a helper who can help you align the drill as you are drilling, all the better. They can check that the drill bit is lined up with the try square and the bevel gauge as you drill. Alternatively, you could place a mirror alongside you – a quick glance will tell you whether you're lined up correctly. Go slow, and always check your alignment often.

1 Transfer the sight lines and drilling points from the template to the underside of the chair, ensuring the sight lines are marked clearly in pencil and the drilling points are made with a bradawl.

2 Clamp your seat to a low bench if you have one. It's a good idea to include a thick piece of leftover plywood between the seat and the bench to drill into once the auger tip emerges from the other side of the seat. The seat should be underside up, so the sight lines and drilling points marked on this underside will be visible.

3 Set your bevel gauge to an acute angle of 24 degrees. Place it so it is sitting along the sight line and the metal side angled to point towards the centre of the chair (remember the chair is upside down). Now place a try square or engineer's square at a right angle with the upright aligned with the line.

4 Start drilling by placing the lead screw of the drill at the drilling mark, and glancing from the side, line the angle of the drill up to the bevel gauge, but make sure it doesn't tilt by also keeping it aligned with the try square. Drill slowly, stop and check your angle.

5 You should also be able to step to the side and look up the sight line towards the auger bit, and the try square should line up with both the sight line and the centre of the auger's length (this is where a helper can be useful). If you need to, adjust the tilt or splay of the drill.

6 Again, proceed slowly and check angles often! Drill all the way through into the sacrificial plywood. Repeat for the other back leg, then adjust your bevel gauge to 15 degrees (or the angle for the specific project) for the front leg, and follow the same steps.

SIDE STRETCHER MORTICES

The back and front legs of the two chairs and the bench are at different angles, which means the centres of the swells are at slightly different heights when measured vertically down from the seat. This means the mortices for the side stretchers in the legs need to be angled towards each other.

To do this, first clamp the seat on top of a pair of blocks to the bench. This will stop the protruding leg tenons from getting in the way. If you're drilling the mortice first, have the back pair of legs furthest away from you.

The drill body or bit should be resting on the side of the corresponding front leg, so twist the rear leg very slightly towards the centre of the chair so you can aim the drill at its centre.

To align the drill, the bit should be pointing from the drill mark in the front leg towards the drill mark in the rear leg. A mirror to the side of you can help you with this alignment, or just move to the side while holding the drill steady against the leg.

Drill slowly, being careful to hold the drill or bit steadily against the front leg. To double check that you are drilling the leg centrally, look carefully at how the drill bit starts to cut. It should be cutting the hole evenly. If the drill cutter starts to score the cut, it is scoring to one side only, so stop drilling and twist the leg ever so slightly, until the bit is scoring evenly.

Once the rear pair are drilled, twist the legs back to their alignment.

Unclamp the seat, turn it around, reclamp it to the bench. This time, drill the mortices in the front pair of legs using the same method.

USING A REAMER FOR MAKING LEG MORTICES

If you happen to already have a tapered reamer, and you know how to use one, you could drill ⅝in (16mm) holes and then ream them with a 6-degree reamer. Follow the same technique as for using a drill, but adjust the bevel gauge to 3 degrees less than the drilling angle – so 21 degrees and 12 degrees – and sight from above the reamer, lining up its point with both the try square and the sight line as well as setting the angle to the bevel gauge.

DRILLING SPINDLE MORTICES FOR SEATS WITH ARM BOWS

One of the trickier processes in chairmaking is 'sighting' for drilling, when you need to ensure that the drill's alignment is straight from one point to another. This is particularly challenging when drilling the mortices for spindles through an arm bow and down into or through the seat. The main issue is that because you are drilling through the bow, the drill point you are aiming at on the seat is obscured by the arm bow itself. While it is usually easy to align the drill's direction from the side by moving your head so you can see the drill point on the seat, it's very difficult to drill at the correct angle when looking from the front.

The solution is to draw a line from the drill point on the arm bow (A) towards the drill point on the seat (B), and then make a second line from the drill point on the seat that is the same length and in the same direction as the line you've just drawn on the arm bow. Point C is where the line on the arm bow touches the inside edge of the bow, and point D is the end of the line you drew on the seat.

You can then hold the edge of a ruler between points C and D, and you will have your exact drill alignment – shifted inwards from points A and B – which you can use when drilling the mortices. You will need to clamp or rest this edge in position while drilling, so make sure your ruler or straightedge is rigid. I often use a framing square.

At the front of the chair, where the opposing sides of the arm bow are parallel, drawing the drilling sight lines and points A and B is straightforward. You can join pairs of drill points from arm to arm with a ruler and strike a pencil line across the arms, making a note of the distance between the drill mark and where the line touches the edge of the bow. On the seat you can join the corresponding pairs of drill points with a ruler, and draw lines from the drill points towards each other. The lines on the seat should be the same length as the corresponding lines on the bow.

However, you can't do this on the curved sections of the arm bow; instead you'll need to use an alternative method. First, imagine a line that connects the drill point on the arm (point A) and the corresponding drill point on the seat (point B) – you may find placing an object on the seat at point B will help. Draw a line from point A to the inside edge of the bow where this imaginary line crosses it (point C), and note down how long this line is.

Next, draw a second line along this imaginary line away from point B (the mortice drill hole on the seat). This line should be the same length as the corresponding line on the arm bow. You may find it helps to look at the bow and the seat from above so you can see the angle of the line you drew on the top of the bow. Your imaginary line should be straight from points A through to D.

Once you have marked points C and D for all the mortices, you can drill them as described above.

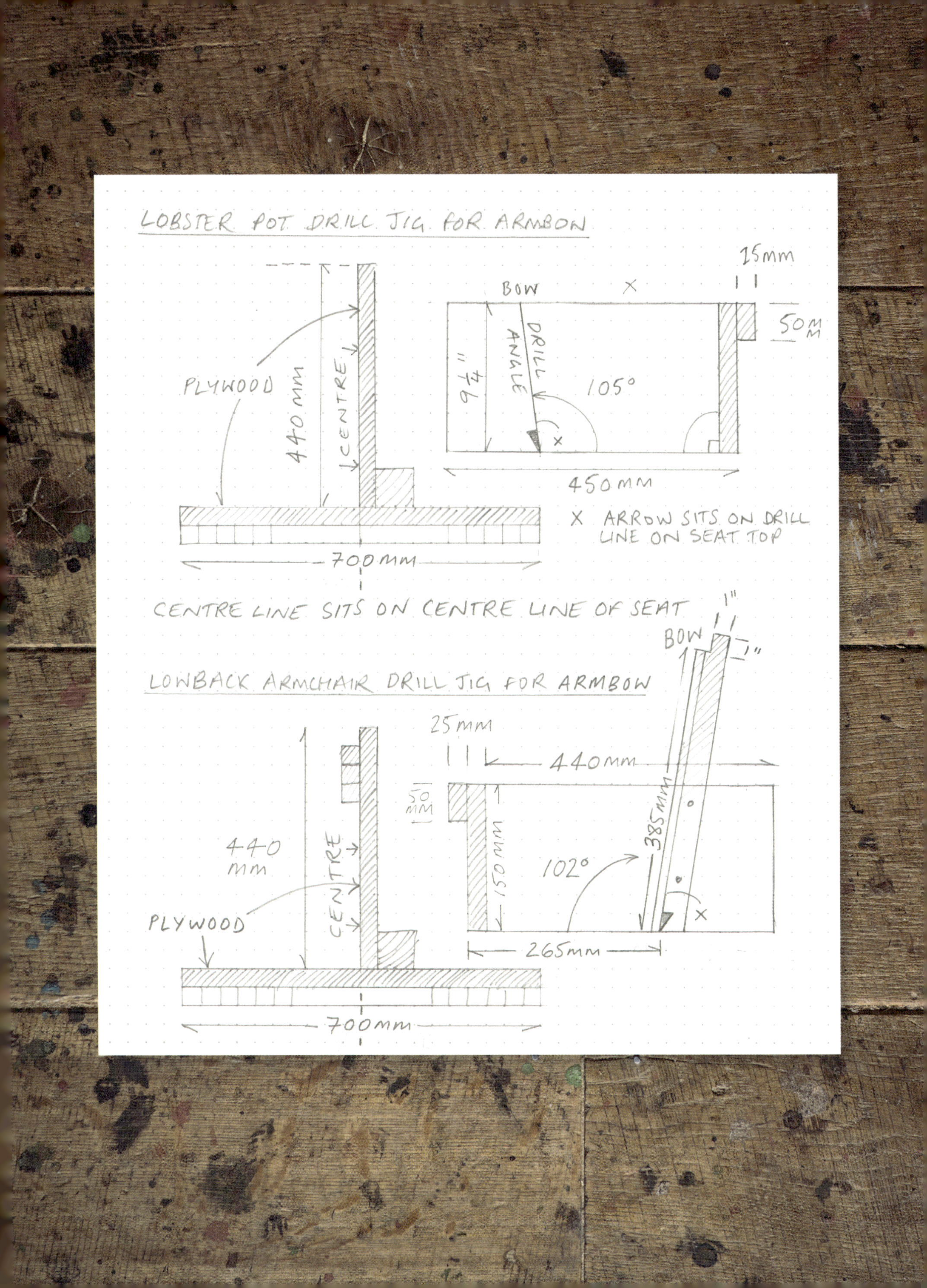

LOBSTER POT DRILL JIG FOR ARMBOW

PLYWOOD
440 MM
CENTRE
700MM

BOW
X
15MM
50MM
DRILL ANGLE
9½"
105°
X
450MM

X ARROW SITS ON DRILL LINE ON SEAT TOP

CENTRE LINE SITS ON CENTRE LINE OF SEAT

LOWBACK ARMCHAIR DRILL JIG FOR ARMBOW

440 MM
CENTRE
PLYWOOD
700MM

1"
BOW
1"
25MM
440MM
50 MM
150MM
385MM
102°
X
265MM

JIGS FOR ARM BOWS

Where a chair project includes an arm bow, it is helpful to use a drilling jig to set up and drill the mortices in the arm bows through to the seats. You may need a drill bit extension to drill all the way to the seat when using the jig. Each jig has a drill angle line drawn on it, and when positioned on the seat, it terminates on the spindle deck of the seat, on the drill line marked on the seat. The arm bow should be aligned to the jig and both should be fastened securely with clamps before you begin to drill.

The jigs are made from two pieces of ¾in (20mm) thick plywood constructed into a T shape, ideally held together by a 2in (50mm) square section of softwood, but anything similar would be fine as long as it is square. Follow the jigs' plans for the dimensions, making sure to cut out the notch for the low back chair.

The top part of the T shape should sit across the front of the seat, with the centre piece of plywood sitting at the back centre point of the seat. One side of this piece of plywood will be the centre face of the jig (see the project's plan). Screwed to the upper front edge of the jig is a length of 2 × 1in (50 × 25mm) timber. It has a central mark, and like a ruler there should be 1in (25mm) marks from this central mark towards either end. It will help align the bow centrally on the jig.

The upright on the jig for the low back chair is where the bow's rear centre point sits. The notch for supporting the arm bow is 1in (25mm) square.

The upright can be made from 2 × 1in (50 × 25mm) plywood or pine. The important thing is that the upright is attached to the jig at the correct angle, and that the drill point and sight line X are correctly drawn onto the upright, ⅜in (10mm) from the front edge of the upright. For the lobster pot armchair, the drill angle and X are drawn on the centre face of the jig.

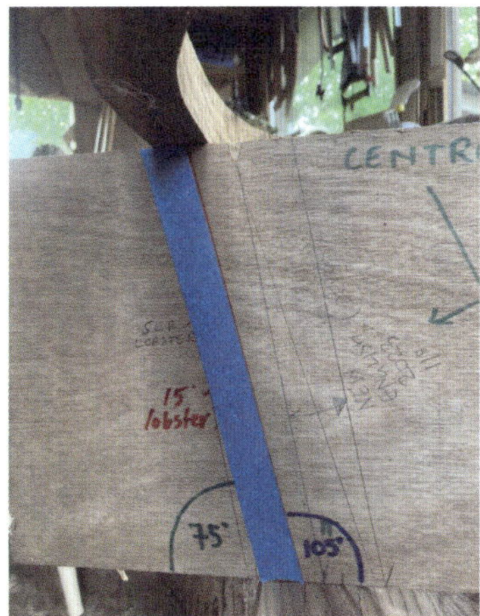

CARVING A SEAT

One of the distinctive features of Windsor chairs, and also Welsh stickleback chairs, is that they usually feature a carved seat. These are sometimes quite heavily carved, but more often they are quite shallow carves. A very heavily carved seat is not necessarily comfortable unless the shape is really good. A shallowly carved seat can be comfortable if the ergonomics of the whole chair are good.

I like to carve a seat so that it is ¾in (20mm) at the deepest point, which is in between the back leg mortices. This is a generous bit of carving, which is why my seats are usually made with blanks that are at least 2in (50mm) thick. Nevertheless, carve only as deeply as you feel confident or as your tools allow. Be careful not to carve through the bottom of the seat, particularly if your seat is as thin as 1½in (38mm).

Before you start: remember that you should always drill and fit the undercarriage before carving a seat. Whether you want to also drill the mortices for the spindles and arm posts before carving the seat or afterwards is up to you.

Using an adze

You'll need to use an adze to carve out the seat shape. When using the adze, hold it with both hands at the end of the handle and allow your hands to pivot from the wrist. The adze should make a shallow 'trough' cut. Experiment with the height that you are sitting at – it's best that your head height is higher than the top of the seat blank.

Don't go over border lines such as the chalk circle when cutting with the adze. The border needs to remain clean of any cuts. If you are 'adzing' for the first time, start in the middle of the seat until you get used to it.

WOOD

1

4a

4b

CARVING THE SEAT

You'll need to mark and carve the seat in stages, starting with a basic shape and getting more precise as you proceed. The tools you'll need for my method are a short-handled adze and a travisher, but you could instead use a large carving chisel.

As the adze will be used across the grain of the seat, make sure you look at your seat blank and mount it accordingly. My seat blank has a side-to-side grain direction, so the seat is mounted with the grain running horizontally, which means I can cut in a downward direction with the adze.

When working with the travisher, if you have a bench vice with dogs, then use that to clamp your work flat to the bench. A good alternative method is to screw a batten to the centre line on the underside of the seat, then you can clamp the batten in a vice, allowing you to work on the topside. I hold my travisher with my thumbs behind the blade, but find your way with this tool.

1 Using a piece of chalk, mark out an area for roughly carving the topside of the seat; it should be 1in (25mm) within the pencil mark marking the edge of the carved area. This is to allow for a margin of error when using the adze. Divide the chalk circle in half: this will be your dividing line and should be in line with the grain on your seat (so it may be side to side or back to front).

2 Use a marking gauge to divide the edge of the seat, drawing a line around it at 1in (25mm) from the top surface of the seat. This line will help you draw the curve in step 10 and mark the arris to be removed in step 18.

3 Mount the seat in a vice (remember to clamp it with the grain running horizontally). You can use a piece of waste timber to create some distance between the work and the vice jaws.

4 Starting just below the chalk line at the top, cut down towards the halfway point first. You are trying to carve a shape that resembles a shallow dish. Adze the top half of the circle. As you reach the outer edges, angle the cuts towards the centre.

5

6

7a

7b

8

9

5 Turn the seat over in the vice, and work on the other half of the chalk circle. Repeat this process until you reach a depth you're happy with. You can check the depth of the cut by laying a ruler across the seat and looking down.

6 Now, give another pass to the back half of the chalk circle, making the deepest carved area towards the back of the seat, where the dotted line marks between the two rear leg mortices.

7 For the legs at the front of the seat, use the chalk to draw two curved areas for carving, but leaving the centre line clear. Now carve this area out towards the back, creating a flat downward slope to the low point of the seat (at the dotted line).

8 Now it's time to use the travisher. First, clean up the rough adzed surface, taking light cuts from the outside towards the centre.

9 Once the surface is smoother, the travisher will cut more easily and you can start to cut closely to the border line. Try to achieve a crisp edge from which the carved seat will drop. Work around the whole seat until it feels balanced and clean, but leave the very front edge for now.

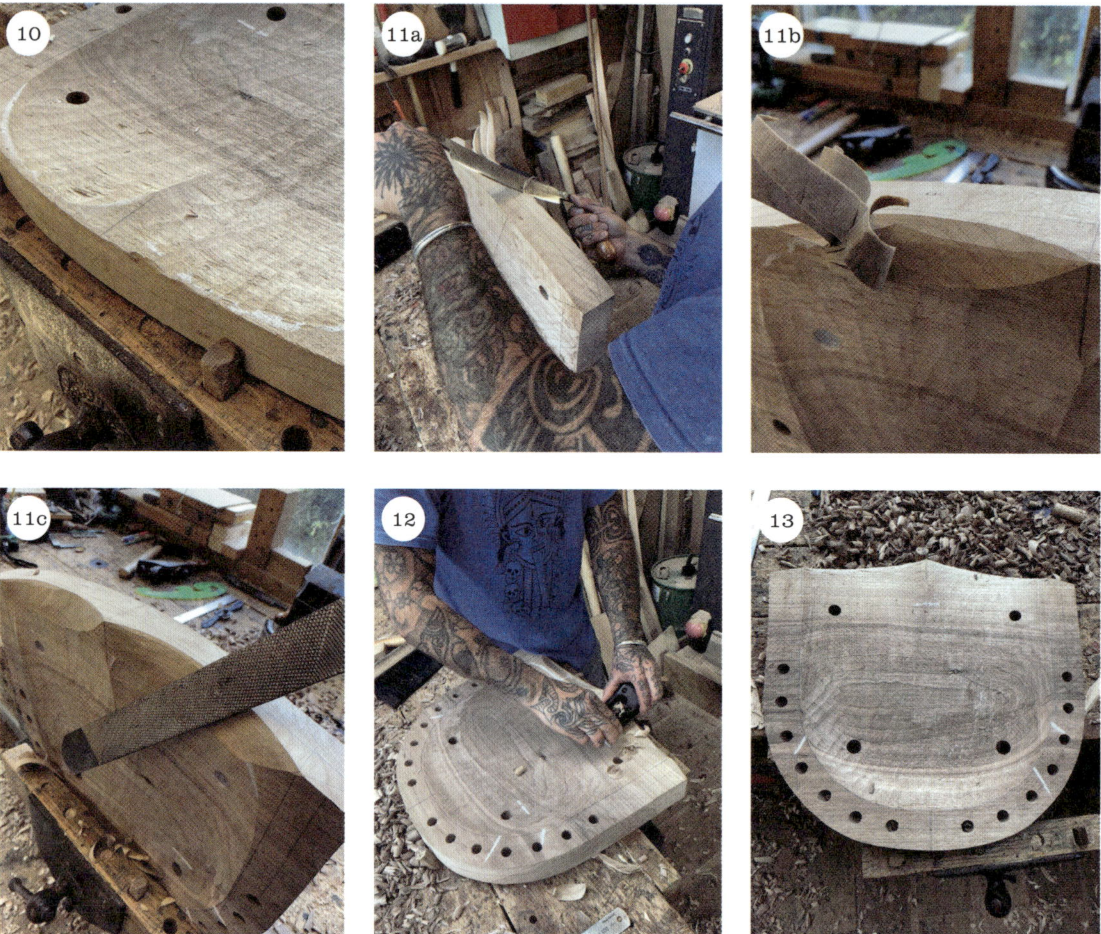

10 Using a French curve, draw the seat shape along the front edge, using the previously marked line as a guide and following the pattern in the specific project plan.

11 Mount the seat sideways. Now remove the front edge of the seat between the 2in (50mm) border lines, carving down to the pattern line to make two curves for the legs. Cut from the outer corners towards the bottom of the pattern, then from the pommel at the centre line (between the curves where the legs meet) to these cuts. You can use either a drawknife, a rasp file or a spokeshave to make these cuts, but use a rasp file to refine the shape.

12 Remount the seat in the vice and, going back to the travisher, remove the material between this carved front edge and the rest of the seat carve.

13 Have a look at the seat profile drawings: they show a 'high' point, between where the seat slopes subtly to the front edge and back towards the deepest part of the seat. The last detail will be to carve a sharp and precise pommel at the front of the seat.

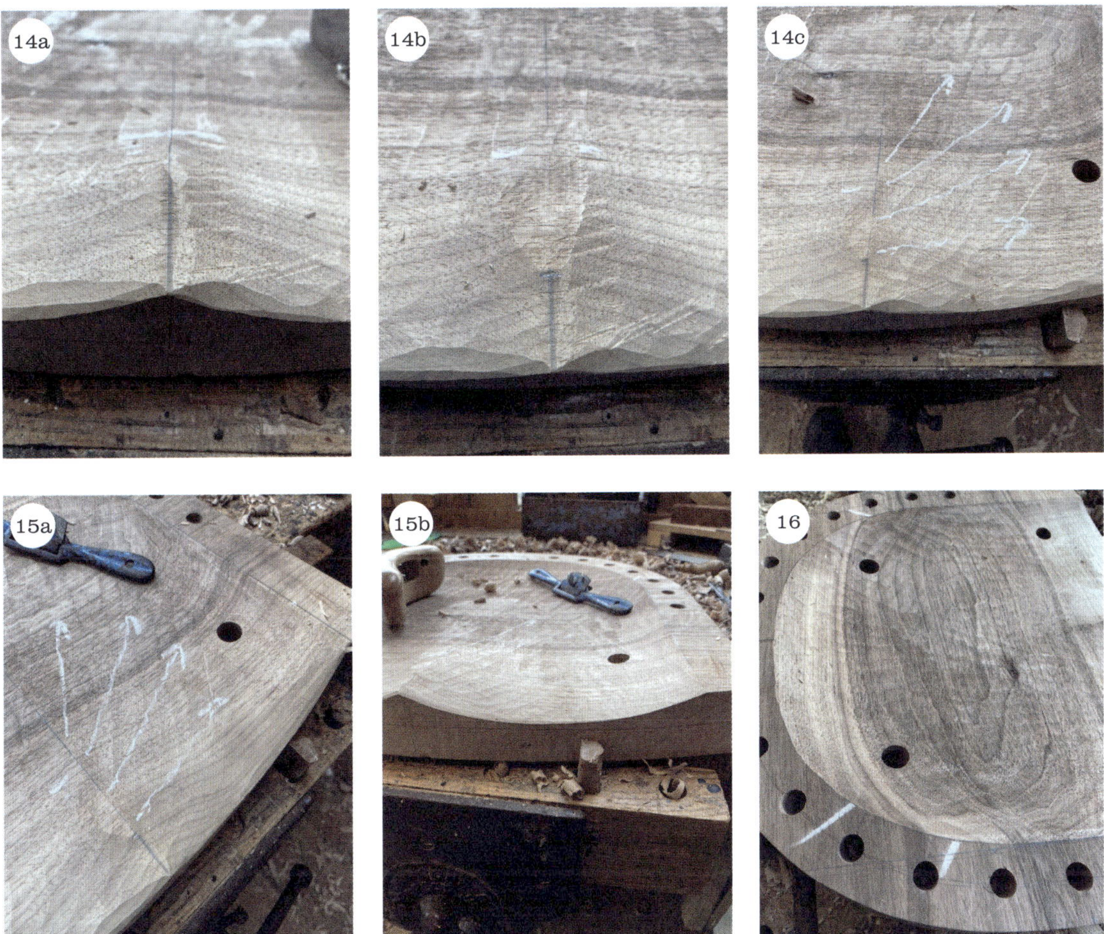

14 Restrike the centre line on the seat with a sharp pencil. Using the travisher, cut down and away from this line. You will end up with a sharp ridge with the pencil line sitting on top of that.

15 You now need to make this sharp ridge drop gently into the dish of the seat. Use a small block plane to remove the lump between the pommel and the dish, starting 1in (25mm) from the front edge. This will leave a flat spot and you'll need to restrike the centre line on this flat spot again. Carve away from this line so you have a crisp pommel that drops into the dish of the seat.

16 Next, use a curved soled spokeshave and a cabinet scraper to achieve a smoother surface over the whole seat.

17 Now mark up the underside of the seat, using the marking gauge to draw a line 1in (25mm) from the seat edge, all the way around the seat.

18 Remove the whole underside corner edge from the dividing line on the seat's side from step 2 to the underside line from step 17. Work on one surface at a time and draw lines through the material to be removed to ensure you remove the correct wood. Use a combination of drawknife, smoothing plane and spokeshave to remove the material, starting with the underside corner edge and taking a little off at a time. Work all the way around the seat until you get to the corner edge on the other side of the front of the chair.

19 Repeat this along the lower front edge of the seat, making sure the two edges meet crisply.

21 For the low back and lobster pot chairs, the top corner edge of the seat should also be removed. Mark it ¼in (6mm) from the corner edge of the seat on the top and the side. Remove the material in between the marks with a block plane.

22 Finally, mark on the front edge of the seat from the top of the carved curve of the seat to the bottom of the chamfer you've just made, and mirror this line on the top edge. Carefully remove this corner with a block plane, retaining the sharp corner of the carved front profile.

ASSEMBLING A CHAIR

When it comes to putting the parts of a chair together there are certain stages that should always be followed. It is essential to do a dry fit and make any necessary adjustments to ensure all the components will fit together well before adding even just a drop of glue. Once you're happy with the final dry fit, it will be time to add wedges to kerfs and glue up the chair.

DRY FITTING THE PARTS

Often, a chair will need to be put together and knocked apart again several times before the final assembly can take place. Perhaps the shoulder of a tenon needs to be slightly reduced to ensure a snug fit in a mortice or a clean line, or there's a pattern of grain that you particularly wish to see but it's hidden behind the chair. For these and other reasons, you'll find that as you progress through the various steps of making a chair, you'll need to assemble certain parts to see how they fit, and then knock them apart again to make adjustments or smooth the finish. At this stage, you don't use glue so you can take apart and assemble the pieces as often as needed: this is known as a dry fit.

If a tenon doesn't seem to be fitting snugly into a mortice, it may be because there is a 'shoulder' on the tenon where it meets the main area of the part. You will need to remove the shoulder: I do this by holding the piece, such as a spindle, flat in a vice and using a small block plane, but you could do the same job using a spokeshave and gripping the part in the jaws of a shave horse.

Positioning the components

When deciding on their positions, you should choose the best or cleanest pair of legs for the front of the seat, with a flat facet face on the leg facing forward. You can lay a ruler across the front faces to get them flat. Take the opportunity to twist the legs to show the best pattern at the front, or perhaps to hide a flaw! Each pair of front legs and each pair of back legs should match in their orientation of grain pattern.

Dry fit the legs so they 'squeakily' fit in the mortices in the seat, twisting their tenons into the mortices. If they don't quite fit, you can 'ease' the tenon by reducing it ever so slightly with a spokeshave, knife or a piece of sandpaper. Using a metal hammer, tap the legs firmly into the mortices until at least ⅜in (10mm) protrudes above the seat – you may need to cut the tenon at the top of a leg a little further if it doesn't. Once you are happy with the orientation of the legs, give each leg a sharp tap with a metal hammer to ensure they fit snugly, then mark up the leg positions (see box, 'Marking').

Try to choose the best and straightest spindles for the back of the seat – the chair will look better, again twisting them to fit the tenons into the mortices. Once you have finalized their positions and marked them, to refine the spindles before glue up, you can clamp them into a vice and plane the facets until you have an elegant taper up to a cut tenon. To avoid planing the tenon itself, wrap it in masking tape.

MARKING

Once you've decided on their positions during a dry fit, the legs, stretchers, spindles and arm posts will have to be taken apart again, so you need a way to keep track of which tenon fits in which mortice, which way the part should be oriented and how deeply it should be tapped in. You can do this by making marks clearly and neatly; for example, where the leg touches the sight line on the seat, add a letter, number or symbol on the leg and on the seat next to that leg's mortice. Keep these marks small neat and precise – you will need them to glue up calmly!

I usually mark the tops of spindles with clear numbers, usually with a fine permanent marker pen, and I mark the orientation of each spindle with a small pencil dot facing towards the front centre of the seat. I also make a few clear pencil marks showing where the bow sits on the spindles.

You may want to tidy up the underside of a seat after it has been marked, but first ensure you transfer all alignment marks to the inside of the mortice with a pen before planing or scraping!

KERFS AND WEDGES

Adding a wedge to a tenon will make it a stronger joint. Wedges are often found where leg tenons go through a seat and tenons go through bow arms. A slot known as a kerf is made into the tenon almost all the way through, then when the chair is glued up, a wedge is inserted into the kerf to form a tighter joint.

Cutting the kerfs

A kerf in a tenon should always be cut so that it is in opposition to the grain direction of the material that holds the mortice. So, if the seat grain is running back to front, the wedge kerf should be running side to side, or vice versa. This is because a wedge that is driven into a kerf that lines up with the seat grain could split or 'pop' the seat open! In opposition, the force of the wedge acts upon the end of the grain.

1 Once you have dry fitted the undercarriage of the chair – the legs, stretchers and seat – check how much of the leg tenons is protruding from the top of the seat. If it's more than ⅜in (10mm), then trim them to that height.

2 Make a pencil mark across the ends of the tenons so the wedges will sit across the grain of the seat.

3 Knock out the legs with a metal hammer and saw the slots for the kerfs using a tenon saw or Japanese rip-cut pull saw. The slots should be cut down the length of the tenon to almost as far as the depth mark.

4 Hold off fitting the wedges until after the legs have been glued in place (see page 115).

Follow the same method for making kerfs in tenons on other parts such as bow arms. However, if you're making the lobster pot armchair, the tops of the short spindles will need to be split in situ with the chisel and then wedged. The same is true for all the spindles on the low back armchair.

Making wedges

Wedges should be made from a dense hardwood. I favour walnut, ash or oak, depending on the colour of the tenon end, and whether I want the wedge more visible or less.

1 Start by cutting a 1in (25mm) cube from a small 1in (25mm) square of hardwood, then using a wide chisel and mallet, split this block into 5⁄32in (4mm) strips.

2 Make a small jig as pictured, using two blocks of wood held in a vice with one providing a flat working surface and the other a bit higher to support the work as you shape it.

3 Place a hardwood strip flat on the jig, then the flat side of the chisel down on the strip. Hold the chisel handle in your lead hand, then rest your stomach against your hand holding the handle. With your other hand flat on top of the chisel, press downwards as you push the chisel forwards. This will produce a flat side on the wedge.

4 Turn the wedge over and repeat the cut, but this time take a heavier cut as you push forwards, creating a wedge shape with a thin end.

5 Trim the sides carefully, and remove the sharp corners of the lead edge. The wedges are ready for glueing up.

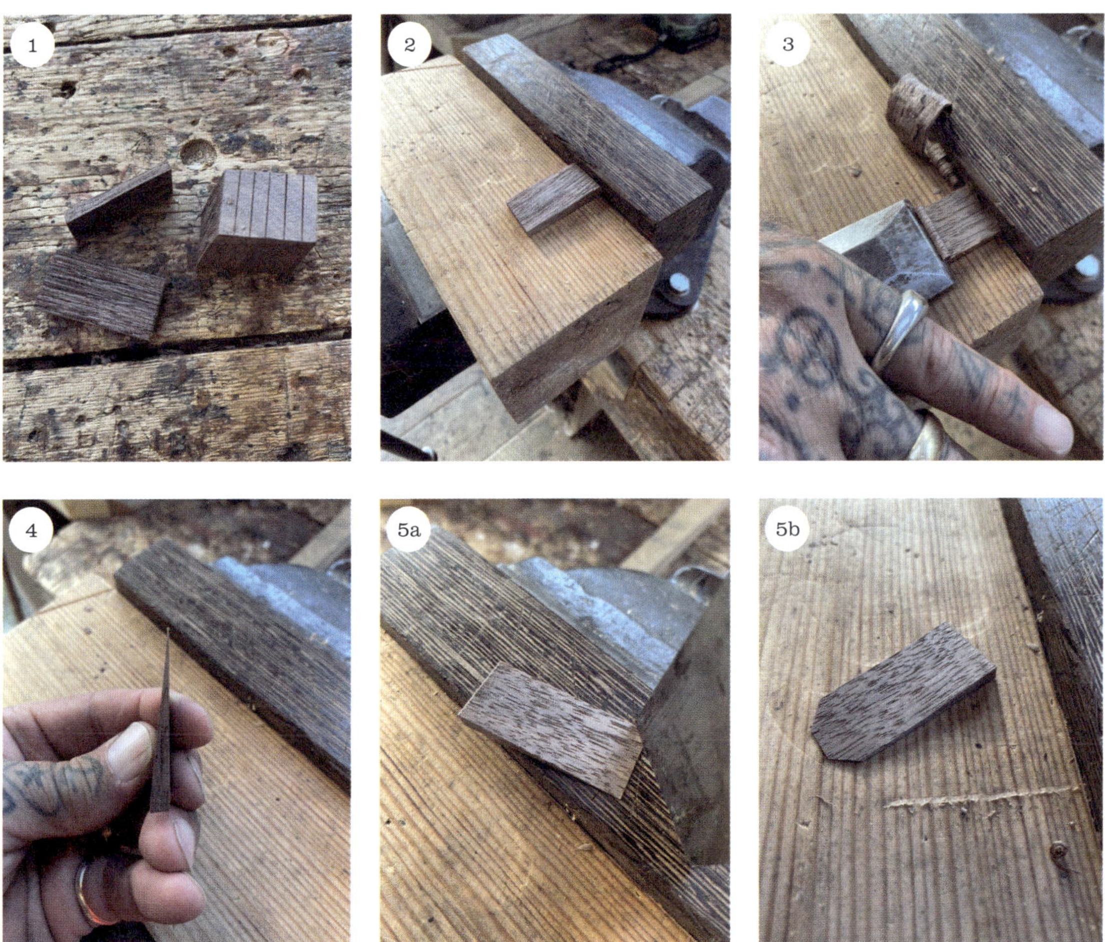

FACET CUTS

The final cuts and details you make to your chair can help elevate it from being a functional piece of furniture to something really very special. If you want the legs, stretchers or spindles to have a faceted finish, you will need to do this after you have dry fitted the undercarriage but before the final glue up. When you've knocked the undercarriage apart, run a very sharp spokeshave over the surfaces of each part, starting at a swell and running to the end of the piece. This will give you a very subtle but identifiable faceted finish.

Be very careful to retain alignment marks, and re-mark them if they are removed. It's very difficult to work on the surfaces after glue up, so take the time to check all your components are finished to your satisfaction at this stage.

Final facet cuts on a leg

GLUEING UP

I use either PVA wood glue or hide glue to glue up with. The advantage of hide glue is the 'open' time – that is, the time it takes to set – is 10–15 minutes, and it cleans up nicely with water. Hide glue also lubricates the joints well before drying, so your chair should go together more smoothly. However, it is made from animals – albeit waste from meat production – so it may not be suitable for some folks. PVA is an okay alternative, but it is sticky to use and has a slightly shorter open time. Don't overglue: it just squeezes out of the joint messily and has to be cleaned up. A thin layer on both the tenon and mortice will suffice.

Before you begin to glue up, I recommend that you have a nice tidy area to work in, and that you are not in a rush. Turn your phone off! Lay out all the parts that you will be glueing. And get your glue ready: if you're using a hide glue, it will need to be warmed up. I usually have the bottle standing in a large jar of very hot water.

You'll also need a metal hammer, a medium ¾in (20mm) chisel, a brush for the glue, and an old toothbrush and a rag to clean up excess. A 2 × 1in (50 × 25mm) block of softwood is useful to act as a barrier between your hammer and an arm bow when fitting and hitting the bow, otherwise you could damage the surface quite significantly.

Undercarriage glue up

Before glueing up, make sure all the components are finished nicely, and do a final dry fit, making sure all your markings are very clear. If you find re-marking any of the parts will give you a better chair at the end, then take the time to do so. Lay out all the parts on the bench.

With the underside of the seat facing you, brush the legs mortices with a thin layer of glue. Then, taking each leg in turn, brush the tenon with glue, and place it lightly in the correct mortice and aligned to the marks. The legs should be loosely in place.

Next, brush a thin layer of glue into the stretcher mortices. Take each stretcher, add a thin layer of glue to each tenon and fit the tenons lightly to the correct mortices. Once both side stretchers are in place, brush glue into the mortices for the centre stretcher and on its tenons. Position the centre stretcher tenons into their mortices.

Make sure all the parts are lined up how you want them and all your marks match up! Now pull everything together: the glue will lubricate the joints to allow this. Once all the tenons of the stretchers are tight, knock the legs firmly in with the hammer until the depth mark is reached. Clean any excess glue away before it sets.

If something seems wrong, check your marks. You may have to knock the undercarriage apart and refit if something has gone wrong – and the clock will be ticking!

Glueing wedges into tenons

Stand the chair on its legs. You need to tap the wedges in now. Take a wedge, add a thin layer of glue on one face, and tap it carefully into the top of the kerf. If the kerf is closed shut, use the chisel to reopen it by tapping it sharply with the hammer in the top of the slot. This should open the kerf enough to enable you to start tapping the wedge home. Remember, you are hitting the wedge in the direction of the leg's axis, not just straight down into the seat. Once the tap sound changes to a dull sound, that's far enough.

If the wedge snaps, it is usually because it won't go any further into the kerf. If it snapped because of a misdirected tap, then simply find the broken-off piece, try to fit it in its original place and tap it further.

TRIMMING WEDGED TENONS

1 Once the glue has dried after a few hours (or preferably overnight), the ends of the wedges that protrude from the seat (or any other part) can be trimmed using a Japanese pull saw. It's best to leave about 3⁄16in (5mm) protruding, which can be trimmed using a sharp carving chisel.

2 Tapping the chisel with a mallet, work from the outside edge in towards the centre of the protruding tenon and wedge, working all the way around, rather than cutting from one side straight through to the other. This helps avoid tear out. Try not to dig a hole while using the chisel: keep the blade's bevel flat to the chair surface when starting the cut, and maintain that angle throughout the cut.

3 Once you have a relatively flush surface, it can be cleaned up using a cabinet scraper.

Topside glue up

Again, make sure you can dry fit all the parts easily and that everything is marked clearly and neatly. Put a thin layer of glue in each spindle or arm post mortice, then add glue in each bow mortice. I don't usually put glue on the spindle itself: it just squishes out and makes a mess during fitting.

Put all the spindles and arm posts into the bow first, making sure they are in the correct holes. Next, place the bow with the spindles onto the chair, and if you can, tap the front pair into their mortices first and then the centre spindle or pair of spindles. This will position the bow, and then you can tap each spindle down into its corresponding mortice; I work in pairs from either side of the centre. Once you have everything correct, tap all the spindles firmly home. You will then need to firmly tap the bow down to the correct height noted by your pencil marks.

If you are fitting a crest, apply a thin layer of glue in the crest mortices and then fit it to the spindles and tap them home.

The front pair of spindles or arm posts, depending on the chair you're making, will travel through the seat. You should first wedge the tops of this pair, then the ends protruding from the underside of the seat. You'll need to turn the chair upside down to do the undersides.

If you're making the lobster pot armchair, the tops of the short spindles will need to be split in situ with the chisel and then wedged. The same is true for all the spindles on the low back armchair. Remember, the wedges should always be orientated in opposition to the bow's grain direction, across the bow.

Give the glue time to set, preferably overnight, somewhere warm, before trimming any wedged tenons, levelling up and finishing.

SECURING A CREST

Use pegs to hold the lobster pot chair's crest securely in place. This is done by fitting a pair of pegs through the crest and the spindles and out of the back of the crest. Do this on the second spindle in from either side, ⅜in (10mm) from the bottom edge of the crest.

To do this, mark the drilling points with a bradawl, then drill a 5/32in (4mm) hole. You might find it easier to drill with a 5/64in (2mm) bit first, then go up a drill bit size to 5/32in (4mm). Drill the two small holes with a piece of waste clamped to the backside to avoid splintering.

Now whittle a pair of 5/32in (4mm) round oak pegs for a tight fit. Put some glue in the holes and tap the pegs through. Trim carefully with a Japanese saw and clean up with a knife and cabinet scraper. Trim and tidy all spindle tops in the same way.

LEVELLING UP

Your stool or chair is fully assembled, but that doesn't mean it will sit level on the floor. To get a nice and steady stool or chair that doesn't wobble, you'll need to level it up. I use a technique taught to me many years ago by my first chairmaking teacher, Paul.

LEVELLING UP WITH CHOCKS

The technique I use relies first of all on having a flat and level surface: I use a leftover length of kitchen worktop surface that sits on top of my gnarly but level workbench. I also have a box full of plywood squares and rectangles, which I use for chocks – that is, blocks to steady the work. These are of mixed thicknesses, from 3⁄64–¾in (1–20mm). There are six 2in (50mm) squares of each thickness, and for each thickness of square, you will also need a 4 × 6in (100 × 150mm) rectangle with a 4in (100mm) long notch cut into it. The notch should be a curved V shape so that it fits snugly to different diameter legs.

I use a combination of thicknesses as needed to get a stool or chair level and determine how much the legs need to be trimmed to size. While the height of the stools can be more flexible, the height of the seats for the chairs is more critical and it's likely it will need adjusting.

1 Start by levelling the chair, side to side. Place a spirit level on top of the chair and using the plywood chocks, get it level, side to side. The chair will probably have a chock on one front leg and its opposite back leg, but use whatever is needed.

2 The pommel in the centre at the front of the seat's top surface needs to be 1in (25mm) higher than the back centre top surface. You may need to add further pieces of ply to either the front or back pairs of legs to achieve this. The seat should be level side to side and tilted so the seat is 1in (25mm) higher at the front than at the back.

3 The final height the seat needs to be, as measured from the workbench, is 18in (460mm) at the front and 17in (430mm) at the back; but, at this stage, the seat will be higher than this. So if, for instance, the height is ¾in (20mm) taller than required, then that much will need to be cut from the end of each leg. However, it is more likely that you'll remove different amounts from each leg when doing this, but this is normal — you are trying to level a chair that is uneven to start with.

4 To establish the height of the seat, first place a heavy object on it to keep the seat steady. Using the blocks along with a notched rectangle, create a platform at the bottom of the first leg on either side to support the notched rectangle. The platform, including the notched rectangle, should be the thickness that you want to remove according to your measurement.

5 Use this platform to rest your Japanese rip-cut pull saw on, and saw through the leg, initially pressing the back side of the blade flat to the platform. Once the cut has been established, your spare hand can hold the leg above the saw.

6 Once you have cut all the way through the leg, remove the cut end and any plywood chocks from that leg, then chock up the newly cut leg with

chocks that are the same thickness as the blocks that made up the platform. Repeat for all the legs.

7 Remove all the chocks, and your chair should sit without a wobble on the flat surface. If there is a slight wobble, then the chair is rocking on a pair of opposite legs. Choose one of these opposite legs and hold it firmly pressed to the flat surface, then take a cut with the Japanese saw pressed flat to the surface. This will remove a half millimetre from the end of the leg and should eliminate the wobble.

8 Now turn the seat upside down and, using a sharp knife, make faceted cuts all around the newly sawn ends, which will prevent the legs from splintering and give a nice, very subtle 'floating' look to the chair.

LEVELLING UP A STOOL OR TABLE

The same steps used for levelling a chair can be used for a stool or table, but without tilting the surface. Simply chock up until the surface is level, testing it using a spirit level. Alternatively, measure the height from the bench up to the top surface of the stool or table. Do this all the way around to check it's consistently the same.

FINISHING TOUCHES

Once you have glued up your chair and levelled it, there is a certain amount of cleaning up and finishing that can add a lot of subtle and wonderful detail to your chair such as adding faceted details on plain turnings. Your chair will then be ready for the final stage: either a paint or an oil and wax finish.

CLEANING UP THE SURFACES

Have a final look at the chair to see where you might want to add some final details. In addition, you don't want any splinters at corners or rough, sharp edges. Sit in the chair and feel around with your hands to detect any areas that are sharp or feel rough and unfinished. Anything that feels rough to the touch needs to be either trimmed with a small block plane or scraped smooth using a cabinet scraper.

Sandpaper (and when to avoid it)

There are many greenwood workers who feel that sandpaper is a dirty word and would never use it. It is a fact that a blade-cut surface is the smoothest and most burnished finish, and the facets from the cuts reflect light that sandpaper would destroy. It is also true that tool marks and blade marks add fascination, detail and character to a finished piece, especially if it's painted. However, I think sandpaper does have its place, but mainly in the smoothing of the carved seat.

Often, the first thing a customer does when looking at my chairs is to stroke the seat. It really needs to be silky smooth. So, after scraping the seat with a cabinet scraper, I use sandpaper to thoroughly sand the carved part of the seat, starting with a 120-grit sheet and working through the grits to a 400 grit.

I want to keep all bladed and faceted detail throughout the chair, but I also don't want any 'sharpness' to the touch. So, I also use the 400-grit sandpaper to soften all the faceted cuts. This isn't visible to the eye, but it makes a subtle difference to the touch.

Finally, I use the 400-grit sandpaper to very gently sand any raised grain in between coats of oil. This produces a super smooth finish.

The finished arm bow

OILING AND PAINTING

In the American Windsor tradition, chairs are very often painted, whereas British chairs tend to be unpainted. This could be because the timbers in the American chairs were very mixed and didn't look so coherent together, or just a difference in styles. Who knows?

I like both natural, unpainted chairs and painted chairs. Painted chairs look very unified and have a strong silhouette. They might sit more easily in a particular colour scheme in a room.

If you want to paint a chair, choose a furniture paint. A chalk paint, milk paint, mineral paint or linseed oil paint will all give good finishes. Acrylic paint is also suitable and easy to apply – but obviously, it is not as natural as the other choices.

I use milk paint. It has its pros and cons, but I like the overall finish. It shows and accentuates detail well. It is a natural pigment paint, it is water soluble and it oils very well. However, it is also laborious and grubby to apply, expensive and fragile when compared to linseed oil paints.

A variety of different finishes for the three-legged stool

MILK PAINT APPLICATION

Milk paint is available as a powder. Don't mix it all at once but make up small batches as you need it. If you want an undercolour, such as a green under a black, you will need two thick coats of green and two thinner coats of black. Avoid overworking the paint as it causes streaks and will eventually disturb any previous dried layer.

Put 4–5 tablespoons of milk paint powder into a clean food tin, add 2–3 tablespoons of warm water and stir it with a wooden stirrer – a stick will do – until it starts to bind into a paste, keeping the paste loose by adding small dribbles of water as you stir. Try to stir out all the lumps. Now add water until it is the thickness of double cream. Pass it through the tea strainer into a jam jar with a lid.

Apply a first coat to your chair. If there is an area to remain unpainted, first mask it off with masking tape. The first coat needs to be applied smoothly, working the paint into the wooden surface with a 1in (25mm) flat artist's brush. If the paint seems gummy, add a little water to ease it. Then clean your brush and seal the jar with the lid. Leave to dry somewhere warm for 8 hours.

Once dry, rub all the painted surface thoroughly with a Scotch-Brite ultra-fine hand pad to burnish the painted surface. Repeat twice, so that you have applied and rubbed down three coats.

The final painted surface, once dried, can be oiled and waxed.

OIL AND WAX

One traditional method for finishing a chair is to use Danish oil, which is linseed oil mixed with a thinner. It is a nice oil to use. Apply a generous coat to the chair, rubbing it in with a clean lint-free cloth, wait 10 minutes and then remove any excess with another clean cloth. Leave to dry for 8 hours. Repeat three or four times.

In between coats, feel the chair's surface for any roughnes – this is grain that has been raised by the oil. You can use 400-grit sandpaper lightly over the roughness before applying the next layer of oil. After the oiling, you could apply a furniture or beeswax as an extra layer of protection.

Alternatively, you can use one of the newer all-in-one products, which are wax-oil combinations. You can apply these, let them dry, then reapply. They are very easy to apply and come in matt, satin and gloss options.

PROJECT NO. 1

A SIMPLE THREE-LEGGED STOOL

This basic stool, often referred to as a milking stool, follows a classic design in which a seat is balanced on only three legs. Not only is its construction one of the easier ones for making something to sit on, but having just three legs provides better stability on uneven or rough surfaces. I made this stool using octagonal shaved legs, but it works equally well with simple turned legs.

ALLOW 2 DAYS, PLUS A WEEK FOR DRYING

MATERIALS

From a 20in (505mm) green ash log, cut:

- 3 square billets for the legs, each 20 × 2 × 2in (505 × 50 × 50mm)

You will also need:

- For the seat, 10¼–12¼ × 10¼–12¼ × 2⅛–2⅜in (260–310 × 260–310 × 55–60mm) kiln- or air-dried hardwood board such as ash or oak
- Scrap plywood for clamping the seat
- 3 wedges: 1 × 1 × ⅛in (25 × 25 × 3mm) hardwood strips
- PVA wood glue or hide glue

see page 208 for the plans

METHOD:

Making the parts (allow a week for drying)

1 Cut the rough 2in (50mm) square billets into 1¾in (45mm) square blanks using a drawknife, or turn them into 1¾in (45mm) diameter blanks on a lathe (see pages 65–69). To shape a leg, mark 8in (200mm) from one end, which is where the 1¾in (45mm) swell will be, and from here, taper the 8in (200mm) section so that it's ¾in (20mm) in diameter at the end, which will be the foot. Repeat this in the other direction from the swell, this time tapering it so that it's 1in (25mm) in diameter at the end. Repeat for the other legs.

When the parts are all super dry

2 Use a compass and pencil to mark a circle between 10in and 12in (255–305mm) in diameter on the 2⅛–2⅜in (55–60mm) thick seat blank, then cut the seat out using a bandsaw or jigsaw (see pages 76–77).

3 Choose the side you want for the top and flatten it with a hand plane. With a marking gauge 2in (50mm) from the now flat underside of the seat blank as reference, draw a line around the side of the blank to mark for an even thickness around the seat. Use this reference line to plane the top side of the seat until it is roughly flat (see pages 78–79).

4 Use a pencil and straightedge to divide the seat in half by drawing a straight line from edge to edge, passing it through the centre point where the compass was. Place the 60-degree angle of a set square at the centre point on the dividing line and mark a second line to the edge of the seat, then move the set square to this new line and mark another line to the edge. Repeat until the seat has been divided into six equal segments.

5 To mark where to drill holes for the legs, on one of the dividing lines, measure 2in (50mm) from the outer edge and make a mark using the pencil. Repeat twice more on every other dividing line so that you have three equally spaced marks. Use a bradawl to make indentations to guide the drill bit.

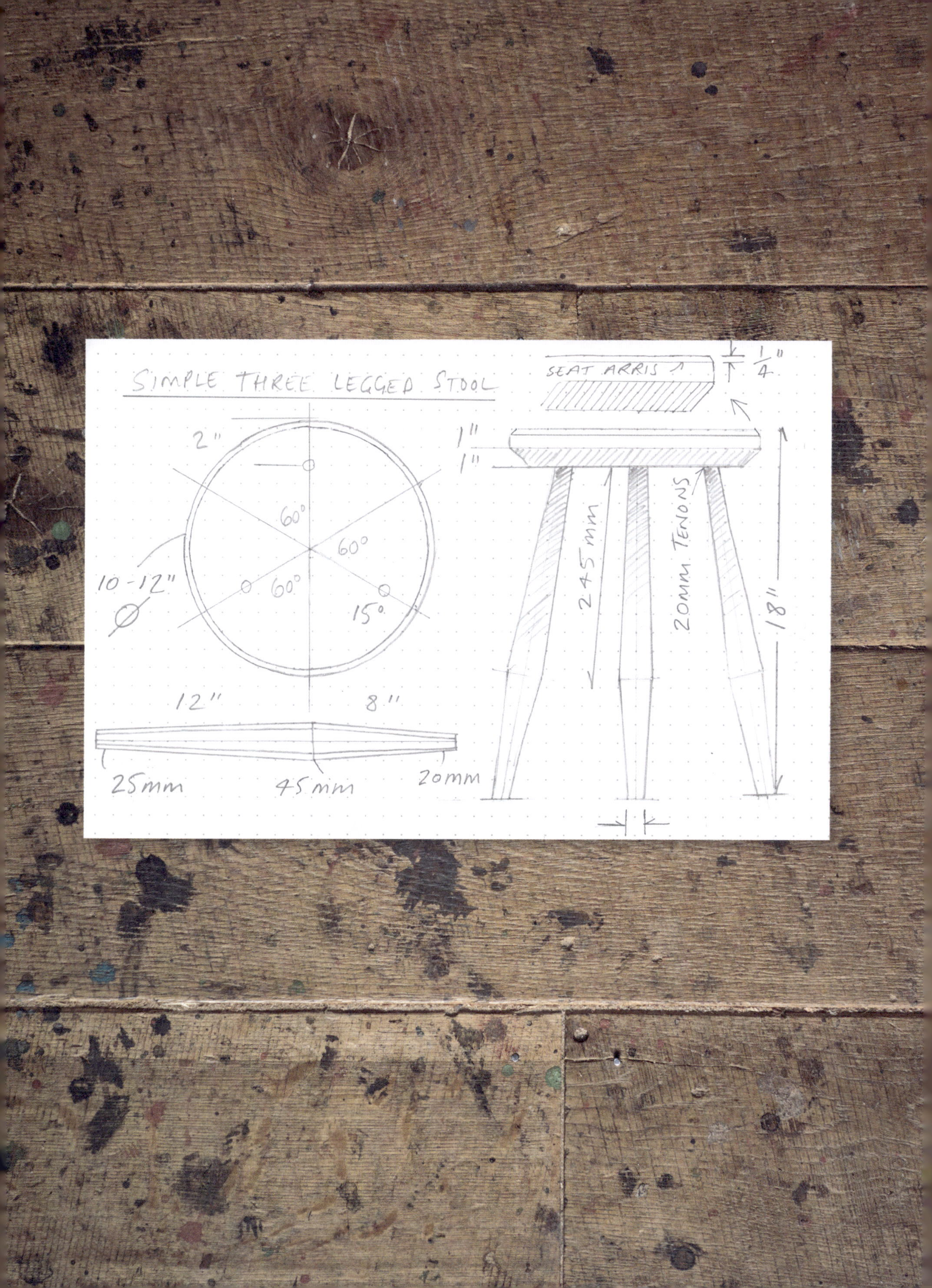
SIMPLE THREE LEGGED STOOL
2"
60°
60°
60°
15°
10-12"
Ø
12"
8"
25mm
45mm
20mm
SEAT ARRIS
1/4"
1"
1"
245mm
20MM TENONS
18"

6 Clamp the seat, topside up, to a workbench or a low table, sandwiching a piece of plywood between the seat and the bench. This is to avoid drilling into the bench's surface, and it reduces tear out on the underside of your work.

7 To make the mortices for the legs of this stool, you'll need to drill them using a ¾in (20mm) drill bit at an angle so the legs can splay out (remember you are working from the top of the seat). Using a bevel gauge set to 15 degrees, place the drill bit at a drill mark, holding the drill with the bit aligned over the dividing line, at a 15-degree angle from the vertical and its tip pointing towards the edge of the seat (see pages 94–95). Drill all the way through the seat. Repeat at the other two marks, ensuring the drill is at the correct angle and aligned along the dividing line for each.

8 The next stage is to create the chamfer on the underside of the seat. Using a marking gauge, mark a line running around the side edge of the seat, 1in (25mm) from the topside. Then, turn the seat upside down and mark a circular line all the way around the base of the seat, 1in (25mm) in from the edge. Remove all of the material between these two lines using a spokeshave or a file and cabinet scraper.

9 Repeat step 8 to make a second chamfer on the top of the seat, but this time make the line around the side edge ¼in (6mm) from the topside, and the circular line around the top of the seat should be ¼in (6mm) in from the edge.

10 Use a lathe or a tenon cutter to make 2½in (63mm) long, ¾in (20mm) diameter tenons on the tops of the legs (see pages 92–93).

11 Check and adjust the fit of the tenons in the mortices (see page 110). Orientate, or twist, the legs into the mortices by hand so that the grain direction on the pairs match, and if you're using octagonal legs, a flat face faces outwards. Tap the legs firmly into the mortices using a metal hammer to seat them. At least ⅜in (10mm) should protrude from the top of the seat; slightly extend the tenon if there is less than this.

12 As you'll be taking apart and reassembling the pieces, to know which leg fits in which mortice, its orientation and how deep it fits into the mortice, make clear marks on the seat and each leg where they touch, label each leg with a letter, number or symbol, and write the same label next to the appropriate mortice (see page 111).

13 If more than about ⅜in (10mm) of the top of a tenon is protruding from the seat, trim it down to that length (use a Japanese pull saw for the best results). Hold the leg that you are trimming from under the seat as you cut across the tenon.

14 Mark the kerfs in the tenons for the wedges, making sure they will sit across the grain of the seat. Knock out the legs and saw the slots for the kerfs (see page 112).

15 One at a time, apply a thin layer of glue to a leg tenon and a mortice in the seat, then insert the tenon into the mortice. Tap with the hammer to ensure a good fit. With the three legs in place, apply a thin layer of glue to one side of each wedge and tap it in place. Leave to dry for at least a few hours (see pages 115–17).

16 Once the glue is dry, use the Japanese pull saw to cut the tops of the wedged tenons so that about ¼in (6mm) is protruding from the top of the seat, then trim them relatively flush with a carving chisel and a mallet before cleaning them up with a cabinet scraper.

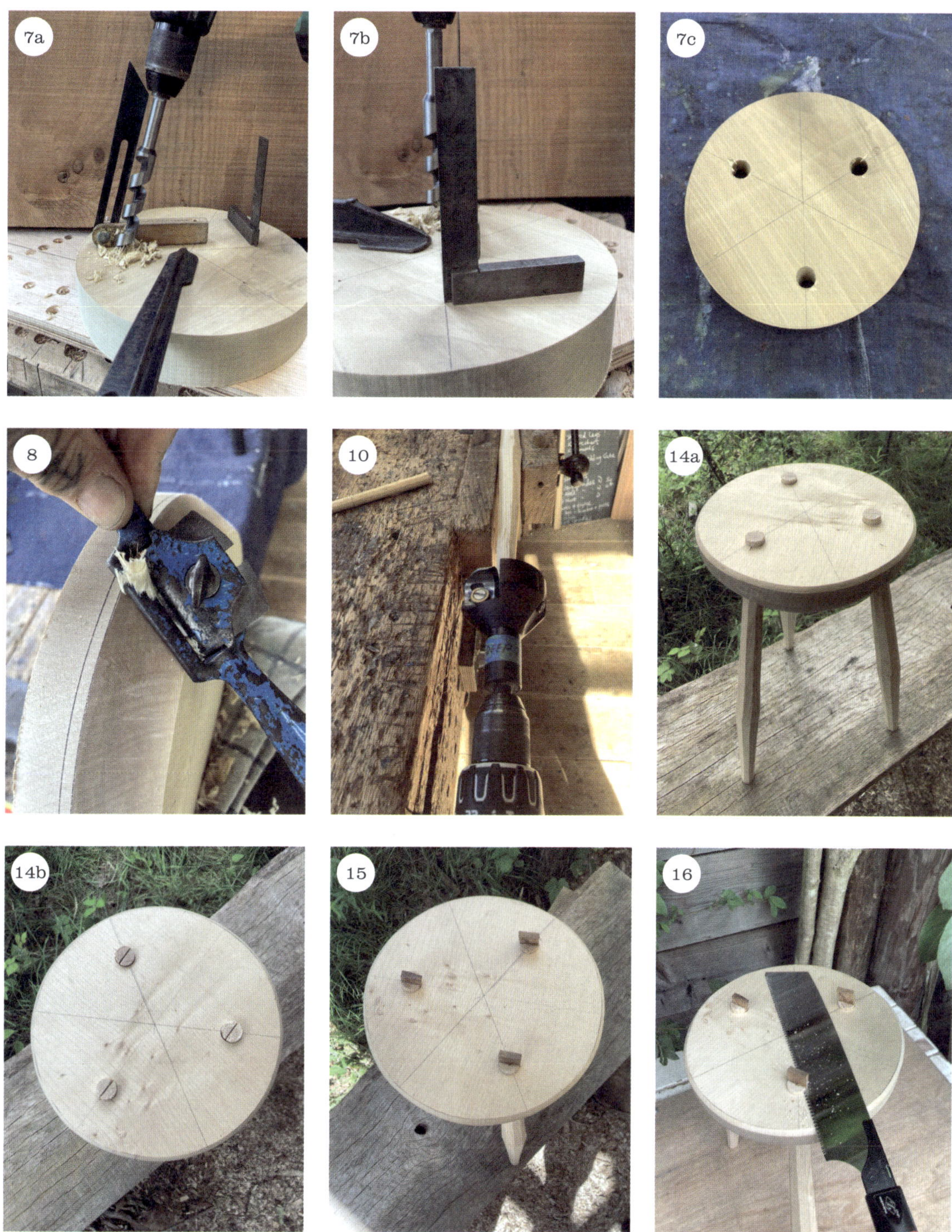
7a
7b
7c
8
10
14a
14b
15
16

17 To support the stool as you work on the top of the seat, wrap one of the legs in a cloth and clamp it in a vice. Alternatively, stand the stool on the floor, butted up against something solid to hold it still as you work on the surface. Using a cabinet scraper, and sandpaper if appropriate, smooth the seat and chair legs.

18 Using a spirit level, check the level of the stool seat to determine which legs need trimming and by how much (see pages 118–19), then trim them using the Japanese saw. Your stool is ready for finishing, whether you choose to paint it or apply an oil and wax finish (see pages 121–23).

PROJECT NO. 2

A STURDY SQUARE STOOL OR TABLE

This is an adaptable and useful household object which can be used as a stool or a side table. Building on the techniques used in the first project, this square stool has a slightly more complex undercarriage. It comprises an octagonal stretcher, pierced at 90 degrees by a dowel, giving the stool more stability and strength. The pattern could be scaled up to create larger square pieces of furniture. You could make this stool with turned parts, but I really like the look of octagonal parts made with a drawknife.

ALLOW 3 DAYS, PLUS A WEEK FOR DRYING

MATERIALS

From a 20in (505mm) green ash log, cut:

- 5 square billets for 4 legs and 1 stretcher, each 20 × 2 × 2in (505 × 50 × 50mm)

You will also need:

- For the dowel, 20 × 1 × 1in (505 × 25 × 25mm) kiln- or air-dried hardwood board such as ash or oak
- For the seat, 14¼ × 14¼ × 2⅛–2⅜in (360 × 360 × 55–60mm) kiln- or air-dried hardwood board such as ash or oak
- Scrap plywood for clamping the seat
- 4 wedges: 1 × 1 × 5⁄32in (25 × 25 × 4mm) hardwood strips (see page 113)
- PVA wood glue or hide glue

see page 209 for the plans

METHOD:

Making the parts (allow a week for drying)

1 Cut 4 of the rough 2in (50mm) square billets into 1¾in (45mm) square blanks for the legs using a drawknife, or turn them into 1¾in (50mm) diameter blanks on a lathe (see pages 65–69). To shape a leg, mark 8in (200mm) from one end, which is where the 1¾in (45mm) swell will be, and from this mark, taper the 8in (200mm) section so that it's about ¾in (20mm) in diameter at the end, which will be the foot. Repeat this in the other direction from the mark of the swell, this time tapering it so that it's 1in (25mm) in diameter at the end, which will be the top of the leg. Repeat for the other legs.

2 Cut or turn the 2in (50mm) square billet for the stretcher in the same fashion, but to a 1½in (38mm) square blank (see pages 65–69). To shape the stretcher, mark the centre of the blank for the 1½in (38mm) swell, and taper it to a diameter of about ⅞in (22mm) at each end. Cut the 1in (25mm) square billet for the dowel to a ¾in (20mm) round blank (see pages 72–75).

3 Place all the parts in a drying kiln for a week until they are super dry.

When the parts are all super dry

4 Use a set square and a ruler to mark a 14in (305mm) square on the 2⅛–2⅜in (55–60mm) thick seat blank, then cut the seat out using a bandsaw, jigsaw or panel saw (see pages 76–77).

5 Choose the side you want for the top and flatten it with a hand plane. With a marking gauge 2in (50mm) from the now flat underside of the seat blank as reference, draw a line around the side of the blank to mark for an even thickness around the seat. Use this reference line to plane the top side of the seat until it is roughly flat (see pages 78–79).

6 On the topside, draw pencil lines between the opposite corners. Measure 5in (125mm) down each line from the centre towards the corner and mark these four points with a bradawl – this will be where you drill mortices.

7 Clamp the seat, topside up, to a workbench or a low table, sandwiching a piece of plywood between the seat and the bench. This is to avoid drilling into the bench's surface, and it reduces tear out on the underside of your work.

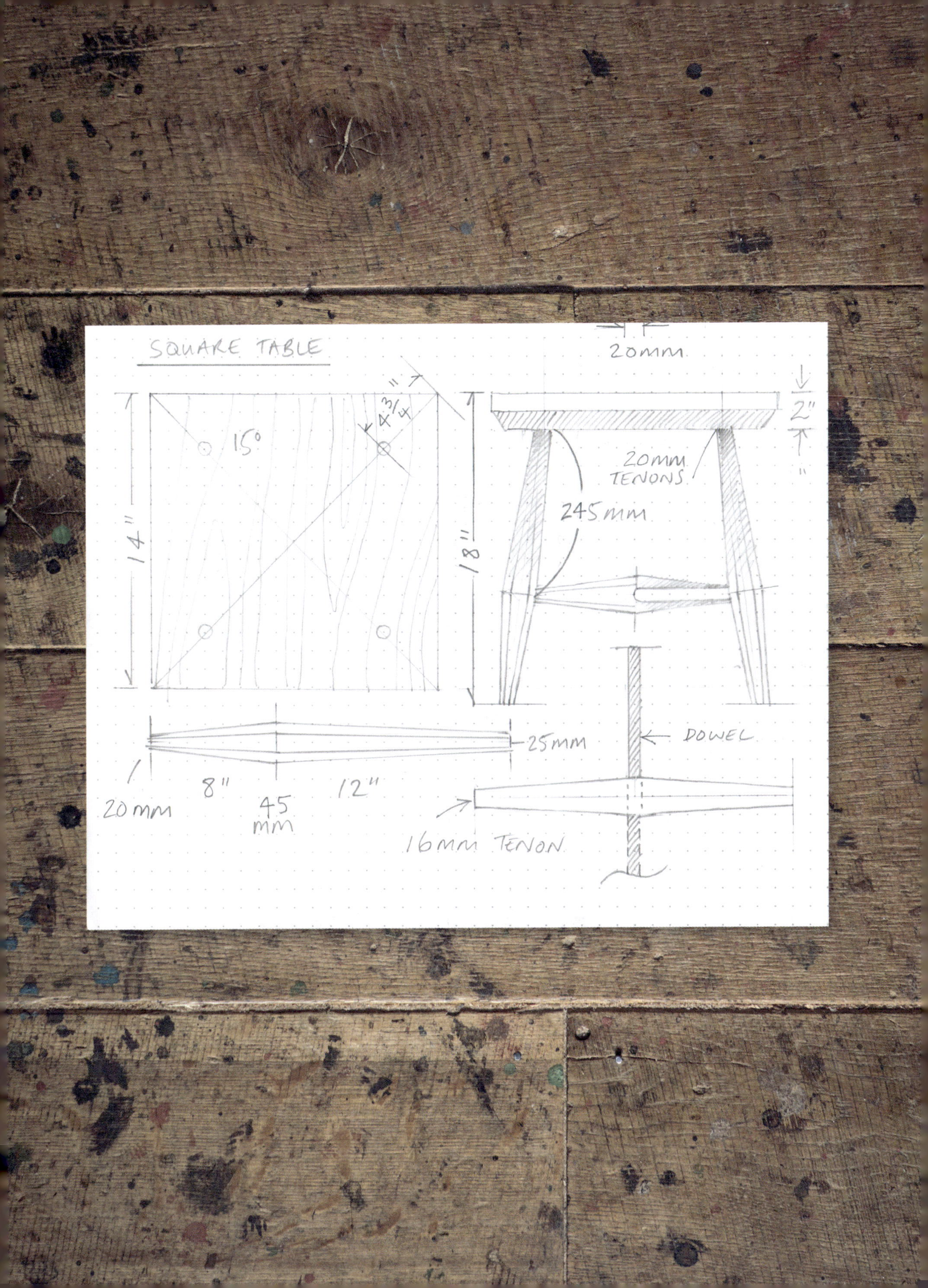

SQUARE TABLE
15°
4 3/4"
14"
20MM
2"
20MM TENONS
245MM
18"
25MM
DOWEL
20MM
8"
45 MM
12"
16MM TENON

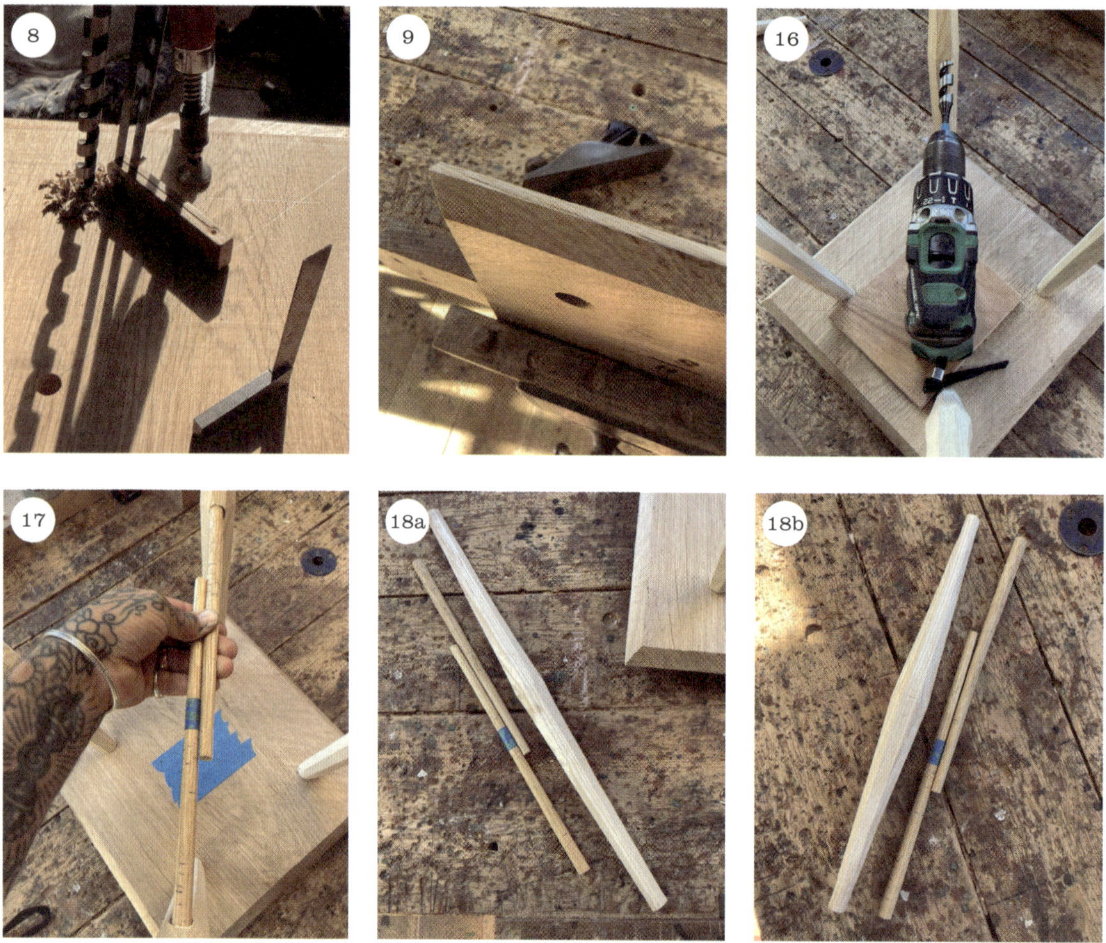

8 To make the mortices for the legs of this stool, you'll need to drill them using a ¾in (20mm) drill bit at an angle so the legs can splay out (remember you are working from the top of the seat). Using a bevel gauge set to 15 degrees, place the drill bit at a drill mark, holding the drill with the bit aligned over the dividing line and its tip pointing towards the edge of the seat at the correct angle (see pages 94–95). Drill all the way through the seat. Repeat at the other three marks, ensuring the drill is at the correct angle and aligned along the dividing line for each.

9 Next, create a chamfer on the underside of the seat. Using a marking gauge, mark a line running around the side edge of the seat and 1in (25mm) from the top. Now turn the seat upside down and mark a line ½in (12mm) in from the edge of the seat. This will create a square drawn on the underside of the seat. Remove the material between these two lines using a spokeshave or a file and cabinet scraper.

10 Use a lathe or a tenon cutter to make 2½in (63mm) long, ¾in (20mm) diameter tenons on the tops of the legs (see pages 92–93).

11 Check and adjust the fit of the tenons in the mortices (see page 110). Orientate, or twist, the legs into the mortices by hand so that the grain direction on the pairs match, and if you're using octagonal legs, a flat face faces outwards. Tap the legs firmly into the mortices using a metal hammer to seat them. At least ⅜in (10mm) should protrude from the top of the seat; slightly extend the tenon if there is less than this.

12 Check that the swells on the legs are around 9–9½in (230–245mm) from the underside of the seat, measured up the shortest side of each leg. Make a small horizontal mark. The measurement must be the same for all the legs – if needed, remove some of the shoulder from a tenon with a block plane until they all match.

13 As you'll be taking apart and reassembling the pieces, to know which leg fits in which mortice, its orientation and how deep it fits, make clear marks on the seat and each leg where they touch. Label the legs A to D working clockwise or anticlockwise and write the same letter next to the appropriate mortice (see page 111).

14 Join the diagonally opposite legs A and C with an elastic band at the height of your marks. Looking down on the leg from above, choose the point horizontally midway between the elastic bands on the marked surface of leg A. Make a small vertical mark. Repeat for leg C.

15 Before removing the elastic band, place a straightedge flat on the underside of the seat, between legs A and C and lined up parallel with the elastic band. It is helpful to close one eye while doing this sighting. Draw a line along the straightedge to make sight line X.

16 Using a ⅝in (16mm) auger drill bit, drill slowly 1in (25mm) into the crosshair on leg A, using the sight line X to help you line up your drill bit. A small drill and short bit may fit between the legs, but if you need to, remove one leg to drill into the opposite leg. To help steady the drill, place some small squares of plywood under it, ensuring that the drill bit is parallel to the seat. Repeat for leg C.

17 Now measure to find the length needed for the stretcher and dowel. Using measuring sticks (see page 93), measure the distance between the depth of the holes in legs A and C. Add 3⁄16in (5mm) to this measurement to create some tension and write that number between the corresponding legs.

18 Mark the stretcher so it will fit in between legs A and C. Divide the measurement you wrote down in half, and mark that distance in both directions from the centre swell of the stretcher. This is the final cut length of the stretcher.

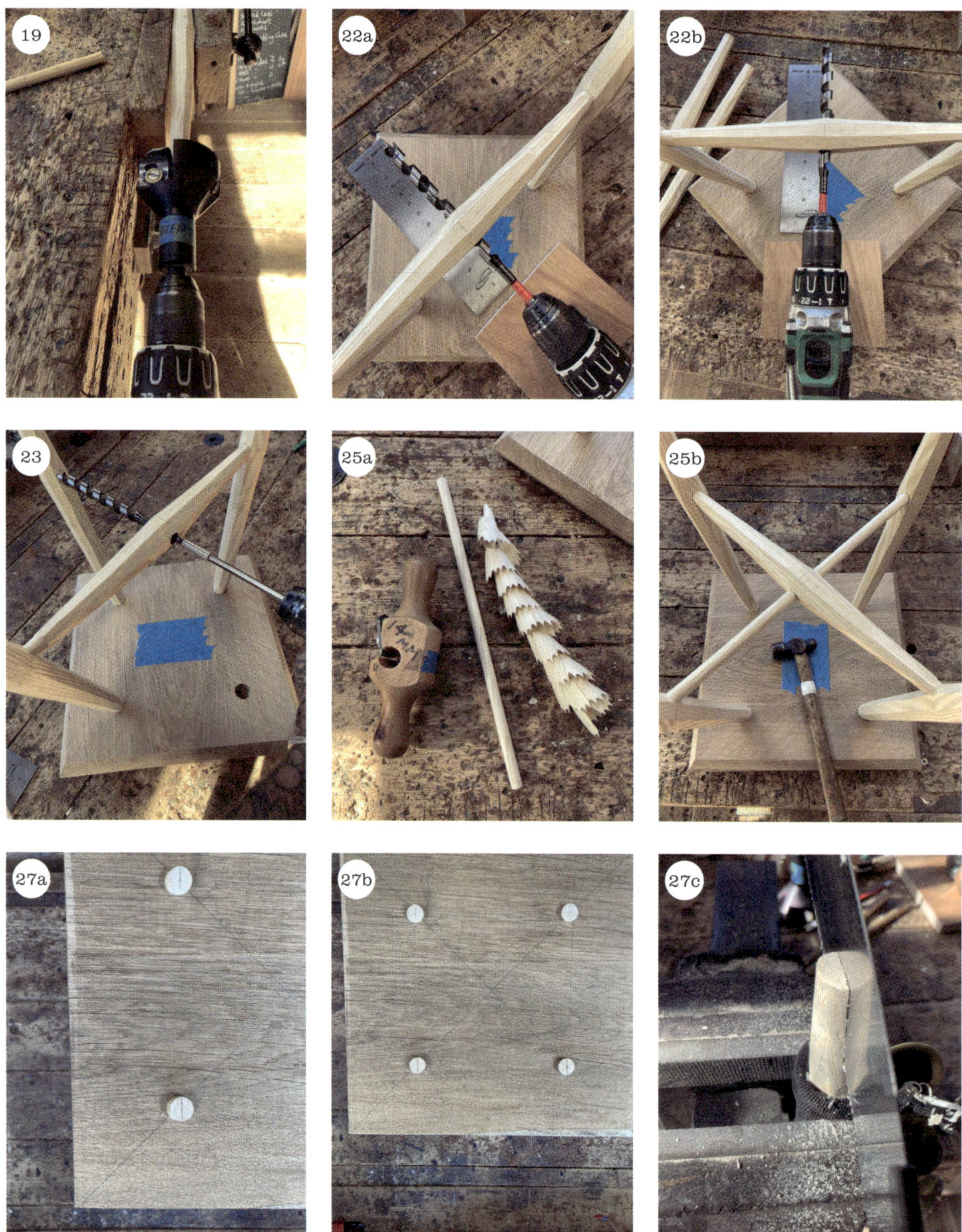
19
22a
22b
23
25a
25b
27a
27b
27c

19 Using a ⅝in (16mm) tenon cutter or your lathe, cut a 1in (25mm) long tenon on both ends of the stretcher. If using a lathe, turn the tenon first and cut the stretcher to size using a Japanese pull saw or standard tenon saw afterwards; if using a tenon cutter, cut the stretcher to size first and then make the tenon.

20 Using a metal hammer, knock legs A and C loose, fit the stretcher between them and knock the legs back in to their depth marks. Pull the legs tight onto the stretcher. Orientate the stretcher so that a flat side is parallel to the seat. Mark clearly where the stretcher aligns on each leg, marking 'A' and 'C'.

21 With all four legs in place, put an elastic band between legs B and D, from swell to swell, across the A–C stretcher. Using a small ruler, make a mark in between and in line with the bands, where they cross the stretcher. This is your B–D sightline. Knock out legs B and D.

22 Drill a hole using a 9⁄16in (14mm) bit, parallel to the seat and through the centre of the stretcher. To make a drill mark, measure directly down from the underside of the seat to the middle of the mortice in leg A, then make a mark on the centre of the stretcher at the same height from the underside of the seat. Drill slowly, taking care to avoid the 'tear out' that can occur as the drill point emerges: stop drilling before going through the stretcher, then drill from the other side into the drill hole.

23 Replace leg B, tapping it home with the hammer. Use an extension to drill through the stretcher mortice into leg B, drilling a 1in (25mm) deep mortice with the 9⁄16in (14mm) drill bit. Now knock out leg B, replace leg D and drill a mortice in leg D using the same method.

24 With all the legs tapped back in place, use measuring sticks to measure the distance between mortices B and D (see page 93). Write the measurement on the underside of the seat. Add 3⁄16in (5mm) to the measurement and write it underneath.

25 Cut the dowel blank to the above length. Wind the piece through a 9⁄16in (14mm) tenon cutter. Tidy with the spokeshave or a block plane. Knock all the legs loose, fit the dowel through the stretcher mortice, fit the legs to the dowel and knock it all together into the seat. Mark all the parts and alignments clearly, so that you know what goes where at glue up.

26 Trim the tops of the tenons, leaving about ⅜in (10mm) protruding, using a Japanese pull saw for the best results. Hold the leg that you are trimming from under the seat as you cut across the top of the tenon.

27 Mark the kerfs in the tenons for the wedges, making sure they will sit across the grain of the seat. Knock out the legs and saw the slots for the kerfs (see page 112).

28

29

30

28 Before glueing up, check that every element of the seat fits well. Using a spokeshave, clean up the octagonal facets of all parts, and remove most of the 'shoulders' on any tenons. Beware of losing important marks. Lay out the parts ready for fitting everything together.

29 One at a time, apply a thin layer of glue to a leg tenon and a mortice in the seat, then loosely insert the tenon into the mortice. Do the same for the stretcher and then the dowel. With all the parts in place, tap with the hammer to ensure a good fit. Apply a thin layer of glue to one side of each wedge and tap it in place. Leave to dry for at least a few hours.

30 Once the glue is dry, use the Japanese pull saw to cut the tops of the wedged tenons so that about ¼in (6mm) is protruding, then trim them with a sharp carving chisel and a mallet before cleaning them up with a cabinet scraper.

31 To support the stool as you work on the top of the seat, wrap one of the legs in a cloth and clamp it in a vice. Alternatively, stand the stool on the floor, butted up against something solid to hold it still as you work on the surface. Using a cabinet scraper, and sandpaper if appropriate, smooth the seat, legs, stretcher and dowel.

32 Using a spirit level, check the level of the stool seat to determine which legs need trimming and by how much (see pages 118–19), then trim them using the Japanese saw. Your stool is ready for finishing, whether you choose to paint it or apply an oil and wax finish (see pages 121–23).

PROJECT NO. 3

LOW BACK ARMCHAIR

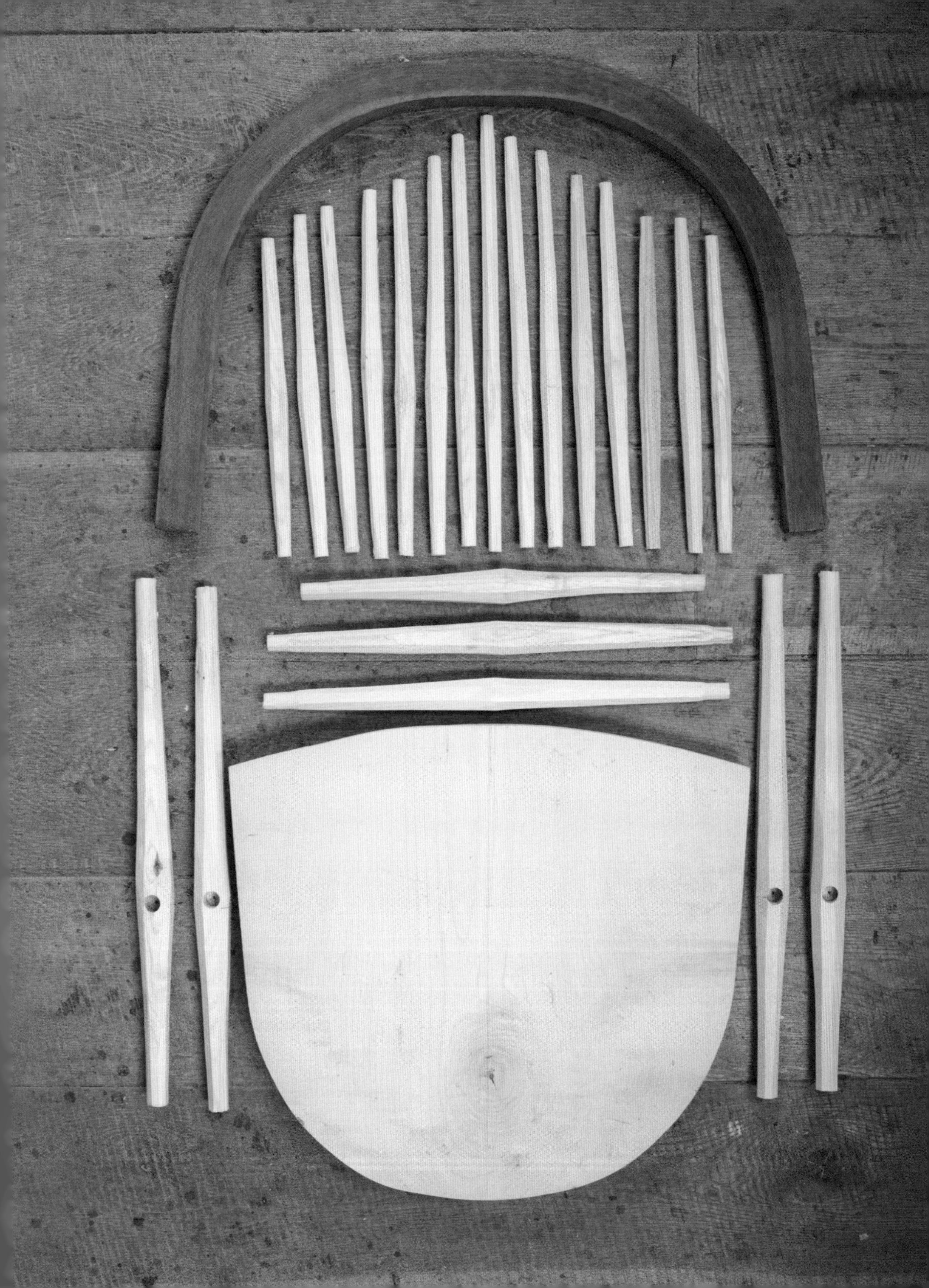

Here is a chair that I love: it is the perfect size for using at a table or a desk, but it still remains comfortable and supportive. This chair is a good example of how you can use octagonal parts instead of lathe-turned parts, plus it's adaptable. This example has a full array of spindles, 15 in total, but it can be made with fewer spindles if you wish, or with turned parts. If you would prefer to make a high-back chair, use the drilling jig from the lobster pot chair (see page 219) and drill through the bow parallel to the seat so it can take taller spindles through it to some form of crest. For this chair, I have used a walnut seat and arm bow along with ash parts.

ALLOW 8 DAYS, PLUS A WEEK FOR DRYING

MATERIALS

From 20in (505mm) green ash log(s), cut:

- 7 square billets for 4 legs and 3 stretchers, each 20 × 2 × 2in (505 × 50 × 50mm)
- 15 square billets for the spindles (plus extras for spares), each 20 × 1 × 1in (505 × 25 × 25mm)

You will also need:

- For the arm bow, 54¼ × 1½ × 1½in (1380 × 38 × 38mm) green or air-dried hardwood board such as oak
- For the seat, 20¼ × 18¼ × 2⅛–2⅜in (515 × 465 × 55–60mm) in kiln- or air-dried hardwood board, such as ash or oak
- Plywood for template and jig
- 21 wedges: 1 × 1 × 5⁄32in (25 × 25 × 4mm) hardwood strips (see page 113)
- PVA wood glue or hide glue

see pages 210–11 for the plans, 216 for the seat and arm bow bending form templates and 219 for the arm bow drilling jig

METHOD:

Making the parts (allow a week for drying)

1 Cut 4 of the rough 2in (50mm) square billets into 1¾in (45mm) square blanks for the legs using a drawknife, or turn them into 1¾in (45mm) diameter blanks on a lathe (see pages 65–69). To shape a leg, mark 8in (200mm) from one end, which is where the 1¾in (45mm) swell will be, and from this mark, taper the 8in (200mm) section so that it's about ¾in (20mm) in diameter at the end, which will be the foot. Repeat this in the other direction from the mark of the swell, this time tapering it so that it's 1in (25mm) in diameter at the end, which will be the top of the leg. Repeat for the other legs.

2 Cut or turn the remaining 2in (50mm) square billets for the stretchers in the same fashion, but to 1½in (38mm) square blanks (see pages 65–69). To shape the stretchers, mark the centre of the blanks for the 1½in (38mm) swell, and taper them to a diameter of about ⅞in (22mm) at each end.

3 Cut the 1in (25mm) square billets for the spindles to ¾in (20mm) square blanks using a drawknife (see pages 72–75). To shape the spindles, mark 6in (150mm) along the length of each blank for the ¾in (20mm) swell. Taper them from the swell mark down the 6in (150mm) length to a diameter of about ⅝in (16mm) at the end, which will be the bottom of the spindle, then taper from the swell mark to the opposite end to a diameter of about 9/16in (14mm), which will be the top of the spindle.

4 Place all the parts in a drying kiln for about a week until they are super dry.

Steam bending (allow two days for drying)

5 Make the arm bow bending form using the plans on page 216, then make the 54 × 1¼ × 1⅛in (1380 × 32 × 28mm) arm bow blank (see pages 80–81). Steam bend the arm bow blank (see pages 82–89). Set aside to air dry for a couple of days. Remove the strap and batten and lightly nail another batten to both ends of the arm bow.

When the parts are all super dry

6 Using the plan on page 216, create the template for the seat on a sheet of plywood, then use this to draw the shape of the seat on the blank. Cut out the shape using a bandsaw or jigsaw (see pages 76–77).

3

5a

5b

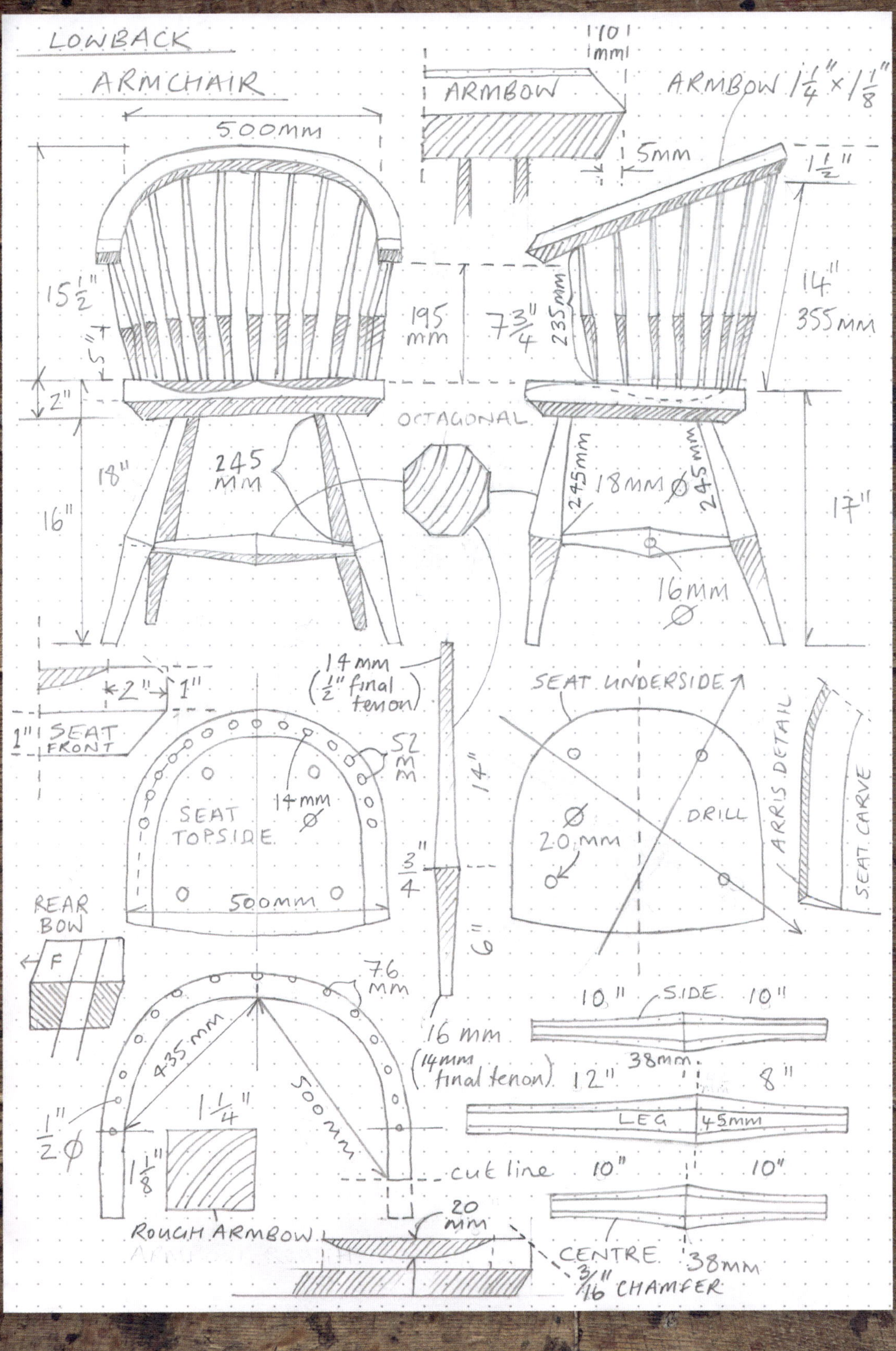

LOWBACK
ARMCHAIR
500MM
10 mm
ARMBOW
ARMBOW 1 1/4" x 1 1/8"
5MM
1 1/2"
15 1/2"
5 1/4"
2"
195 mm
7 3/4"
235mm
14"
355MM
18"
16"
245 MM
OCTAGONAL
245mm
18MM Ø
245mm
17"
16MM Ø
2"
1"
1"
SEAT FRONT
14mm (1/2" final tenon)
SEAT UNDERSIDE
52 MM
14mm Ø
SEAT TOPSIDE
500MM
14"
DRILL
20 MM Ø
ARRIS DETAIL
SEAT CARVE
3/4"
REAR BOW
F
6"
76 MM
435 MM
500MM
1/2" Ø
1 1/4"
1 1/8"
16 mm (14mm final tenon)
ROUGH ARMBOW
cut line
20 MM
10" SIDE 10"
38mm
12" 8"
LEG 45mm
10" 10"
CENTRE 38MM
3/16" CHAMFER

7 Level the underside of the seat blank using a hand plane. To gauge if the seat is flat, place a pair of rulers or straightedges on opposite sides the blank and look at one in relation to the other. This will show you if the seat has any twist. If it does, plane the higher parts of the seat to eliminate it (see pages 78–79).

8 Use a marking gauge to draw a line all around the seat 2in (50mm) from the now flat underside. Use this reference line to plane the top side of the seat until it is roughly flat and the seat is an even thickness on all sides.

9 Transfer the drilling sight lines from the plywood template to the underside of the seat blank and mark the centres of the leg mortices. Then, using a marking gauge, draw a dividing line around the sides of the blank, making it 1in (25mm) from the top surface of the blank (you will use this later for carving the seat).

10 Clamp the seat, underside up, to a workbench or a low table, sandwiching a piece of plywood between the seat and the bench. This is to avoid drilling into the bench's surface, and it reduces tear out on the top of your work.

11 The mortices for the legs are made using a ¾in (20mm) drill bit and drilled at an angle so the legs can splay out (remember you are working from the underside of the seat). For the front legs, set your bevel gauge to a 16.5 degree angle and for the back legs set it to 24 degrees. Place the drill bit at a drill mark, holding the drill with the bit aligned along the drilling guideline and its tip pointing towards the edge of the seat (see pages 94–95). Drill all the way through the seat. Repeat at the other three marks, ensuring the drill is at the correct angle and aligned along the dividing line for each.

12 Use a lathe or a tenon cutter to make 2½in (63mm) long, ¾in (20mm) diameter tenons on the tops of the legs (see pages 92–93).

7a

7b

7c

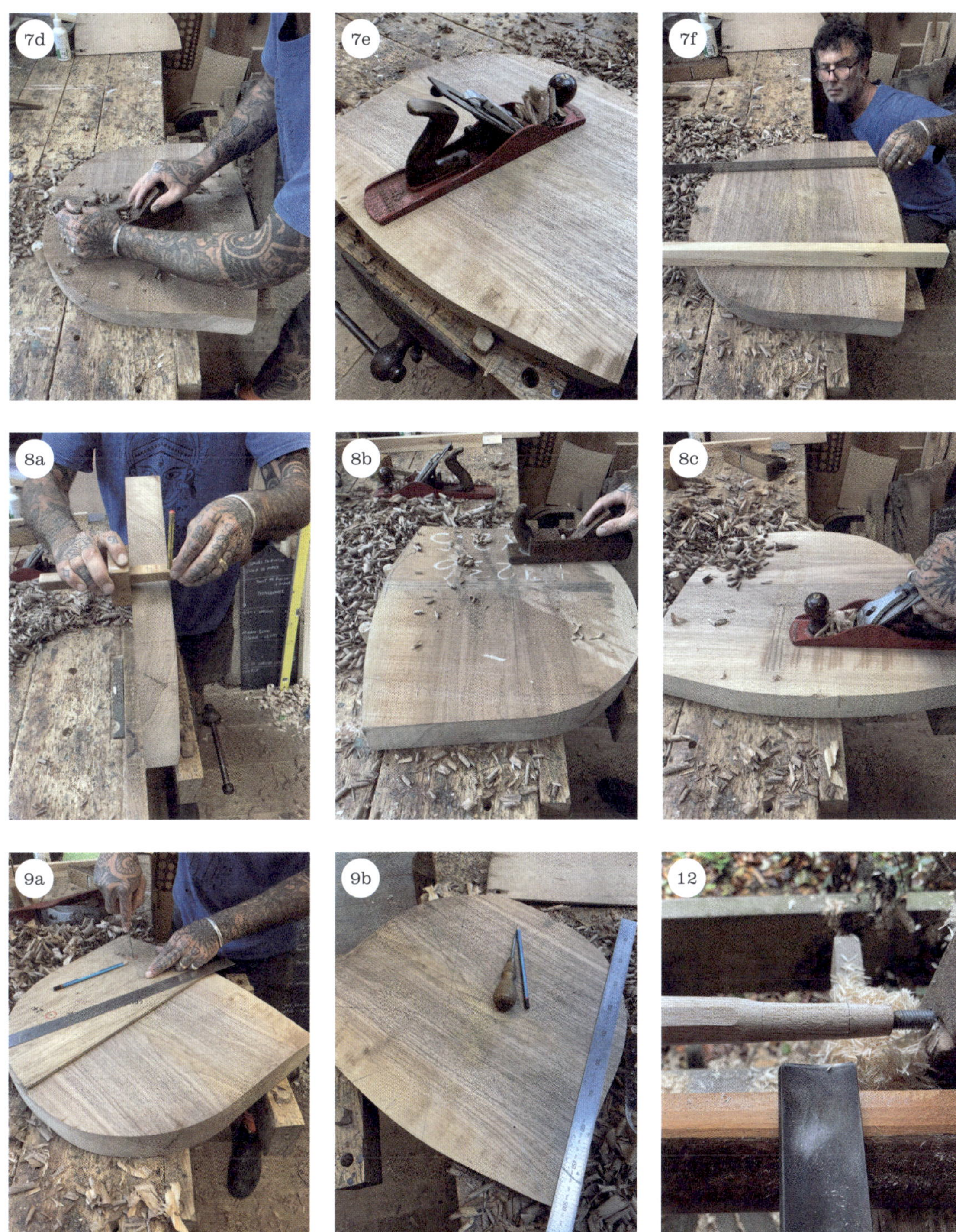
7d
7e
7f
8a
8b
8c
9a
9b
12

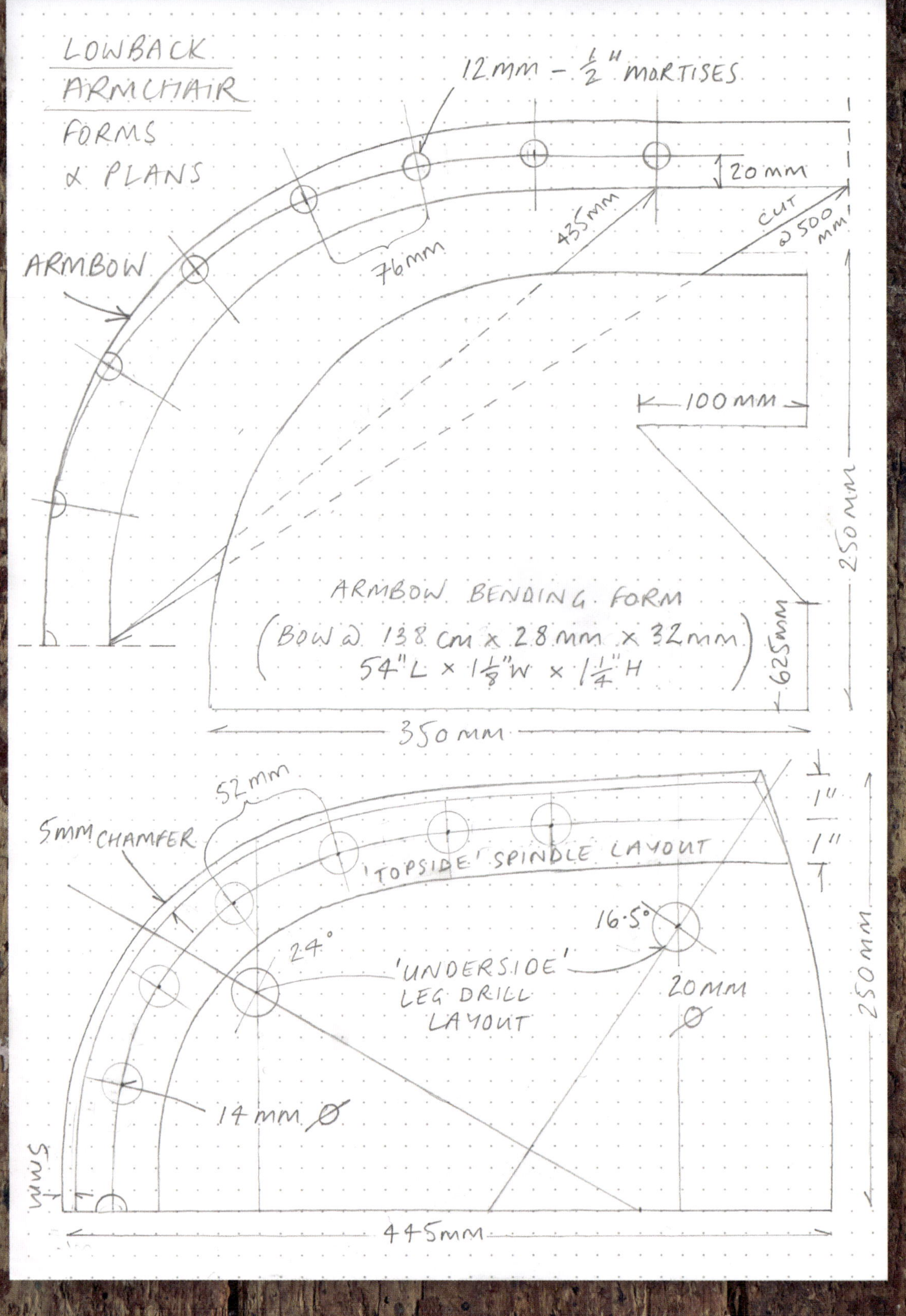

LOWBACK
ARMCHAIR
FORMS
& PLANS
12 MM – 1/2" MORTISES
20 MM
ARMBOW
76 MM
435 MM
CUT
⌀ 500 MM
100 MM
250 MM
ARMBOW BENDING FORM
(BOW @ 138 CM × 28 MM × 32 MM
54" L × 1 1/8" W × 1 1/4" H)
625 MM
350 MM
52 MM
5 MM CHAMFER
1"
1"
'TOPSIDE' SPINDLE LAYOUT
16.5°
24°
'UNDERSIDE' LEG DRILL LAYOUT
20 MM ⌀
250 MM
14 MM ⌀
5 MM
445 MM

13 Check and adjust the fit of the tenons in the mortices (see page 110). Orientate, or twist, the legs into the mortices by hand so that the grain direction on the pairs match, and if you're using octagonal legs, a flat side faces outwards. You can lay a ruler across the front faces to check the flat surfaces are aligned correctly. Tap the legs firmly into the mortices using a metal hammer to seat them. At least ⅜in (10mm) should protrude from the top of the seat; slightly extend the tenon if there is less than this.

14 Check that the swells on the legs are around 9–9½in (230–245mm) from the underside of the seat, measured up the shortest side of each leg. Make a small horizontal mark. The measurement must be the same for all the legs – if needed, remove some of the shoulder from a tenon with a block plane until they all match.

15 Clearly mark on the legs where they meet the sight lines on the seat. Write different letters or numbers on each leg, then put the same symbols next to the mortices on the seat. These will tell you which leg belongs in which mortice, how deep to tap and which way to orientate them (see page 111).

16 To make drilling marks for the stretchers, fit elastic bands between the front and back legs at the horizontal marks you made on the swells. Using the bands as sight guides, make a small vertical mark in between the bands on each leg. Mark the points with a bradawl.

17a

17b

19

20

21a

21b

21c

23a

23b

17 Clamp the seat on top of a block to the bench. Slightly twist the back legs so that you can drill into them with the drill body or bit resting against the front legs. Use the drill point on the front leg to angle the drill towards the drill point on the back leg (see page 96). Using a 11⁄16in (18mm) diameter drill bit, make mortices 1in (25mm) deep. Do the same for the front legs.

18 Make sure the legs are correctly oriented in the seat again and tapped home. Using measuring sticks (see page 93), measure the distance between the depths of the front and back mortices on the legs on one side of the chair. Add 3⁄16in (5mm) to this measurement to create some tension and write that number between the legs. Repeat for the other pair of legs; these measurements may vary slightly.

19 Choose a side stretcher to go in between one pair of legs and label each end to match the corresponding leg's label. Take the measurement you wrote down for that pair of legs and mark out the stretcher's final size with the swell at the centre of this measurement. You then need to turn or cut a 1in (25mm) long, 11⁄16in (18mm) diameter tenon at each end of the stretcher. If using a lathe, turn the tenon and cut to size using a Japanese pull saw or standard tenon saw afterwards; if using a tenon cutter, trim first and then cut the tenon. Repeat for the other side stretcher.

20 Knock the legs very loose. Fit the side stretchers into the mortices and orientate them again so that flat sides face each other. Pull the legs tight on the stretchers. Mark the stretchers where they enter the mortices, and ensure they are numbered or named with the legs they stretch between.

21 To make drill marks for the centre stretcher mortices, first lay a ruler between the widest point in the centre of the swells on the side stretchers, aligning it parallel with the front edge of the seat – place another ruler against the front legs so you can check the two rulers are parallel. You may find that the swells aren't perfectly aligned and your drill point will be slightly off the widest part of one of the swells. Draw a line across the top of each swell where the ruler is, then use these marks and a ruler or square to mark the vertical centre of each stretcher at these marks. Mark the centres with a bradawl.

22 On the underside of the seat, measure and mark 8in (200mm) along the side edge of the seat from each front corner. Join these marks across the seat with a piece of tape or a ruler and a pencil. Once a set of legs has been knocked loose, you can line the drill up to this sight line.

23 Knock a set of legs and a stretcher free from the seat, then drill a 1in (25mm) deep mortice into the drill mark on the other side stretcher using the sight line on the seat and keeping the drill bit parallel to the seat, this time using a 5⁄8in (16mm) drill bit. Knock the first pair of legs and the corresponding stretcher back into place and then repeat this step for the legs and stretcher on the other side.

24 Once the pairs of legs and their stretchers are knocked together again, using the sticks, measure the distance between the mortices in the centres of the side stretchers. Again, add 3⁄16in (5mm) and write the number on the seat.

25 Repeat step 19 to make the tenons on the centre stretcher, but this time the tenon should be 5⁄8in (16mm) in diameter. Knock all the legs and stretchers loose, fit the centre stretcher in place and knock all the parts back together into the seat. Pull all the tenons in tightly, then orientate and label the centre stretcher.

26 Trim the tops of the tenons, leaving about 3⁄8in (10mm) protruding, using a Japanese pull saw for the best results. Mark the kerfs in the tenons for the wedges, making sure they will sit across the grain of the seat.

27 Using a measuring gauge, draw a line on the top of the seat 1in (25mm) from the edge, starting at one front corner, working around the side and back and finishing at the other corner. Draw a line down the centre of the seat. Copy the mortice drill points from the plan (see page 216); the first mark should be where the two lines you've just drawn intersect at the back of the seat. On each side of this drill mark, make seven more drill marks on the line around the top of the seat; there should be 21⁄16in (52mm) between each drill mark.

28 Lightly plane the top and bottom surfaces of the arm bow with a block plane.

29 Make the jig for the arm bow (see page 101). Place the jig on the seat, removing the battern holding it in shape and making sure that the centre of the jig sits on the centre line of the seat. Then, carefully line up the bow onto the jig, making sure the ends of the bow are equal distances from the centre of the jig/seat, and the bow looks balanced in relation to the edges of the seat. If the jig is too small for the arm bow, clamp a piece of wood to the jig to support the arm bow. Also check the angle of the back spindle sight line on the jig. When everything is aligned, securely clamp the jig to the seat and the arm bow to the jig.

30 The next stage is to mark the the drilling points for the mortices in the arm bow. Because the bow on this chair is at an angle to the horizontal, these drill points will vary as you move from the back centre to the front pair. At the back centre, the point is on the arris of the bow (the corner where the top surface meets the back surface), 1¼in (32mm) from the inside edge. Draw a line across the bow at this point, using the centre line of the jig to guide you.

31 The spindles then gradually get closer to the inside edge as you move towards the ends of the bow, with the front pair of spindles ¾in (20mm) from the inside edge. Using a measuring gauge, draw a line around the entire length of the top of the bow, ¾in (20mm) from the inside edge. Next, using dividers set to 3in (76mm), mark seven evenly spaced points towards one end of the bow, starting from the centre line of the jig at the back of the bow. Repeat this to make seven more marks towards the other end of the bow.

32 It is important that the front pair of mortices are parallel to the front corners of the seat. To check this, lay one ruler on the seat, aligned with the front corners, then lay a ruler on the bow, and check your front pair of drill points. If they are out of alignment, it could be to do with the regularity of the bow's bend. This isn't a big problem – there is a lot of tolerance in chairmaking – but you may want to adjust one of the front drill points so that they align with the ruler on the front of the seat. If

24

26

29a

29b

29c

30

you are moving the point by around ½in (12mm) or more, you might want to add about 5⁄64in (2mm) to all the 3in (76mm) gaps on that side of the bow, in order to disguise the difference. Don't worry, the eye won't pick this difference up.

33 Next, draw a smooth curve from the final mark you've made on one end of the bow to the mark at the back of the bow in the centre, then repeat this on the other side. Now make new marks on these curved lines where the original marks on the line ¾in (20mm) from the inside edge are. These new marks will be the drill points for the mortices on the arm bow.

34 The next stage is to mark the arm bow and the seat with the sight lines to allow you to drill at the correct angle. Start by laying a ruler across the front pair of arm bow drill points, and strike a line across the bow at these points. Lay a ruler across the front pair of points on the seat, and join these with a straight pencil line. Make marks on this line on the seat that are ¾in (20mm) from each drill point and towards the centre of the seat. Mark the remaining drill sight lines on the arm bow and the seat (see pages 98–99).

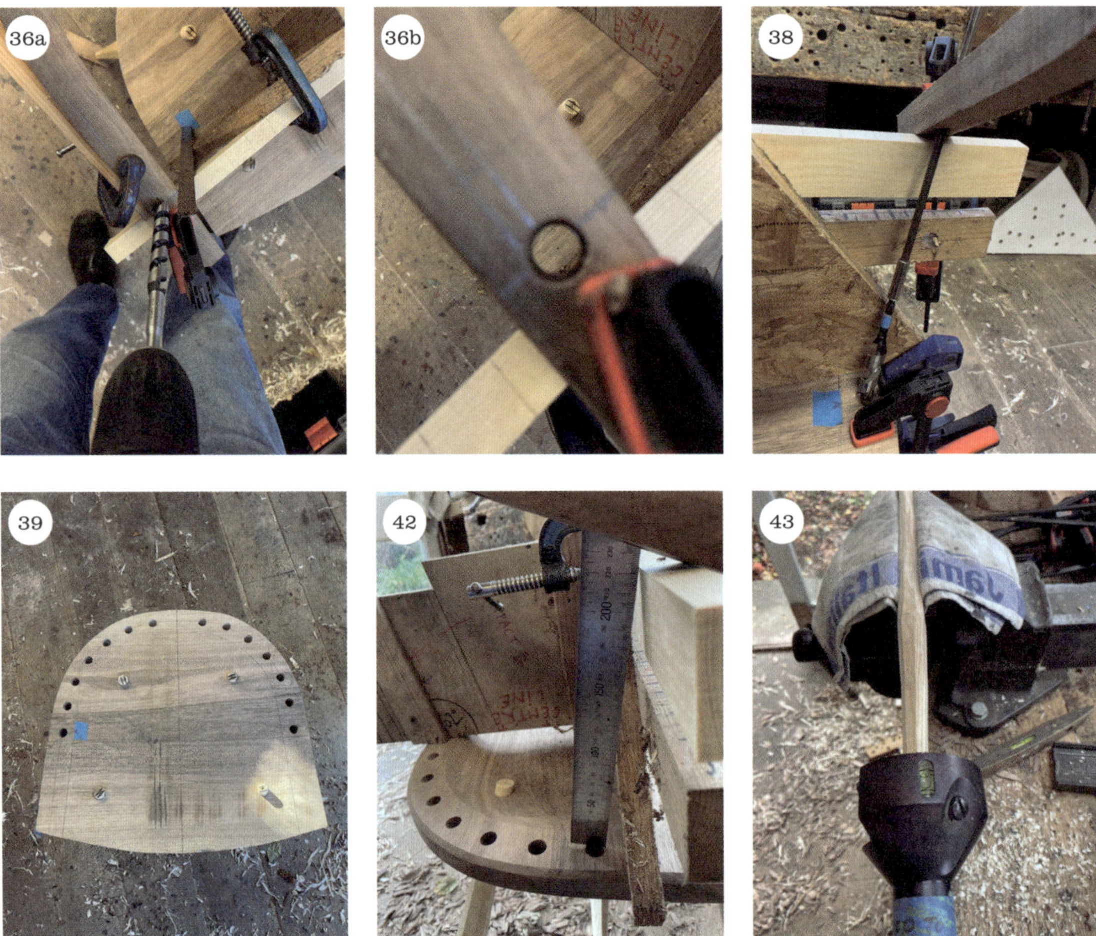

35 Once all the drill points and sight lines have been marked on the arm bow and the seat, you can drill the mortices. They will go all the way through the thickness of the bow, so clamp a piece of waste material under the bow where you will be drilling, so that as the drill bit emerges it doesn't tear out any splinters.

36 Starting with the front pair of spindle holes, place a stiff ruler against the ends of the sight lines you marked, then use this to drill through the bow using the ½in (12mm) drill bit at the correct angle. Check your drilling by sighting through the hole.

37 Keep drilling all the arm bow mortices, making sure that you are lining them up with the correct corresponding seat drill marks. The jig will obstruct the centre drill holes; just wait until the spindles are fitted, then you can drill that last pair.

38 When you've finished drilling the mortices in the arm bow, drill the mortices in the seat. For the front pair only you'll be drilling the spindle holes completely through the seat, so clamp a piece of scrap wood under the seat in these areas to avoid 'tear out' splinters as the drill bit emerges. With the bow still clamped to the jig, pass an extension with a 9⁄16in (14mm) drill bit through the arm bow hole and drill all the way through the seat.

39 Still using the extension, continue to drill the remaining seat mortices for the other spindles, but make them only 1in (25mm) into the seat.

40 The next stage is to carve the seat. First, disassemble the undercarriage, transferring the leg labels to the insides of the leg mortices, in case you lose them when planing the seat underside clean.

41 To determine the area for carving the seat, first draw the edge of the carved area 2in (50mm) from the one corner of the front of the seat all the way around the back to the other corner using a measuring gauge and a pencil, then draw a circle with a piece of chalk that it is 1in (25mm) within the carved area at the back and the sides – it will be further away from the pencil line as it curves towards the centre of the front of the seat. Use an adze followed by a travisher to carve out the seat (see pages 102–8).

42 Refit the legs and stretchers and knock them in place. Place the jig back on the seat, ensuring it's aligned to the centre line laterally and to the mortice in the centre of the back of the seat. On one side of the seat, measure the distance from the frontmost mortice in the seat to the bottom of the corresponding hole at the front of the arm bow. Write this measurement on the seat – it should be about 9¼in (235mm).

43 The next stage is fitting the spindles in place. For the front pair of spindles, cut longer 2½in (63mm) tenons using a 9⁄16in (14mm) tenon cutter at the base end of one of the spindles. You'll then need to measure from the shoulder of the tenon up the spindle the same distance you recorded in the previous step; make a mark at this point. Now measure a further 2in (50mm) beyond that and make another mark. Trim the spindle at the final mark using a Japanese saw, then use a ½in (12mm) tenon cutter to make a tenon on the top 2in (50mm) section of the spindle. Repeat this step for the other front spindle.

44 First ensure the base ends of this front pair of spindles fit all the way through the mortices to below the seat, then ensure the tops fit easily through the bow. If they fit, place the spindle tops into the bow, then position the bow above the chair and tap them into their seat holes. Make sure that the bow sits at the same height on both sides, at 8⅞in (225mm) from the top edge of the seat to the bottom edge of the front of the bow.

45 Turn a tenon on the base end of all the remaining spindles, giving them a 9⁄16in (14mm) diameter and making them 1in (25mm) long to fit in the seat mortices. Ideally, once fitted, the centre of the bow should sit directly above the centre of the seat when viewed from the front – you may have to twist the front pair of spindles until the bow sits centrally.

46 Next, cut a piece of 2 x 1in (50 x 25mm) board the same length as the gap between one of the pairs of mortices on either side of the central spindle at the back of the seat and use it to support the arm bow. Drill the missing mortice for the centre spindle that was obstructed by the jig.

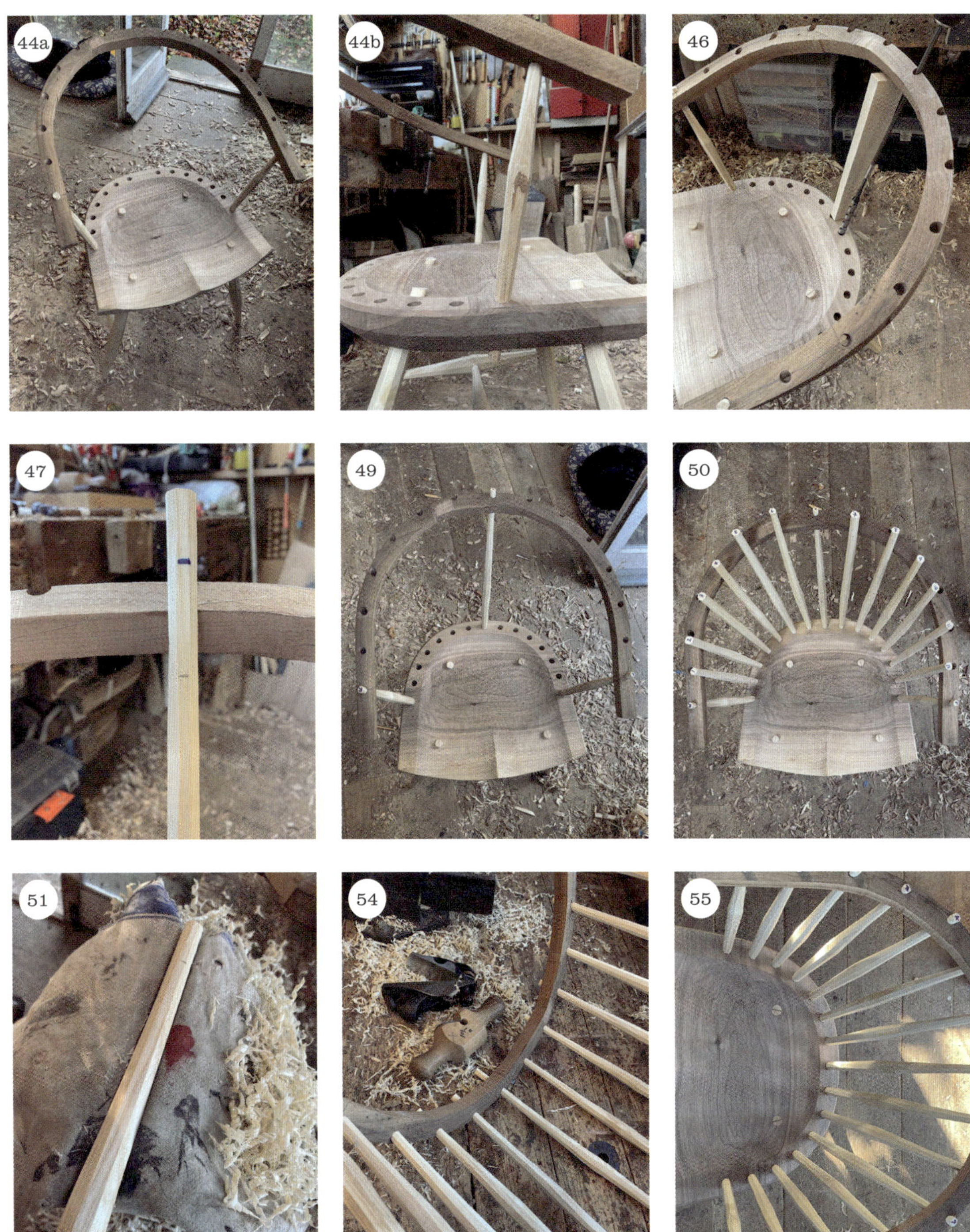
44a
44b
46
47
49
50
51
54
55

47 Now fit the centre spindle. Choose the nicest and straightest spindle, then knock it into the seat, but just in front of the bow. Sighting across the bow, make a mark on the spindle 2in (50mm) above the bow.

48 Carefully remove the spindle from the seat, holding it firmly with both hands around the base and twisting it up. Trim the spindle to the line. Cut a ½in (12mm) diameter tenon on the top 2½in (63mm) of the spindle.

49 Knock the bow loose from the seat. Fit the top of the centre spindle. With the front pair of spindles in the seat, drop the bow onto this pair and tap the centre spindle into the seat mortice.

50 With the bow suspended on the centre and two front spindles, place the remaining spindles just slightly into the mortices in the seat, leaning them against the front of the bow. Duck down so that your sight line is at the height of the bow, and sighting each spindle in turn, make a clear pencil mark on each spindle 2in (50mm) above the bow. Label everything clearly, marking L and R on the front pair, then numbering the rest 1 through 13.

51 Keeping the centre and front pair of spindles in place, remove all the other spindles. Trim the top of the loose spindles to the marked lines, then cut ½in (12mm) diameter tenons on the top 2½in (63mm) of these spindles. You'll need to relabel the spindles after trimming them.

52 The next stage is to glue up the undercarriage. Disassemble the legs and stretchers, then saw the slots for the kerfs in the top of the legs (see page 112).

53 One at a time, apply a thin layer of glue to a tenon and a matching mortice, then loosely insert the tenon into the mortice, starting with the legs, then the side stretchers and finally the centre stretcher. With all the parts in place, tap with the hammer to ensure a good fit. Apply a thin layer of glue to one side of each wedge and tap it in place. Leave to dry for at least a few hours. Once the glue is dry, use the Japanese pull saw to cut the tops of the wedged tenons so that about 3⁄16in (5mm) is protruding, then trim them relatively flush with a carving chisel and a mallet before cleaning them up with a cabinet scraper.

54 It's time to dry fit the rest of the spindles into the arm bow. Knock the bow loose, using a metal hammer to make sharp taps. Fit all the loose spindles into the bow, making any necessary adjustments, then place the bow back on the front pair of spindles, tapping and twisting all the spindles down into their mortices. Now tap the bow down – the bow needs to sit in such a way that the length of the exposed spindles between the seat and the arm bow is 8⅞in (225mm) on the front pair and 14in (355mm) on the centre spindle at the back.

55 You might find that the bow doesn't move down far enough. Make sure all the spindles are hammered into the seat, then see which spindle tops need a little more tenon length, mark them, knock apart and cut the tenons further as needed. Assemble again, with spindles into bow and bow onto the front pair, then tap the spindles home and knock the bow down. Do this until you have the desired height. Ensure all the tops of the spindles still have clear numbers.

56 Now with the chair fully fitted and assembled, mark the ends of the bow for trimming. Measure 19¾in (500mm) in a straight line from the inside centre of the back of the bow to a point on the inside of one arm. Mark this length on the arm, then place a ruler from this mark across to the other arm, moving the loose end of the ruler until it lines up parallel to the front of the seat. It helps to close one eye when lining it up, and it might help to lay a ruler or a level onto the seat.

57 Strike a line across both 'handholds'. Now mark the ends of the bow using a bevel gauge so that they line up with the slight angle of the seat front. Cut the ends with a Japanese saw, then smooth them with a cabinet scraper and sandpaper.

58 It's now time to refine the parts before glueing up the arm bow and spindles. Clamp a spindle into a vice, then plane the facets until you have an elegant taper up to the cut tenon. Repeat this for all the other spindles. Go over the seat one last time, adding faceted details to the front edge and giving the seat a scrape with a cabinet scraper before sanding until very smooth and giving one final scrape.

59 Turn your attention to the bow. Clamp it flat to your bench or in a vice, and plane the top and bottom surfaces again. Clean up the outside edge using a sharp spokeshave with a flat sole; the inside edge is best worked on with a curved spokeshave and a cabinet scraper. Then, using the marking gauge, strike a line around the edges of the bow about 9⁄16in (14mm) down from the top edge, dividing it in two. On the inside edge of the entire length of the bow, angle the top half inwards, which will be easier on the back. On the outside edge of the bow, taper the bottom edge inwards. On the handholds, make a mark across the top of the armbow ⅜in (10mm) from the front edges, and on the bottom make a mark across 3⁄16in (5mm) from the front edge. Use these marks to carve a pointed taper at the front. All the corners should be finely faceted, using a spokeshave.

60 You are ready to start glueing the spindles. Apply glue only in the holes of the seat and the bow. Fit the front pair of spindles into the seat, then the remaining spindles into the bow. Place the bow onto the front pair of spindles, and hammer the spindles firmly into their mortices in the seat, then hit the bow down to the correct height, using a block between the hammer and the bow to prevent damage.

61 Ensuring they are going against the grain of the wood in the seat, split the tops of the tenons protruding from the bow with a sharp chisel, striking it with a hammer, and also the underside ends of the front pair of spindles. Glue and tap in the wedges.

62 After the glue has set, trim the tenons just as you did with the legs (step 53). Scrape and sand the bow until silky smooth.

63 Using a spirit level, check the level of the chair seat to determine which legs need trimming and by how much (see pages 118–19), then trim them using a Japanese saw.

64 Your chair is ready for finishing, whether you choose to paint it or apply an oil and wax finish (see pages 121–23).

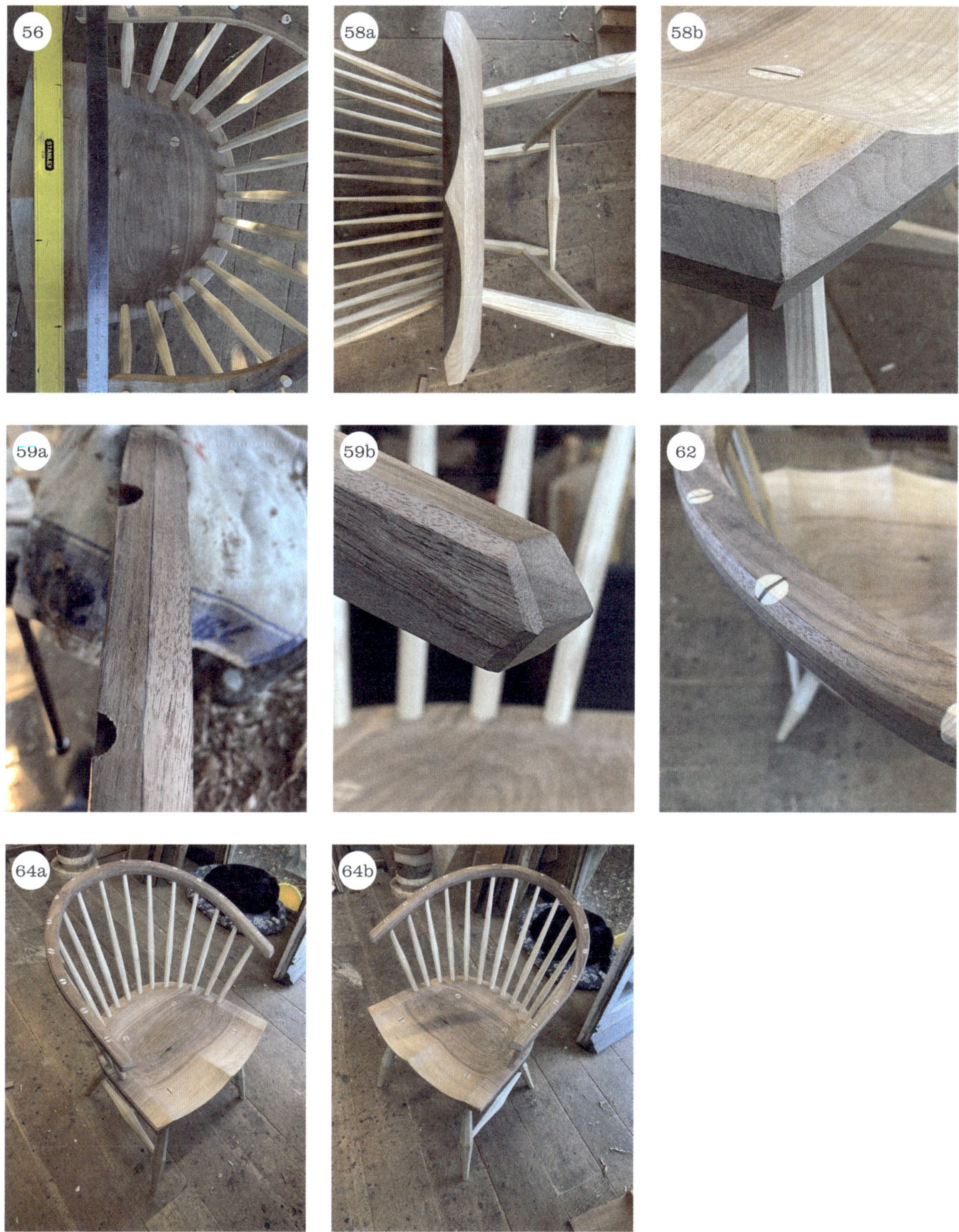
56
58a
58b
59a
59b
62
64a
64b

PROJECT NO. 4

SHAKER BENCH

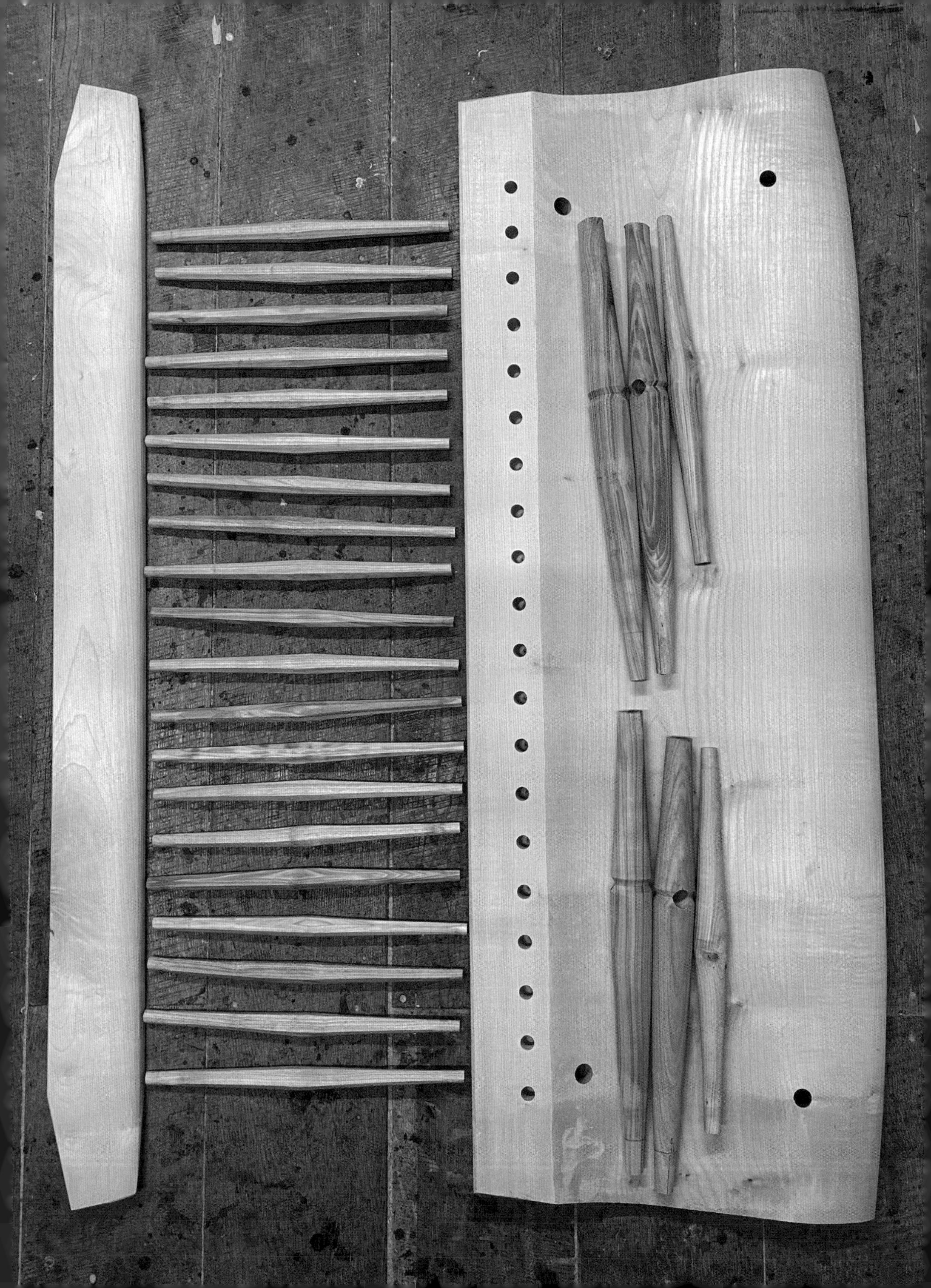

This is my version of a Shaker-style bench. The Shakers are famous for their beautiful furniture, which is both austere and utilitarian. My version of this bench is made with a little more flair than would have met their approval, but it still retains a simple design that relies on fluid lines and well-made uniform spindles. The length of the bench can be altered to fit a particular space, but if it exceeds 5ft (1.5m) it might need a central pair of legs to support the weight of three or more persons. For the sake of this project, the bench is 47¼in (1200mm), making it a comfortable two-seater, but you could opt for a smaller 43in (1090mm) bench with 18 spindles if you prefer.

ALLOW 10 DAYS, PLUS A WEEK FOR DRYING

MATERIALS

From 20in (505mm) green cherry log(s), cut:

- 6 square billets for 4 legs and 2 stretchers, each 20 × 2 × 2in (505 × 50 × 50mm)
- 20 square billets for the spindles (plus extras for spares), each 20 × 1 × 1in (505 × 25 × 25mm)

You will also need:

- For the seat, 47½ × 18¼ × 2⅛–2⅜in (1205 × 465 × 55–60mm) kiln-dried hardwood board such as sycamore, ash or oak
- For the crest, 47½ × 4¼ × 1¼in (1205 × 110 × 32mm) kiln-dried hardwood board such as sycamore, ash or oak, to match or nicely contrast with the seat
- Plywood for template and jig
- 4 wedges: 1 × 1 × 5⁄32in (25 × 25 × 4mm) hardwood strips (see page 113)
- PVA wood glue or hide glue

see pages 212–13 for the plans and 218 for the seat template

METHOD:

Making the parts (allow a week for drying)

1 Cut 4 of the rough 2in (50mm) square billets into $1\frac{3}{4}$in (45mm) square blanks for the legs using a drawknife, or turn them into $1\frac{3}{4}$in (45mm) diameter blanks on a lathe (see pages 65–69). To shape a leg, mark $7\frac{1}{2}$in (190mm) from one end for the $1\frac{3}{4}$in (45mm) swell, and from this mark, taper the $7\frac{1}{2}$in (190mm) section so that it's $\frac{3}{4}$in (20mm) in diameter at the end, which will be the foot. Repeat this in the other direction from the swell, this time tapering it so that it ends 1in (25mm) in diameter. If you are using a lathe, carve out a 'V' at the swell, making cuts $\frac{5}{16}$in (8mm) above and below the swell so that it's $1\frac{3}{8}$in (35mm) in diameter in the centre. Repeat for the other legs.

2 Cut or turn the remaining 2in (50mm) square billets for the stretchers in the same fashion, but to $1\frac{1}{2}$in (38mm) square blanks (see pages 65–69). To shape the stretchers, mark the centre of the blanks for the $1\frac{1}{2}$in (38mm) swell, and taper them to a diameter of about $\frac{7}{8}$in (22mm) at each end.

3 Cut the 1in (25mm) square billets for the spindles to $\frac{3}{4}$in (20mm) square blanks using a drawknife (see pages 72–75), then trim them to 14in (355mm). To shape the spindle, mark 6in (150mm) along the length of each blank for the $\frac{3}{4}$in (20mm) swell. Taper them from the swell down the 6in (150mm) length to a diameter of $\frac{5}{8}$in (16mm) at the end, which will be the bottom, then taper from the swell to the opposite end to a diameter of $\frac{9}{16}$in (14mm), which will be the top.

4 Place all the parts in a drying kiln for about a week until they are super dry.

When the parts are all super dry

5 Using the plan on page 218, create the template for the seat on a sheet of plywood, then use this to draw the shape of the seat on the blank (see pages 76–77). For a $47\frac{1}{4}$in (1200mm) wide bench, once you've drawn the first end, you'll need to add a $11\frac{1}{4}$in or a 300mm long section and then use the template again to add the other end. Cut out the shape using a bandsaw or jigsaw.

6 Use a scrub plane or bench plane to flatten the underside of the seat (see pages 78–79). On a long piece of timber like this, check for any twist or 'wind' in the board over its length and adjust accordingly.

1

5

6

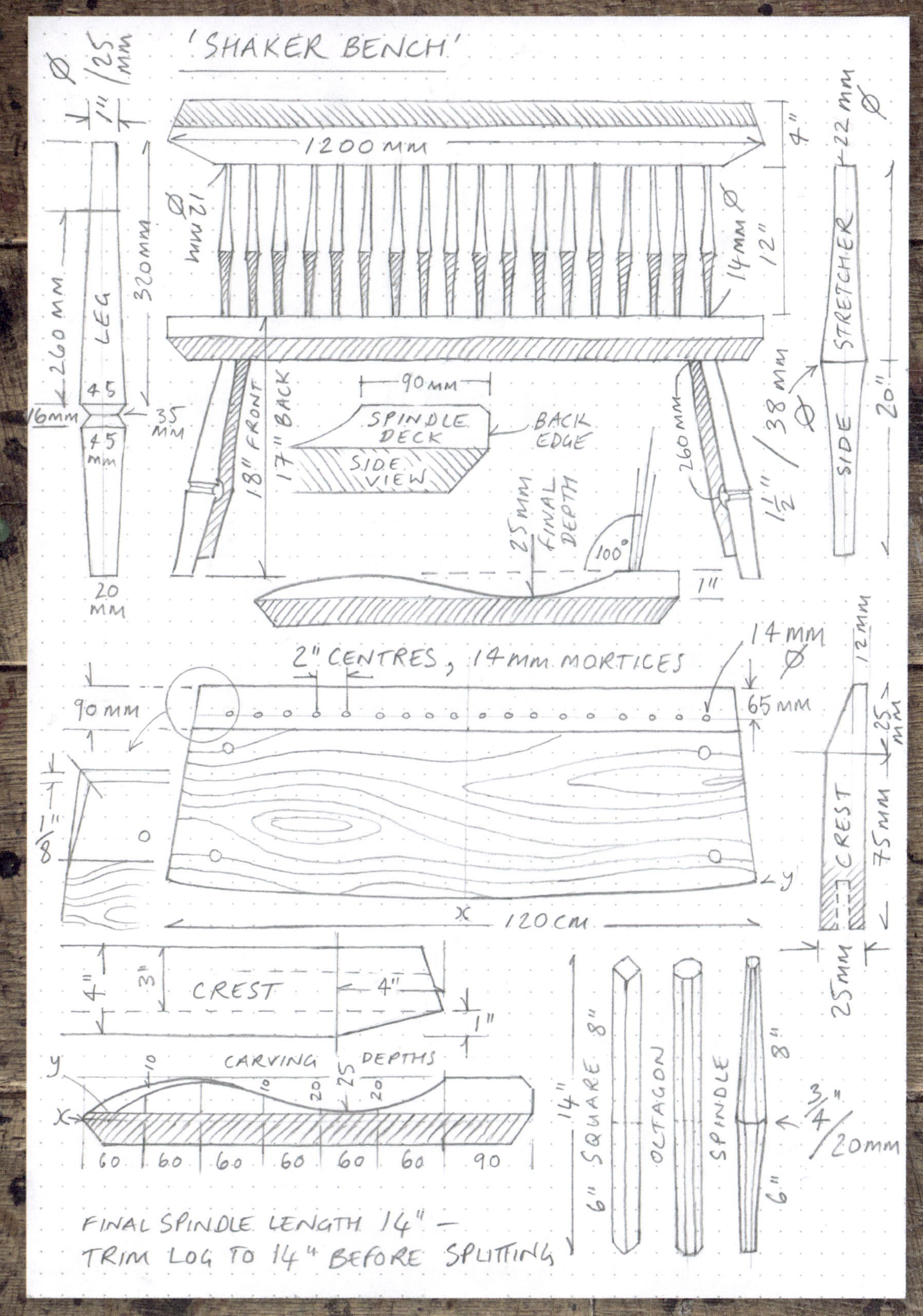

'SHAKER BENCH'
1200 MM
4"
12"
14MM Ø
12MM Ø
22 MM Ø
STRETCHER
SIDE
20"
1½" / 38 MM Ø
LEG
260 MM
320 MM
45
45 MM
35 MM
16MM
20 MM
1" / 25 MM Ø
90MM
SPINDLE DECK
BACK EDGE
SIDE VIEW
18" FRONT
17" BACK
260MM
25MM FINAL DEPTH
100°
1"
2" CENTRES, 14MM MORTICES
14 MM Ø
65 MM
90 MM
1⅛"
120 CM
12MM
25 MM
75MM
25MM
CREST
4"
3"
1"
CARVING DEPTHS
10
20
25
60
90
14"
8"
6"
SQUARE
OCTAGON
SPINDLE
¾" / 20MM
FINAL SPINDLE LENGTH 14" –
TRIM LOG TO 14" BEFORE SPLITTING

7 Use a marking gauge to draw a line all around the seat 2in (50mm) from the now flat underside. Use this reference line to plane the top side of the seat until it is roughly flat and the seat is an even thickness on all sides.

8 Transfer the drilling sight lines and mark the centres of the leg mortices from the plywood template to the underside of the seat blank. Then, using the marking gauge, draw a dividing line around the sides of the blank, making it around 1in (25mm) from the top surface of the blank.

9 Clamp the seat, underside up, to a workbench or a low table, sandwiching a piece of plywood between the seat and the bench. This is to avoid drilling into the bench's surface, and it reduces tear out on the top of your work. If the seat is too large for your workbench, place it on the floor and hold it in place with your foot when drilling.

10 The mortices for the legs are made using a ¾in (20mm) drill bit and drilled at an angle so the legs can splay out (remember you are working from the underside of the seat). For the front legs, set your bevel gauge to an 11-degree angle and for the back legs set it to 18 degrees. Place the drill bit at a drill mark, holding the drill with the bit aligned along the drilling guideline and its tip pointing towards the edge of the seat (see pages 94–95). Drill all the way through the seat. Repeat at the other three marks, ensuring the drill is at the correct angle and aligned along the dividing line for each.

11 Use a lathe or a tenon cutter to make 2½in (63mm) long, ¾in (20mm) diameter tenons on the tops of the legs (see pages 92–93).

12 Check and adjust the fit of the tenons in the mortices (see page 110). Orientate, or twist, the legs into the mortices by hand so that the grain direction on the pairs match, and if you're using octagonal legs, a flat side faces outwards. Tap the legs firmly into the mortices using a metal hammer to seat them. At least ⅜in (10mm) should protrude from the top of the seat; slightly extend the tenon if there is less than this.

13 Check that the swells on the legs are around 9–9½in (230–245mm) from the underside of the seat, measured up the shortest side of each leg. Make a small horizontal mark. The measurement must be the same for all the legs – if needed, remove some of the shoulder from a tenon with a block plane until they all match.

14 Clearly mark on the legs where they meet the sight lines on the seat. Write A and C on the front legs and B (behind A) and D (behind C) on the rear legs. Put the same letters next to the mortices on the seat. These will tell you which leg belongs in which mortice, how deep to tap and which way to orientate them (see page 111).

15 To make drilling marks for the stretchers, fit elastic bands between the front and back legs at the horizontal marks you made on the swells or the V. Using the bands as sight guides, make a small vertical mark in between the bands on each leg. Mark the points with a bradawl.

16 Place a ruler on the seat next to the pair of legs. Close one eye, and looking through the bands from above, line the ruler up so that it is parallel to the bands. Strike a strong line along the ruler's edge onto the seat. Repeat this for the other pair of legs. These will be your sight lines for drilling when one of the legs from each pair is removed from the bench.

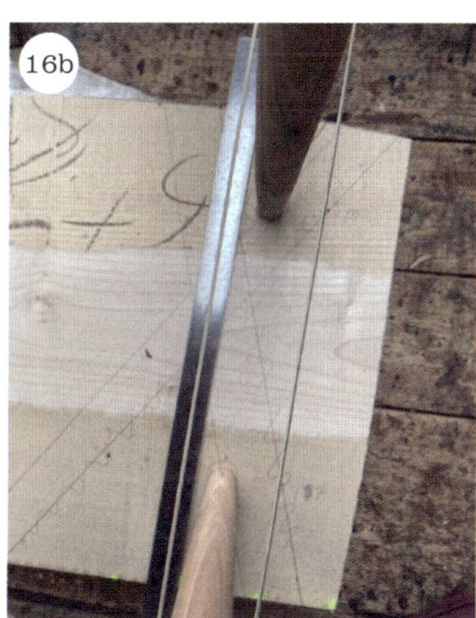

17 To drill mortices in the legs for the stretchers, you will need to remove a front leg to have room to drill the rear leg, then remove the rear leg and fit the front leg back in to make the front leg's mortice, then repeat for the other pair of legs. Use the sight line on the seat to ensure the direction of drilling is correct and use the elastic band around the swells on the other pair of legs to ensure you're drilling at the correct angle. Make 1in (25mm) deep mortices using a 11⁄16in (18mm) bit.

18 Make sure the legs are correctly oriented in the seat again and tapped home. Using measuring sticks (see page 93), measure the distance between the depths of the front and back mortices on the legs on one side of the bench. Add 3⁄16in (5mm) to this measurement to create some tension and write that number between the legs. Repeat for the other pair of legs; these measurements may vary slightly.

19 Choose a side stretcher to go in between one pair of legs and label each end to match the corresponding leg's label. Take the measurement you wrote down for that pair of legs, and mark out the stretcher's final size with the swell at the centre of this measurement. You then need to turn or cut a 1in (25mm) long, 11⁄16in (18mm) diameter tenon

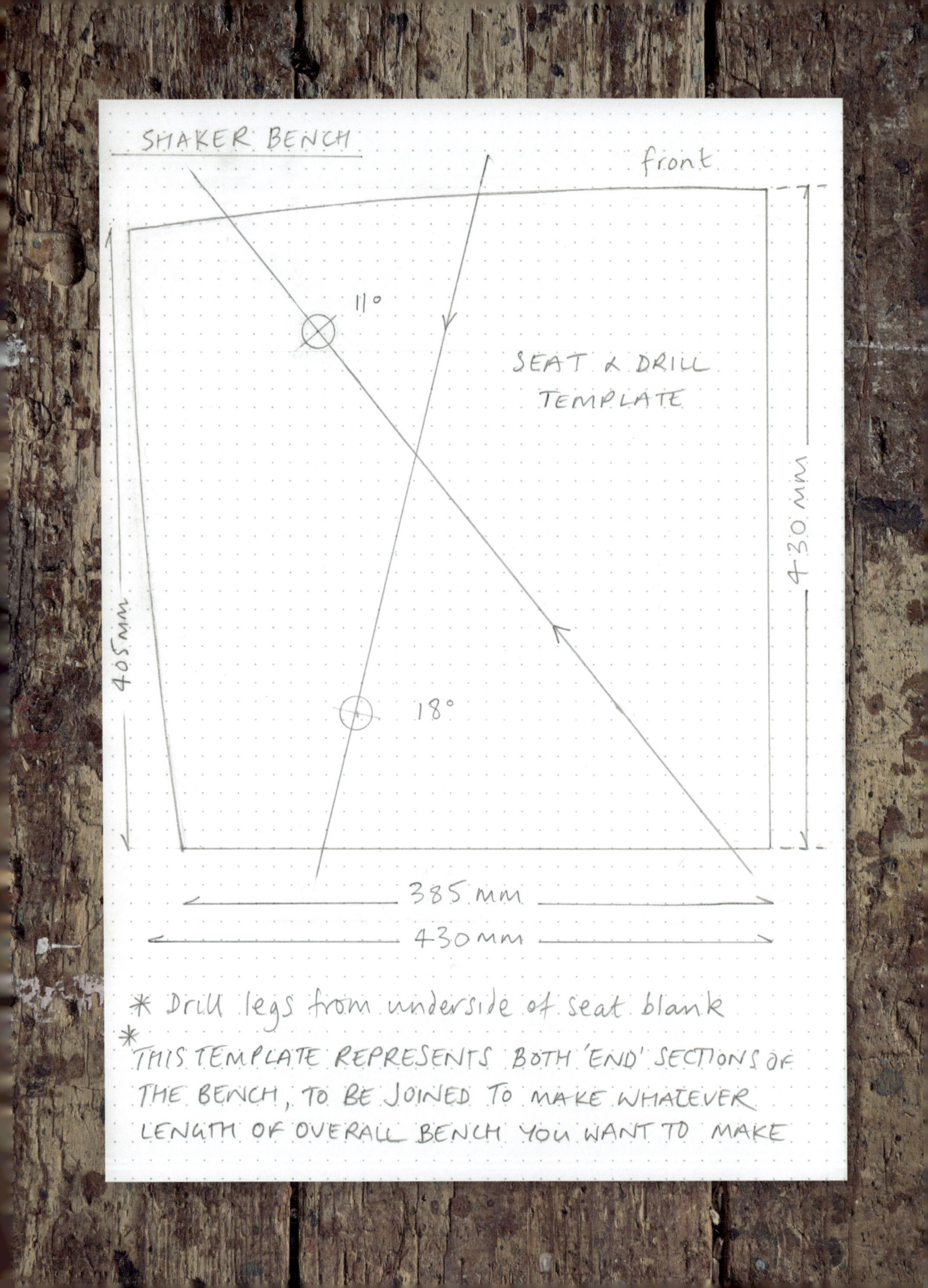

SHAKER BENCH

front

11°

SEAT & DRILL TEMPLATE

430 MM

405 MM

18°

385 mm

430 mm

* Drill legs from underside of seat blank

* THIS TEMPLATE REPRESENTS BOTH 'END' SECTIONS OF THE BENCH, TO BE JOINED TO MAKE WHATEVER LENGTH OF OVERALL BENCH YOU WANT TO MAKE

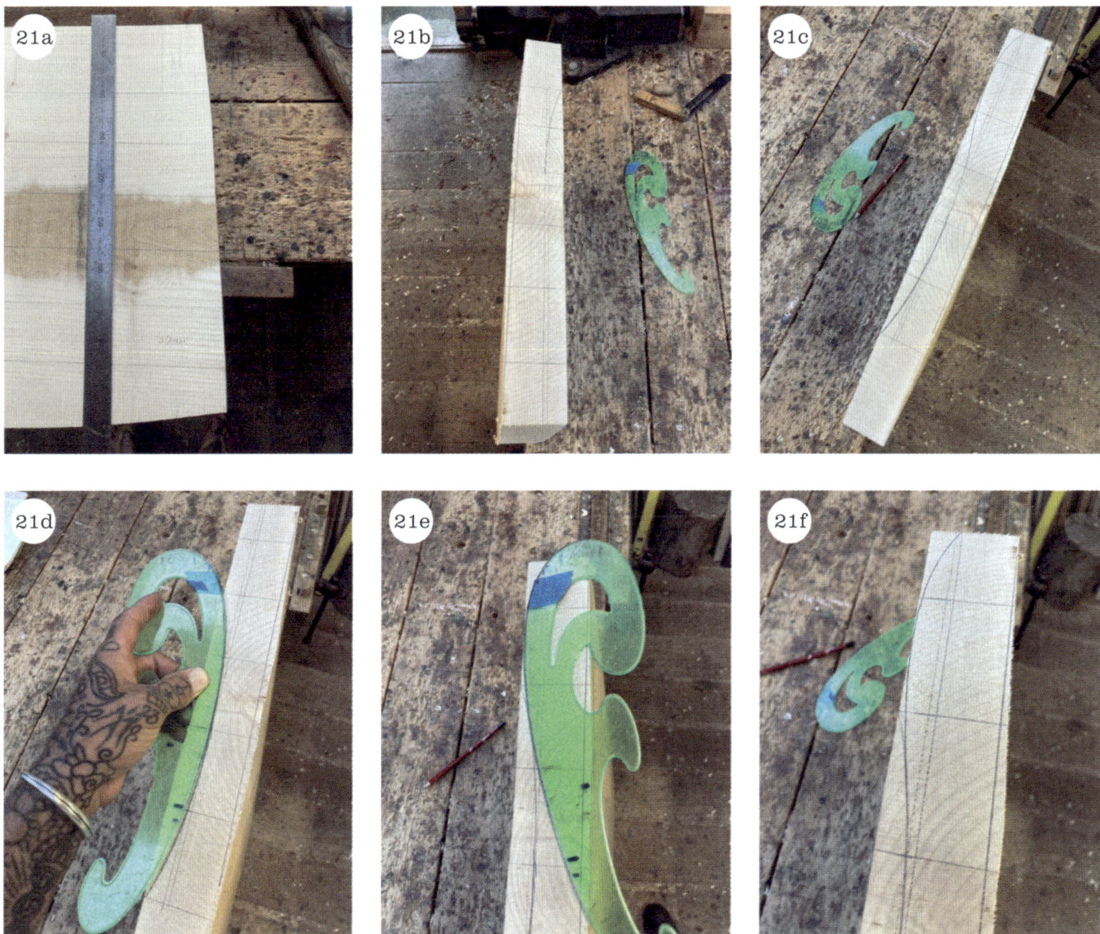

at each end of the stretcher. If using a lathe, turn the tenon and cut to size using a Japanese pull saw or standard tenon saw afterwards; if using a tenon cutter, trim first and then cut the tenon. Repeat for the other side stretcher.

20 Knock the legs very loose. Fit the side stretchers into the mortices and orientate them again so that flat sides face each other. Pull the legs tight on the stretchers. Mark the stretchers where they enter the mortices, and ensure they are labelled to match the legs they stretch between.

Trim the tops of the tenons, leaving about ⅜in (10mm) protruding, using a Japanese pull saw for the best results. Mark the kerfs in the tenons for the wedges, making sure they will sit across the grain of the seat. Disassemble the legs and stretchers.

21 Mark the topside and the ends of the seat following the pattern provided in the plan, with the lines on the top continuing down the side edges. Use a French curve to make a nice flowing shape on the ends, making sure they don't dip below the line you drew in step 8.

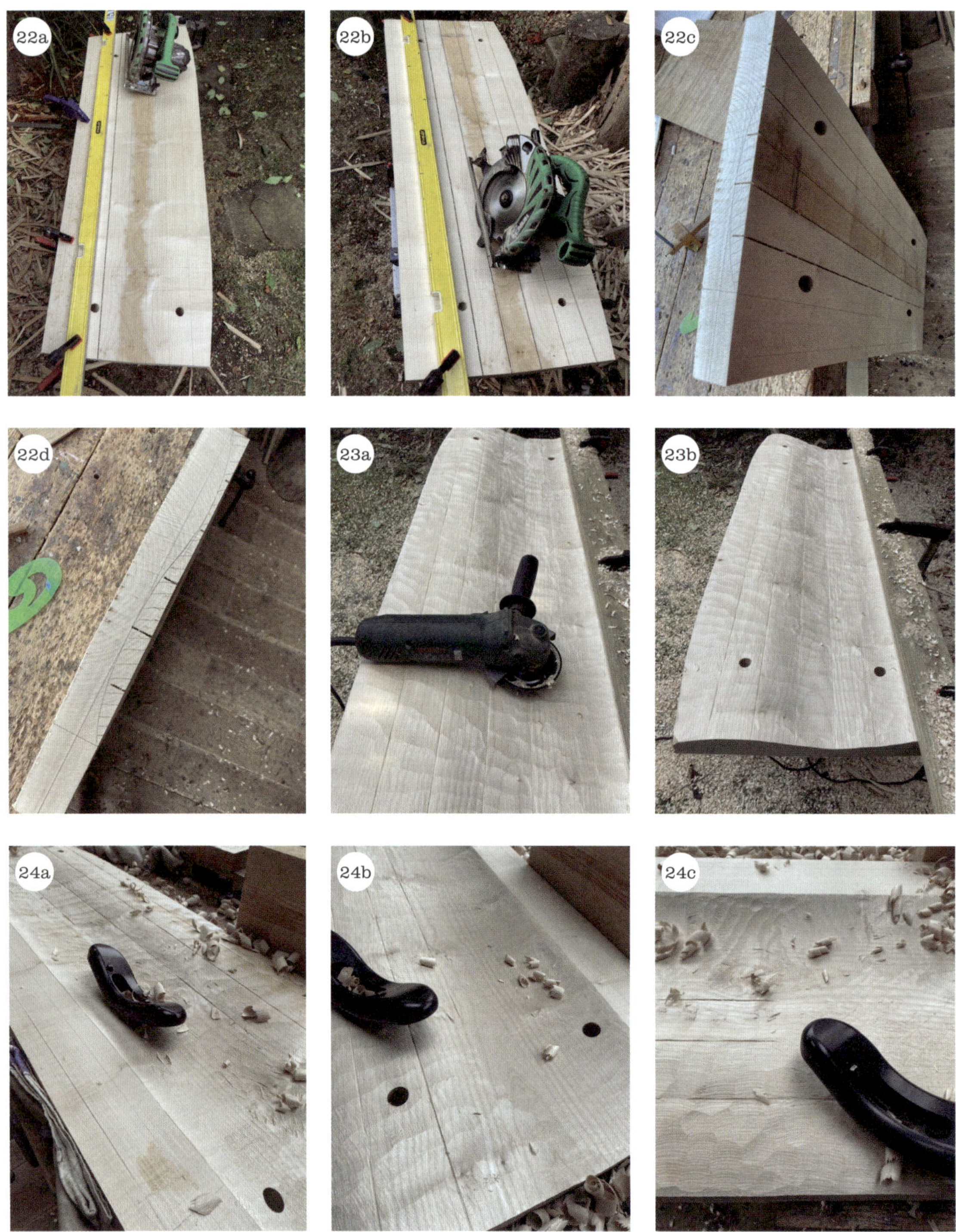
22a
22b
22c
22d
23a
23b
24a
24b
24c

24d

24e

25

22 You will need to make some depth marks along the lines in the pattern on the top of the seat, which will give you a good idea of how deep to carve it. You could drill a series of holes along the lines set to specific depths, or you can use a circular saw to cut slots along the lines to specific depths. I prefer the second method. Clamp a long level to the seat to use as a guide for the saw. Be very careful to adjust the depth of the saw between cuts (or drill between lines of holes).

23 Carve a basic shape down to the depth lines. You can use a wood carving blade such as an Arbortech on an angle grinder if you're experienced in using one, but otherwise mount the seat sideways in a vice and cut the basic shape with a short carving adze (see page 102).

24 Using a travisher, refine the shape. Do not remove the wood entirely to the final depth mark until the final finish, but try to achieve the shape marked on the ends of the seat.

25 Now use a long bench plane to work along the shape to ensure that it is even and that the shape at the front edge meets the line drawn along the front edge of the seat. At this point you could use a belt sander or disc sander to even the shape out.

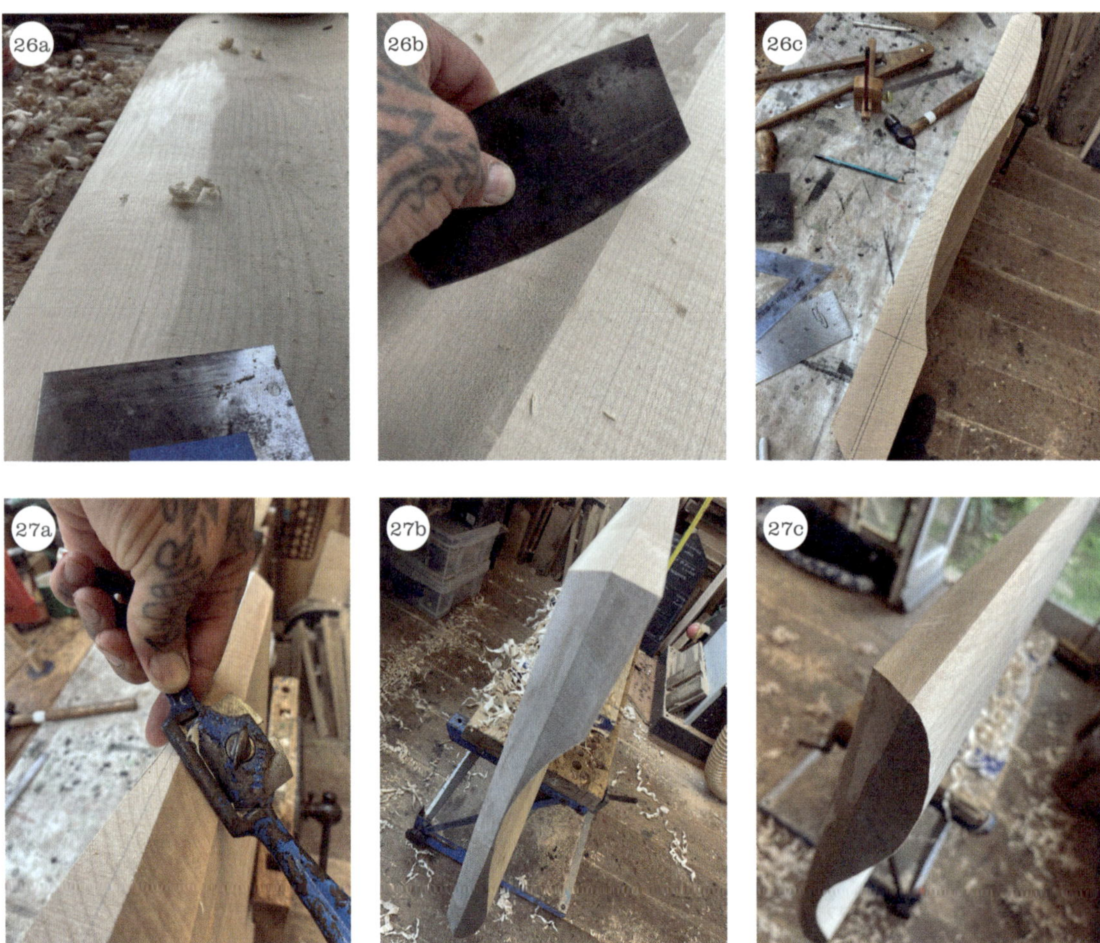

26 Scrape smooth using a cabinet scraper. Try to get a nice crisp 'drop off' where the spindle deck drops into the seat carve.

27 The next stage is to create the chamfer on the underside of the seat. Using a marking gauge, mark a line running all the way around the base of the seat, 1in (25mm) in from the edge. If the line around the edge of the seat you made in step 8 is no longer visible, re-mark that. Remove all of the material between these two lines using a spokeshave or a file and cabinet scraper.

28 Mark the seat for drilling the spindle mortices. First establish the centre line on the board. Make 20 marks for the spindle holes in the spindle deck area 1in (25mm) from where the seat carve starts, working from the centre to the ends, leave 2in (50mm) centres between the holes. The holes on either side of the centre line should be spaced 2in (50mm) apart with the centre line halfway between them, with 10 holes on either side. For a different length bench, simply add or remove a pair of spindles for every 4in (100mm) change in length, keeping the spindles 2in (50mm) apart.

29 Make the 47¼ × 4 × 1in (1200 × 100 × 25mm) crest (see pages 80–81). The board must be totally straight in both axes. You can check this by closing one eye and sighting down its length to look for any bends or twists. If necessary, plane the board until it is flat.

30 Mark the crest for drilling the spindle holes similarly to the how they were marked on the seat (see step 28). Again, mark the centre line, then mark out the drilling points along a midline on the narrow edge of the board, with the centres at 2in (50mm) between the holes.

31 Set a bevel gauge at a 10-degree angle at either end of the spindle deck, raking them backwards. Make sure they align with each other. Drill the 20 mortices 1in (25mm) deep, using a 9⁄16in (14mm) diameter drill bit. Lean the drill backwards to line up with the bevel gauges, and use a small square against the drill bit to make sure they are drilled straight, side to side.

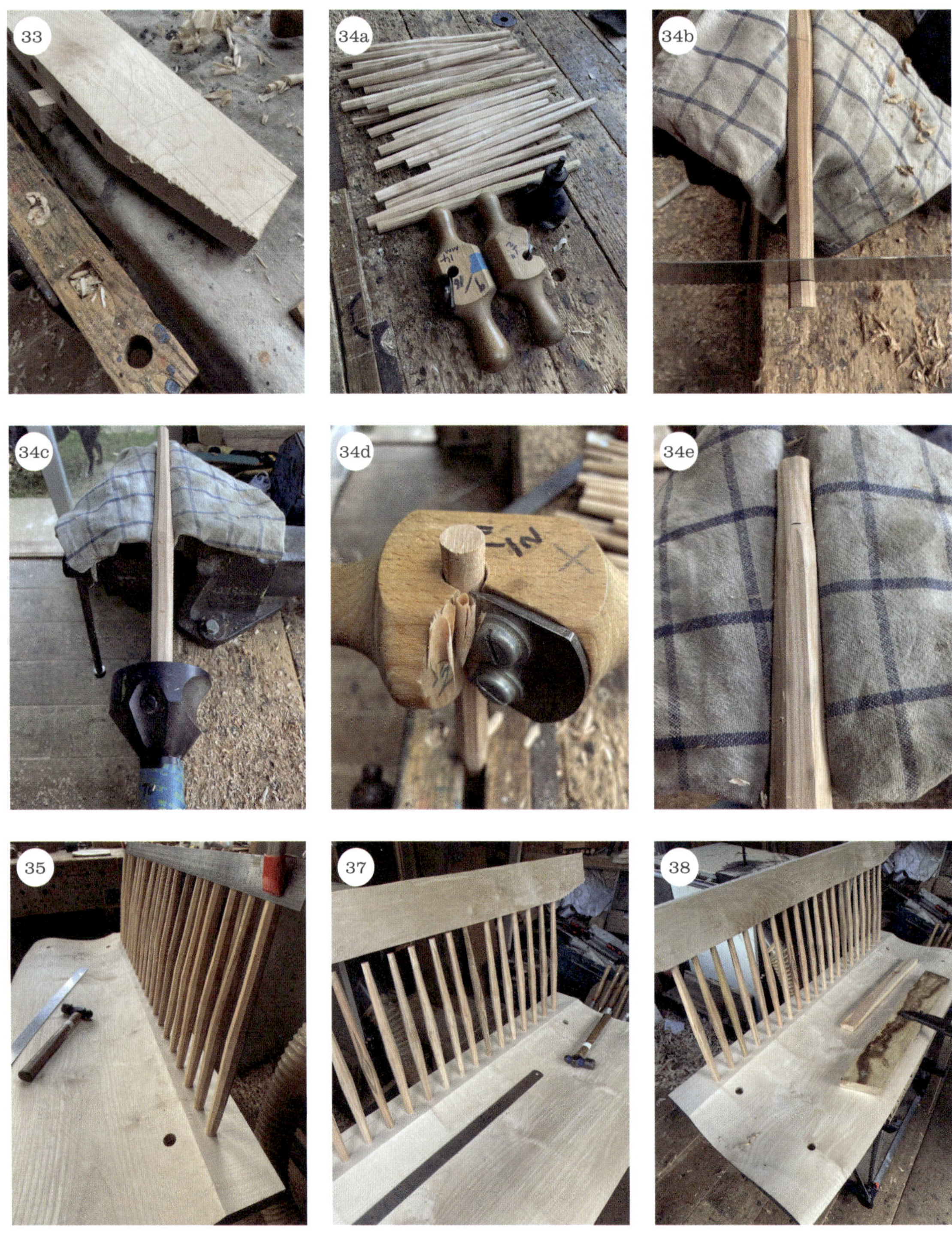
33
34a
34b
34c
34d
34e
35
37
38

32 Now drill the holes in the crest using a ½in (12mm) bit to a 1in (25mm) depth. Mortices should again be straight up and down and in line with the thickness of the board to avoid 'breaking out' of the front or back surfaces – clamping a flat stick or small ruler to the front edge can help in keeping the drill in line.

33 Make marks ½in (12mm) and 4in (100mm) from each end of the crest on the top and bottom edges and draw straight vertical lines between the pairs. On each end of the crest and the inner-most lines you just drew, make marks 1in (25mm) from the bottom edge and join them with straight horizontal lines. Use these lines to cut out the triangles at the ends of the crest using a saw. (As it gets a bit of hammering during the dry fitting stage, the final shaping and smoothing of the crest comes later.)

34 Cut 9⁄16in (14mm) diameter, 1in (25mm) long tenons on the bottom ends of the spindles. Shape the octagonal facets to remove any 'shoulder' where the tenon starts. At this stage, if you prefer, you can glue up the undercarriage so you have the bench on the floor (see step 43), or you can glue up everything at the end.

35 Tap all the spindles into their mortices on the seat. Orientate them so that they align as well as possible. Clamp a ruler to the top of the row of spindles with the top edge at 13in (330mm) above the seat, measured up the length of the spindles. If there is any spindle top standing higher than the edge of the ruler, make a mark and trim the spindle to this length with a Japanese saw.

36 Remove the spindles from the seat. Turn a 1in (25mm) long tenon on the top of all the spindles to a diameter of ½in (12mm). Refit the spindles to the seat.

37 To fit the spindles in the crest, first locate the end spindle in its mortice, tap down until the next spindle can be located, then locate and tap again. Keep doing this and work your way along the length of the crest. This can be very tricky, and some spindles may need a tiny bit trimmed from their tops as you go along – take your time. An extra pair of hands can be useful.

38 Once fitted, tap down firmly with a metal hammer, cushioning the crest with another block to prevent damage. Measure the height from the seat up along the spindles and the crest – it should be 16in (405mm) to the top edge of the crest. If it doesn't measure up correctly, check if your mortices are deep enough. Are the spindles fitting well? If not, adjust accordingly until you get a good fit.

39 Once fitted, you have a chance to twist the spindles so that they align and look their best. If you have kept their octagonal shape, a flat facet should face forwards. Hold a straightedge against the fronts of the spindles to check the alignment of the flat facets. Number each spindle clearly, and put a little pencil dot on the front of each, to ensure correct alignment when glueing.

40

41a

41b

44

45a

45b
ゼットソー
265

40 Refine the parts before glue up, starting with the spindles. Clamp them into a vice, then plane the facets until you have an elegant taper up to the cut tenon. To avoid planing the tenon itself, you could wrap the tenons in masking tape. (You may need to re-mark the number and/or pencil dot if you plane them off.) With the spindles back in place, you will also need to check that the crest is lining up with the back edge of the seat. If the crest is wonky, you can change the twist of the spindles to help line it up.

41 With a marking gauge ⅜in (10mm) from the front of the crest, draw a line along the top of the crest (which you'll use in step 42) and down each side. Make a mark on the top and bottom edges at the back of the crest 4in (100mm) from either end, then draw a vertical line between each pair of marks. Using the pairs of vertical lines you've just drawn at the back and the ends of the crest to guide you, cut a tapered fillet at the back of each end of the crest with a block plane or a drawknife.

42 Next, we are going to create a sloped surface to the top of the front of the crest. Draw a line with a marking gauge along the front of the crest 1in (25mm) from the top. Using this line and the line on the top of the crest to guide you, taper the top section towards the back with a block plane. Plane carefully, and try to get this face entirely flat. You can use a rectangular cabinet scraper to get the final 'flat' finish. Make facet cuts on all the edges; on the shorter end grain you can use a knife or chisel, but it's easier to use a block plane on the longer edges that run in line with the grain.

43 If you haven't already, glue up the undercarriage. Saw the slots for the kerfs in the top of the legs (see page 112). One at a time, apply a thin layer of glue to a tenon and a matching mortice, then loosely insert the tenon into the mortice, starting with the legs, then the side stretchers. With all the parts in place, tap with the hammer to ensure a good fit. Apply a thin layer of glue to one side of each wedge and tap it in place. Leave to dry for at least a few hours.

44 Make facet cuts on the front and back edges of the seat. Make sure to clean and smooth the spindle deck before glueing in the spindles. Apply glue in the mortises only, not on the spindles themselves. Firmly tap the spindles into the seat. Now apply glue to the holes of the crest, and fit it on the spindles in the same way as in step 37, tapping it down using a block in between the hammer and crest top. Measure the height at both ends to make sure it is the same.

45 Once the glue is dry, use the Japanese pull saw to cut the tops of the wedged tenons so that about 3⁄16in (5mm) is protruding, then trim them relatively flush with a carving chisel and a mallet before cleaning them up with a cabinet scraper. Give the seat a thorough scrape with a curved cabinet scraper and then a thorough sand – silky smooth is good! Then, using a 400-grit sheet of sandpaper, give any sharp edges a light buff – everything should feel crisp but not sharp. Be careful not to remove the faceted details with sandpaper, just soften their edges to touch.

46 Using a spirit level, check the level of the bench seat to determine which legs need trimming and by how much (see pages 118–19), then trim them using the Japanese saw. Level to 18in (460mm) to the high point of the carved seat area and to 17in (430mm) to the back edge of the seat.

47 Your bench is ready for finishing, whether you choose to paint it or apply an oil and wax finish (see pages 121–23).

PROJECT NO. 5

LOBSTER POT ARMCHAIR

This chair embodies its primitive roots, while also being elegant and characterful. The seat is generous in size, and it has simple turnings with the addition of a cross stretcher for strength and durability. The spindles are pulled into the crest and form a lobster pot shape, hence the chair's name. There are some fine examples of this chair from the West Country and Wales, often with elm seats.

ALLOW 10 DAYS, PLUS A WEEK FOR DRYING

MATERIALS

From a 28in (710mm) green ash log, cut:

- 10 square billets for the spindles (plus extras for spares), each 28 × 1 × 1in (710 × 25 × 25mm) *

From 20in (505mm) green ash log(s), cut:

- 7 square billets for 4 legs and 3 stretchers, each 20 × 2 × 2in (505 × 50 × 50mm)
- 10 square billets for the spindles (plus extras for spares), each 20 × 1 × 1in (505 × 25 × 25mm)

You will also need:

- For the arm bow, 54¼ × 1½ × 1½in (1380 × 38 × 38mm) green or air-dried hardwood board such as oak
- For the crest, 26¼ × 2¼ × 1¼in (665 × 55 × 32mm) green or air-dried hardwood board such as oak
- For the seat, 18¼ × 22¼ × 2⅛–2⅜in (465 × 565 × 55–60mm) kiln- or air-dried hardwood board such as sycamore, ash or oak
- Plywood for template and jig
- 16 wedges: wedges: 1 × 1 × 5⁄32in (25 × 25 × 4mm) hardwood strips (see page 113)
- 2 pegs: 5⁄32in (4mm) round × 2in (50mm) whittled hardwood
- PVA wood glue or hide glue

** If you haven't used all of the log, you can split it into two 14in (355mm) sections to make some of the spindles listed under the 20in (505mm) log.*

see pages 214–15 for the plans, 217 for the seat and arm bow bending form templates, 219 for the arm bow drilling jig and 220 for the crest bending form template

METHOD:

Making the parts (allow a week for drying)

1 Cut 4 of the rough 2in (50mm) square billets into 1¾in (45mm) square blanks for the legs using a drawknife, or turn them into 1¾in (45mm) diameter blanks on a lathe (see pages 65–69). To shape a leg, mark 8in (200mm) from one end, which is where the 1¾in (45mm) swell will be, and from this mark, taper the 8in (200mm) section so that it's about ¾in (20mm) in diameter at the end, which will be the foot. Repeat this in the other direction from the mark of the swell, this time tapering it so that it's 1in (25mm) in diameter at the end, which will be the top of the leg. Repeat for the other legs.

2 Cut or turn the remaining 2in (50mm) square billets for the stretchers in the same fashion, but to 1½in (38mm) square blanks (see pages 65–69). To shape the stretchers, mark the centre of the blanks for the 1½in (38mm) swell, and taper them to a diameter of about ⅞in (22mm) at each end.

3 Cut the 1in (25mm) square billets for the spindles to ¾in (20mm) square blanks using a drawknife (see pages 72–75). To shape the spindles, mark 8in (200mm) along the length of two of the short blanks for the two front spindles, and 6in (150mm) along the length of the remaining blanks for the side and longer back spindles. These marks are for the ¾in (20mm) swells. Taper each blank from the swell mark down the shorter length to a diameter of about ⅝in (16mm) at the end, which will be the bottom of the spindle, then taper from the swell mark to the opposite end, also to a diameter of about ⅝in (16mm). Whittle the pegs.

4 Place all the parts in a drying kiln for about a week until they are super dry.

Steam bending (allow two days for drying)

5 Make the arm bow and crest bending forms using the plans on page 217, then make the 54 × 1¼ × 1¼in (1380 × 32 × 32mm) arm bow blank (see pages 80–81). Steam bend the arm bow blank (see pages 82–89). Set aside to air dry for a couple of days.

6 Make the 26 × 2 × 1in (660 × 50 × 25mm) crest blank (see pages 80–81), then steam bend it (see pages 82–87, 90). This will also need to air dry for a couple of days.

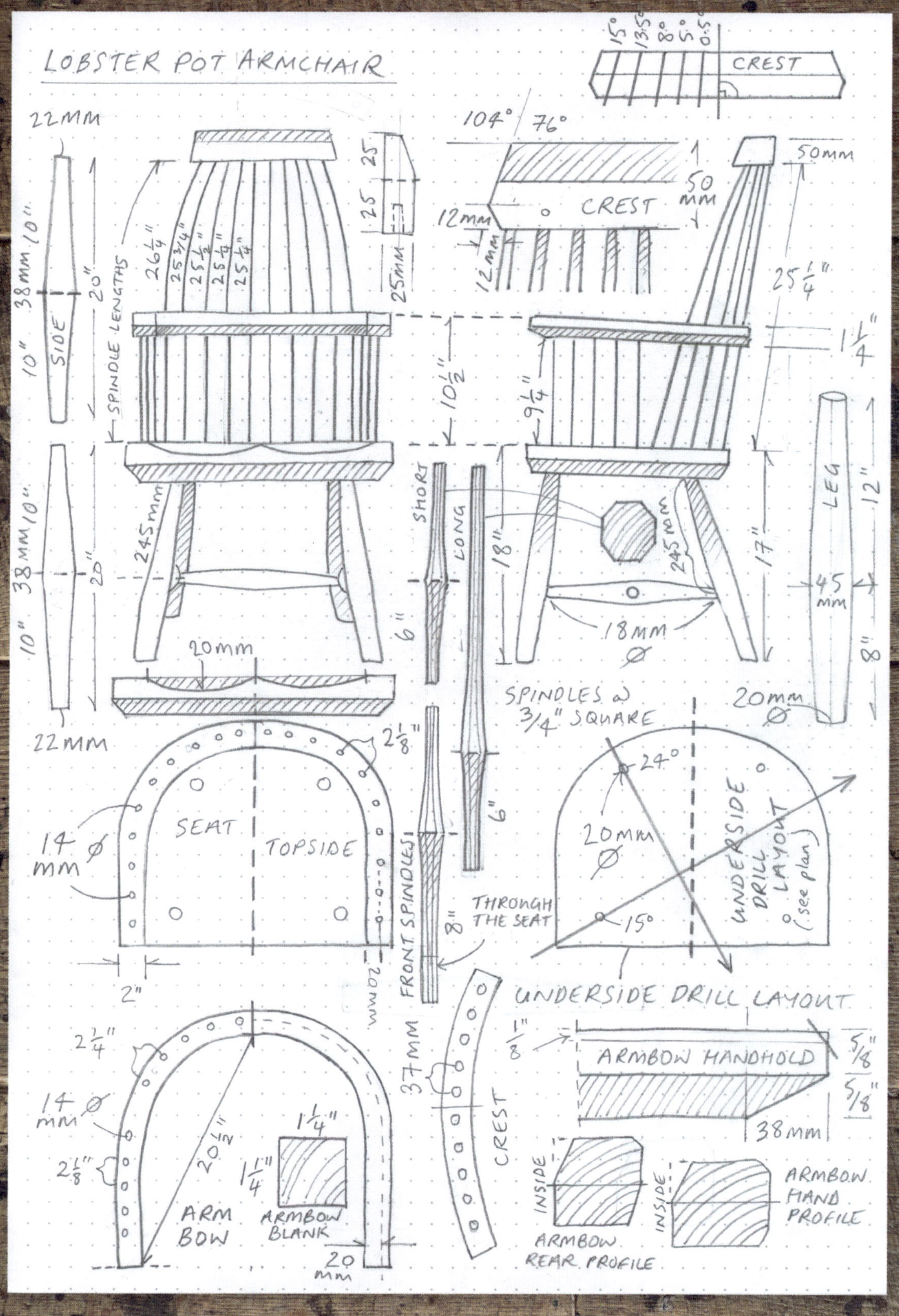

LOBSTER POT ARMCHAIR
CREST
104°
76°
50MM
CREST
50 MM
12MM
12MM
25MM
25
25
22MM
38MM
10"
10"
20"
SIDE
SPINDLE LENGTHS
26¼"
25¾"
25½"
25¼"
25¼"
25¼"
1¼"
10½"
9¼"
245MM
245MM
SHORT
LONG
18"
17"
LEG
12"
45 MM
8"
6"
18MM Ø
20MM
22MM
SPINDLES @ 3/4" SQUARE
20MM Ø
2⅛"
14 Ø MM
SEAT
TOPSIDE
24°
20MM Ø
15°
UNDERSIDE DRILL LAYOUT (see plan)
6"
THROUGH THE SEAT
FRONT SPINDLES
8"
20MM
2"
UNDERSIDE DRILL LAYOUT
⅛"
ARMBOW HANDHOLD
5/8"
5/8"
38MM
2¼"
14 Ø MM
2⅛"
20½"
1¼"
1¼"
ARMBOW BLANK
ARM BOW
37MM
CREST
INSIDE
INSIDE
ARMBOW REAR PROFILE
ARMBOW HAND PROFILE
20 MM

When the parts are all super dry

7 Using the plan on page 217, create the template for the seat on a sheet of plywood, then use this to draw the shape of the seat on the blank. Cut out the shape using a bandsaw or jigsaw (see pages 76–77).

8 Level the underside of the seat blank using a hand plane (see pages 78–79). To gauge if the seat is flat, place a pair of rulers or straightedges on the blank, one each on opposite sides, and look at one in relation to the other. This will show you if the seat has any twist.

9 Use a marking gauge to draw a line all around the seat 2in (50mm) from the now flat underside. Use this reference line to plane the top side of the seat until it is roughly flat and the seat is an even thickness on all sides.

10 Transfer the drilling sight lines and mark the centres of the leg mortices from the plywood template to the underside of the seat blank. Then, using the marking gauge, draw a dividing line around the sides of the blank, making it 1in (25mm) from the top surface of the blank (you will use this later for carving the seat).

11 Clamp the seat, underside up, to a workbench or a low table, sandwiching a piece of plywood between the seat and the bench. This is to avoid drilling into the bench's surface, and it reduces tear out on the top of your work.

12 The mortices for the legs are made using a ¾in (20mm) drill bit and drilled at an angle so the legs can splay out (remember you are working from the underside of the seat). For the front legs, set your bevel gauge to a 15-degree angle and for the back legs set it to 24 degrees. Place the drill bit at a drill mark, holding the drill with the bit aligned along the drilling guideline and its tip pointing towards the edge of the seat (see pages 94–95). Drill all the way through the seat. Repeat at the other three marks, ensuring the drill is at the correct angle and aligned along the dividing line for each.

13 Use a lathe or a tenon cutter to make 2½in (63mm) long, ¾in (20mm) diameter tenons on the tops of the legs (see pages 92–93).

14 Check and adjust the fit of the tenons in the mortices (see page 110). Orientate, or twist, the legs into the mortices by hand so that the grain direction on the pairs match, and if you're using octagonal legs, a flat side faces outwards. Tap the legs firmly into the mortices using a metal hammer to seat them. At least ⅜in (10mm) should protrude from the top of the seat; slightly extend the tenon if there is less than this.

15 Check that the swells on the legs are around 9–9½in (230–245mm) from the underside of the seat, measured up the shortest side of each leg. Make a small horizontal mark. The measurement must be the same for all the legs – if needed, remove some of the shoulder from a tenon with a block plane until they all match.

16 Clearly mark on the legs where they meet the sight lines on the seat. Write different letters or numbers on each leg, then put the same symbols next to the mortices on the seat. These will tell you which leg belongs in which mortice, how deep to tap and which way to orientate them (see page 111).

17 To make drilling marks for the stretchers, fit elastic bands between the front and back legs at the horizontal marks you made on the swells. Using the bands as sight guides, make a small vertical mark in between the bands on each leg. Mark the points with a bradawl.

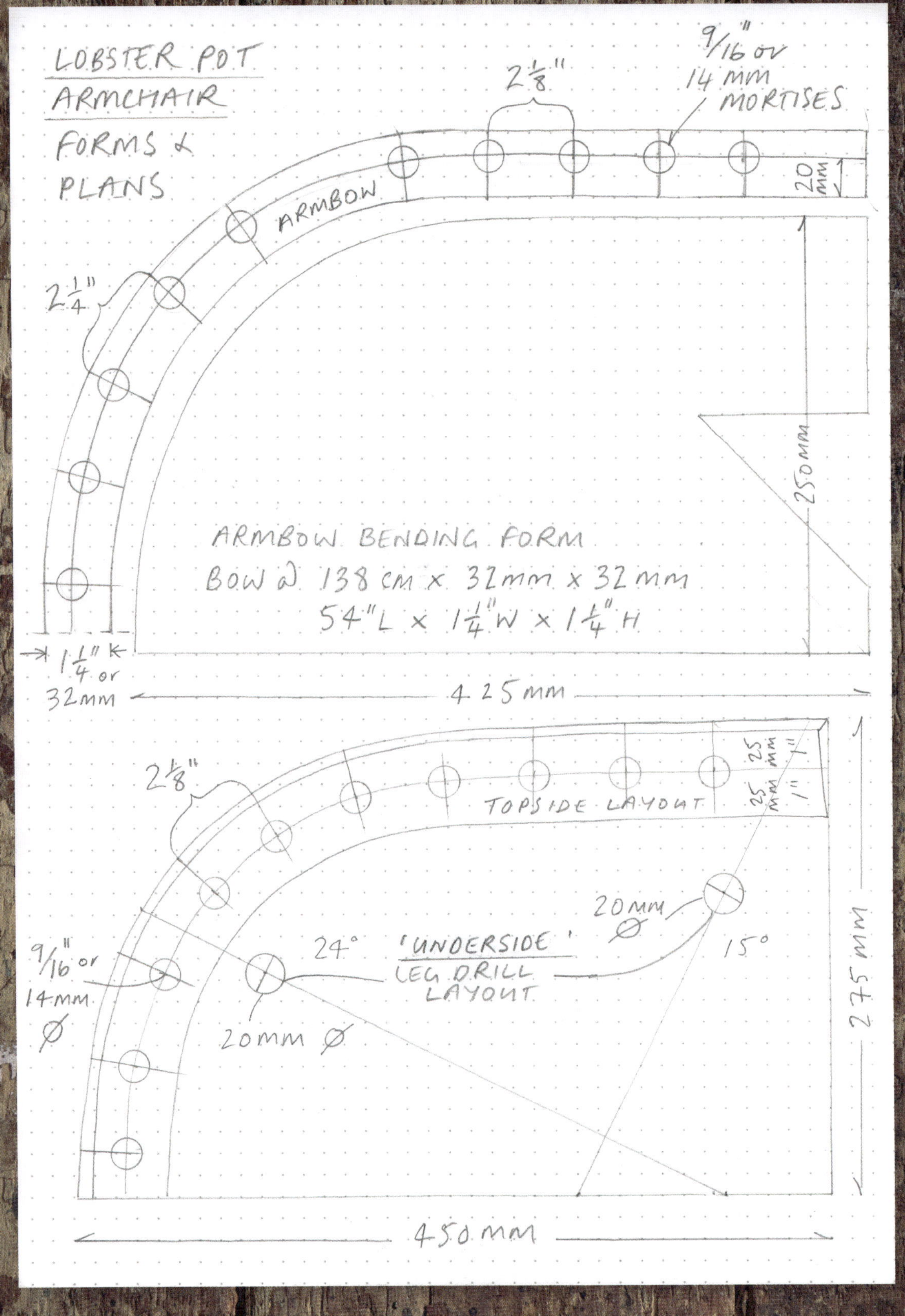

LOBSTER POT
ARMCHAIR
FORMS & PLANS
2 1/8"
9/16" or
14 MM
MORTISES
20 MM
ARMBOW
2 1/4"
250MM
ARMBOW BENDING FORM
BOW @ 138 CM x 32mm x 32mm
54"L x 1 1/4"W x 1 1/4"H
1 1/4" or
32MM
425MM
2 1/8"
TOPSIDE LAYOUT
25 MM
1"
25 MM
1"
20MM
Ø
9/16" or
14MM
Ø
24°
'UNDERSIDE'
LEG DRILL
LAYOUT
15°
20MM Ø
275MM
450MM

18 Clamp the seat on top of a block to the bench. Slightly twist the back legs so that you can drill into them with the drill body or bit resting against the front legs. Use the drill point on the front leg to angle the drill towards the drill point on the back leg (see page 96). Using a 11/16in (18mm) diameter drill bit, make mortices 1in (25mm) deep into both legs. Do the same for the front legs.

19 Make sure the legs are correctly oriented in the seat again and tapped home. Using measuring sticks (see page 93), measure the distance between the depths of the front and back mortices on the legs on one side of the chair. Add 3/16in (5mm) to this measurement to create some tension and write that number between the legs. Repeat for the other pair of legs; these measurements may vary slightly.

20 Choose a side stretcher to go in between one pair of legs and label each end to match the corresponding leg's label. Take the measurement you wrote down for that pair of legs and mark out the stretcher's final size with the swell at the centre of this measurement. You then need to turn or cut a 1in (25mm) long, 11/16in (18mm) diameter tenon at each end of the stretcher. If using a lathe, turn the tenon and cut to size using a Japanese pull saw or standard tenon saw afterwards; if using a tenon cutter, trim first and then cut the tenon. Repeat for the other side stretcher.

21 Knock the legs loose. Fit the side stretchers into the mortices and orientate them again so that flat sides face each other. Pull the legs tight on the stretchers. Mark the stretchers where they enter the mortices, and ensure they are labelled to match the legs they stretch between.

22a
22b
24a
24b
25
26
27a
27b
28

22 To make drill marks for the centre stretcher mortices, lay a ruler between the widest point in the centre of the swells on the side stretchers, aligning it parallel with the front edge of the seat. – place another ruler against the front legs so you can check the two rulers are parallel. You may find that the swells aren't perfectly aligned and your drill point will be slightly off the widest part of one of the swells. Draw a line across the top of each swell where the ruler is, then use these marks and a ruler or square to mark the vertical centre of each stretcher at these marks. Mark the centres with a bradawl.

23 On the underside of the seat, measure and mark 8in (200mm) along the side edge of the seat from each front corner. Join these marks across the seat with a piece of tape or a ruler and a pencil. Once a set of legs has been knocked loose, you can line the drill up to this sight line.

24 Knock a pair of legs and a stretcher free from the seat. Using a ⅝in (16mm) bit, drill a 1in (25mm) deep mortice into the other side stretcher, using the sight line to keep the drill bit parallel to the seat. Knock the first pair of legs and the corresponding stretcher back into place and then repeat this step for the legs and stretcher on the other side.

25 Once the pairs of legs and their stretchers are knocked together again, using the sticks, measure the distance between the mortices in the centres of the side stretchers. Again, add 3⁄16in (5mm) and write the number on the seat.

26 Mark out the centre stretcher's final size with the swell at the centre of this measurement. You then need to turn or cut a 1in (25mm) long, ⅝in (16mm) diameter tenon at each end of the stretcher. If using a lathe, turn the tenon and cut to size using a Japanese pull saw or standard tenon saw afterwards; if using a tenon cutter, trim first and then cut the tenon. Knock all the legs and stretchers loose, fit the centre stretcher in place and knock all the parts back together into the seat. Pull all the tenons in tightly, then orientate and label the centre stretcher.

27 To determine the area for carving the seat, first draw the edge of the carved area 2in (50mm) from one corner of the front of the seat all the way around the back to the other corner using a measuring gauge and a pencil, then draw a circle with a piece of chalk that is 1in (25mm) within the carved area at the back and the sides – it will be further away from the pencil line as it curves towards the centre of the front of the seat. Carve out the seat following the steps on pages 102–8.

28 Refit the legs and stretchers. Trim the part of the leg tenons that protrude from the topside of the seat, leaving ⅜in (10mm) protruding. Mark the kerfs in the tenons for the wedges, making sure they will sit across the grain of the seat. You can either glue and wedge the undercarriage now (see steps 60–61), or wait to glue the whole assembly at the end.

29 Using a measuring gauge, draw a line on the top of the seat 1in (25mm) from the edge, starting at one front corner, working around the side and back and finishing at the other corner. Copy the mortice drill points from the plan (see page 217) onto this line; there should be 2⅛in (54mm) between each drill mark. Draw a line down the centre of the seat.

31a
31b
31c
15°
lobster
75°
105°
32
33a
33b
36
37
38

30 Lightly plane the top and bottom surfaces of the arm bow with a block plane.

31 Make the jig for the arm bow (see page 101). Clamp the jig to the seat, making sure that the centre of the jig sits on the centre line of the seat. Then, carefully line up the bow onto the jig, making sure the ends of the bow are equal distances from the centre of the jig/seat, and the bow looks balanced in relation to the edges of the seat. Also check the angle of the back spindle sight line on the jig. The top of the drill line on the jig should be ½in (12mm) from the front edge of the bow. Mark the front of the bow where it sits on the centre line of the jig; this is the centre of the bow. Carefully clamp the arms and the back of the bow to the jig using quick grip clamps.

32 Strike a line on the top of the bow using the marking gauge, this time ½in (12mm) from the back edge of the bow, all the way along the length of the bow. Your drill points will be on this line. Set your dividers to 2¼in (57mm) and mark out 10 drill points for the long spindles at the back of the bow, 5 on each side. This chair doesn't have a central spindle, so the first pair of marks should be made 1⅛in (28–29mm) either side of the centre mark.

33 For the front pair of mortices, place the corner of a set square at one of the front drill marks on the seat, then draw a line up the edge of the arm bow where the square meets the arm bow directly above. Use a bradawl to make a mark on your pencil line on the arm bow at this point, then repeat this on the other side of the seat. Set the dividers to 2⅛in (54mm) and make four more marks along the pencil line on each side. The gap between the fifth spindle on each side and the back spindles will be larger than the gaps between the other spindles.

34 The next stage is to mark the arm bow and the seat with the sight lines to allow you to drill at the correct angle. Start by laying a ruler across the front pair of arm bow drill points, and strike a line across the bow at these points. Lay a ruler across the front pair of points on the seat, and join these with a straight pencil line. Make marks on this line on the seat that are ¾in (20mm) from each drill point and towards the centre of the seat. Make the remaining drill sight lines on the arm bow and the seat (see pages 98–99).

35 Once all the drill points and sight lines have been marked on the arm bow and the seat, you can drill the mortices. They will go all the way through the thickness of the bow, so clamp a piece of waste material under the bow where you will be drilling, so that as the drill bit emerges it doesn't tear out any splinters.

36 Starting with the front pair of spindle holes, place a stiff ruler against the ends of the sight lines you marked, then use this to drill through the bow using the 9⁄16in (14mm) drill bit at the correct angle. Check your drilling by sighting through the hole. Keep drilling all the arm bow mortices, making sure that you are lining them up with the correct corresponding seat drill marks.

37 When you've finished drilling the mortices in the arm bow, drill the mortices in the seat. For the front pair only you'll be drilling the spindle holes completely through the seat, so clamp a piece of scrap wood under the seat in these areas to avoid 'tear out' splinters as the drill bit emerges. With the bow still clamped to the jig, pass an extension with a 9⁄16in (14mm) drill bit through the bow hole and drill all the way through the seat. Still using the extension, continue to drill the remaining seat mortices for the other spindles, but make them only 1in (25mm) into the seat.

38 Shape and fit the back spindles to the bow. First, wind a 9⁄16in (14mm) tenon cutter along the long spindles from the top end to 10¼in (260mm) from the bottom. Then using the same tenon cutter, cut a 1in (25mm) long tenon on the bottom of the spindles. Do the same for the short spindles. The front pair of spindles are 2in (50mm) longer at the bottom because they travel through the seat, so you'll need to wind the tenon cutter down from the top end to 12¼in from the bottom, then cut a 3in (75mm) tenon on the bottom of the spindles. Fit the spindles to their correct mortices in the bow.

39 Knock all the short spindles loose and set them aside. Loosely place the bow – with all the long spindles still fitted in place as well as the front pair of 'through' spindles – on the seat, push the front pair of spindles through the seat and gently tap. Repeat this with the outside pair of long spindles, followed by the centre pair and then all the rest. Once all of the spindles have been tapped into place, firmly tap the bow down to the 10½in (265mm) pencil marks.

40 Knock apart the spindles from the seat so you can fit the short spindles to the bow, then refit the whole assembly to seat as in the previous step. Twist each spindle to help orientate and align it with the mortice in the seat. Tap the bow firmly down on all spindles so that the arm bows top surface is 10½in (265mm) from the seat. If you cannot get it down to the height, the chances are, that the bow is 'riding' on one or more spindles – check each one carefully and twist them to identify which ones need a further turn through the tenon cutter.

41 Once the spindles and bow fit correctly, trim the tops of the short spindles so that no more than ⅜in (10mm) protrudes above the bow and number them 1–8, and mark the front spindles L and R. Also mark each long spindle where it enters and exits the bow.

42 Make sure the spindles are knocked into their mortices. Measure up from the seat along the length of each long back spindle, marking where they will need to be trimmed at the top according to the plan.

43 Mark the ends of the bow for trimming. The bow will be trimmed in line with the front edge of the seat; place a try square against the front edge of the seat and use the other end of the square to draw a vertical line on the outside edge of the bow. Repeat on the other end of the bow, then lay a ruler across the two points to check they are parallel with the front edge of the seat. Strike a line across each hand held at these points. Make a mark on the top of the arm bow at one end, then knock apart the bow and spindles. Trim the ends at the marked points using a Japanese saw or a bandsaw.

44 Using a measuring gauge, draw a line around each side of the bow, ⅝in (16mm) from the top. At the front of each end of the bow, make a mark 1½in (38mm) from the front on the bottom edge, then draw a straight line from this point to the front of the bow at the centre line. Knock the bow apart, then remove the marked area with a Japanese saw to make a nice undercut. Clean up the top and bottom of the bow with a block plane, and the inside and outside of the curve with a spokeshave. Make facet cuts on all the edges using a block plane or spokeshave.

45 Cut the long back spindles to the marks made in step 42, then use a block plane or a spokeshave to make ¾in (20mm) long, ⅜in (10mm) diameter tenons at the top of each spindle. You can drill a ⅜in (10mm) hole into a piece of scrap wood and use this to check the diameter of the tenons. Refit the spindles and bow to the seat, twisting the spindles so they fit and move easily, and with each spindle having a flat facet facing towards the seat. Check everything is marked clearly and remake any marks that have been lost.

46 Measure 8in (200mm) from the centre of the crest towards one end and make a mark. Trim the end of the crest at this mark with a bandsaw, then repeat on the other side.

47 To mark up the crest for where the mortices should be drilled, first lay it on its back, press a long ruler into the curve and mark the centre point. Next, using a try square, strike a line through this centre on the front face, dividing the crest in half. Use a measuring gauge to draw a line ½in (12mm) from the front edge along the length of the underside. Extend the dividing line from the front face across this new line on the underside of the crest.

48 Set your dividers to 1⁷⁄₁₆in (37mm), then place the two points on the dividing line either side of the centre line. Mark these points with a bradawl, then make four more marks on each side of the dividing line 1⁷⁄₁₆in (37mm) apart so that you have a total of 10 drill points marked.

49 The spindle holes on the crest are at different angles, mirrored either side of the centre. Clamp one half of the crest in a vice, underside up. Using a bevel gauge, set the angles as indicated on the plan and strike lines on the face of the crest, aligned with the bottom of the corresponding drill point. To create a sight guide for the first mortice, clamp a small straightedge or a pencil to the front face of the crest, aligned with the angled drill line on the front face of the crest and with 2in (50mm) proud of the crest.

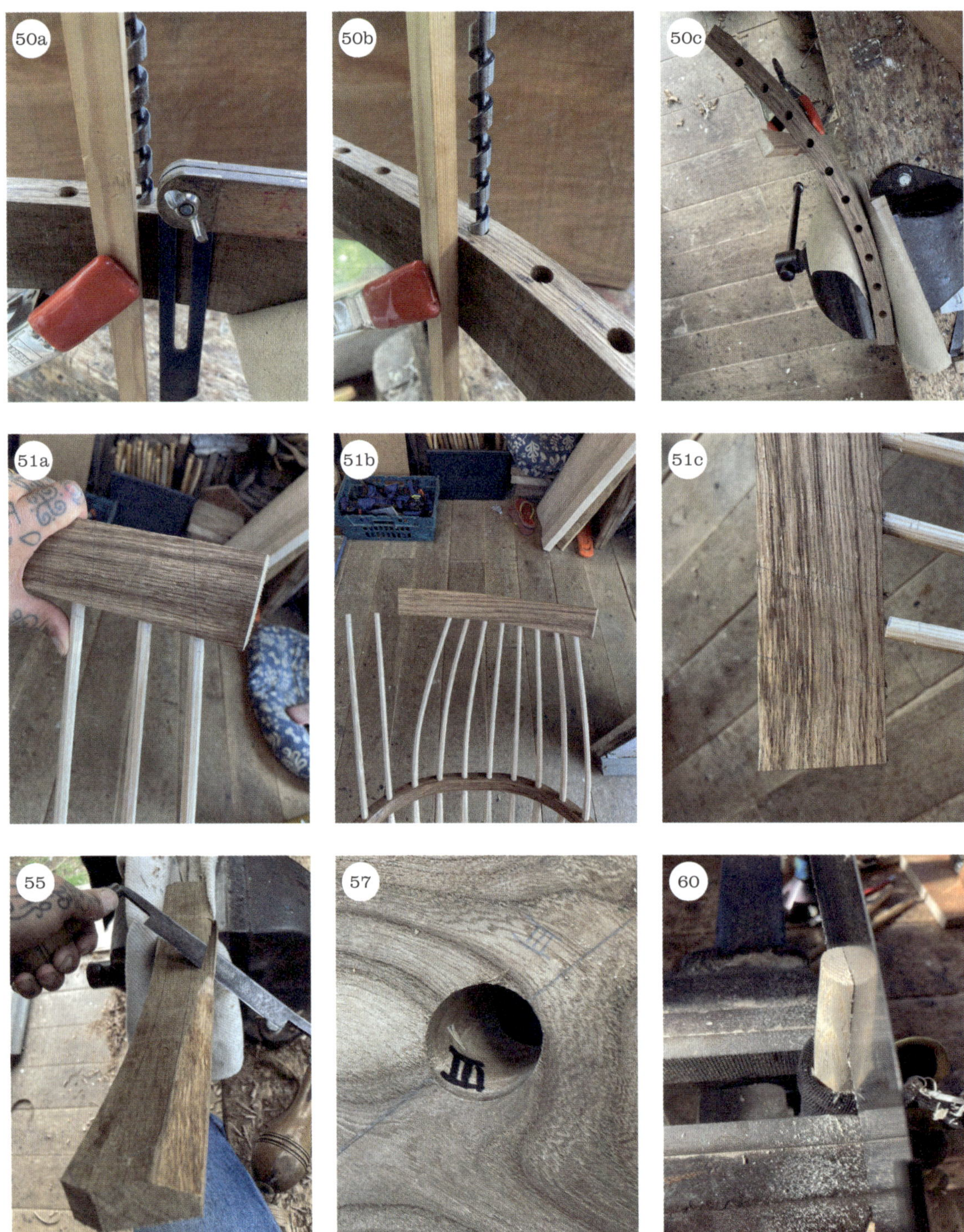
50a
50b
50c
51a
51b
51c
55
57
60

50 Drill a ¾in (20mm) deep mortice using a ⅜in (10mm) drill bit, lining the bit up with the sight guide side to side and back to front. Be very careful to drill centrally down through the mass of the crest, without breaking out of the front or back face. Repeat this for the other four mortices, then clamp the other half of the crest and make the five mortices on the opposite side.

51 Fit the spindles into the crest from one side to the other, pulling in each spindle at a time, and tapping the crest down bit by bit.

52 Once fitted, run a pencil underneath the crest, marking on the spindles where they meet the crest, then knock the crest off the spindles. Each long spindle should have a pencil mark ¾in (20mm) from the top. If this is not the case, trim the spindles that have longer tenons to match the length of the shorter tenons, then make them all ¾in (20mm) long, ⅜in (10mm) diameter tenons.

53 To shape the crest, make marks on the bottom edge of the crest ½in (12mm) from one of the outer mortices. Set a bevel gauge to 14 degrees and use this to draw a line on the front face of the crest from the mark you've just made, tapering inwards. Remove the edge of the crest outside of this line using a Japanese saw. Repeat this on the other side of the crest.

54 Next, make marks ½in (12mm) up from the bottom corner of each edge, then marks just outside the edge of the outer mortices. Draw a straight line between each pair of marks and then remove the triangles with a Japanese saw.

55 Using a marking gauge, draw a line along the front of the crest from one side to the other, 1in (25mm) from the bottom edge. Draw a second line ½in (12mm) from the front edge along the length of the top of the crest. Remove the material between these two lines using a spokeshave to create a backwards sloping surface.

56 Smooth the top and bottom of the crest with a block plane. The back side of the crest can be planed using a small block plane or spokeshave. The front surface can be scraped with a cabinet scraper. All the edges now need to be chamfered using a spokeshave. You could do this using a bench vice or a shave horse.

57 Clean up and mark up the underside of the seat for glue up, transferring the marks into the mortices. Make facet cuts on all undercarriage parts with a sharp spokeshave.

58 Re-establish the octagonal tapers on the spindles. Clean up the spindles swells below the bow, keeping the octagonal facets.

59 Now, with all the elements knocked back in place for a final dry fit, check that everything looks balanced. Disassemble the chair elements, laying them out neatly for reassembly. Give the spindle deck a final clean with a cabinet scraper.

60 Starting with the undercarriage, saw the slots for the kerfs in the top of the legs (see page 112).

61a

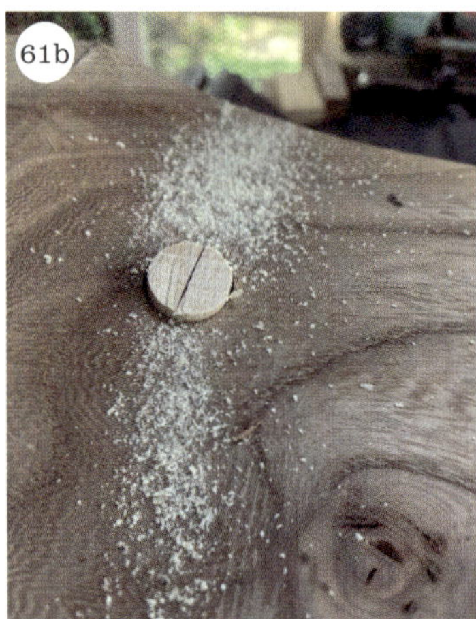
61b

61c

61 Continuing with the undercarriage and working on one leg at a time, apply a thin layer of glue to a tenon and a matching mortice, then loosely insert the tenon into the mortice. Repeat for the side stretchers and the centre stretcher. With all the parts in place, tap with the hammer to ensure a good fit. Apply a thin layer of glue to one side of each wedge and tap it in place. Leave to dry for at least a few hours. Once dry, trim the tops of the wedged leg tenons flush with the seat using a Japanese pull saw, and scrape smooth.

62 For the short spindles, apply glue in the holes of the seat and the bow, and for the long spindles only in the holes for the seat and the crest. Reassemble the spindles in the bow and on the seat (see steps 39–40), and tap home. Check the bow height and tap to adjust it. Check all the spindle orientations.

63 Split the tops of the short spindles with a sharp blow of a chisel. Glue and drive home the wedges. Remember to wedge the underseat ends on the front pair of spindles.

64 Apply glue to the crest mortices, locate and fit the spindles in them, and tap home firmly. Clean up excess glue.

65 Two pegs help to hold the crest in place (see page 117). Locate the second spindle in from one end, and mark a point with a bradawl where the centre of the spindle is and ⅜in (10mm) from the bottom edge. Clamp a piece of waste to the back of the crest, then drill completely through the crest and the spindle using a 5⁄32in (4mm) bit. Repeat on the other end of the crest. Put some glue in the mortices and tap the pegs through.

66 After the glue has set, trim the tenons of the spindles and the pegs flush using a Japanese pull saw, and scrape smooth. Now give the elements a final scrape and sand to remove any sharp edges until silky smooth.

67 Using a spirit level, check the level of the chair seat to determine which legs need trimming and by how much (see pages 118–19), then trim them using a Japanese saw.

68 Your chair is ready for finishing, whether you choose to paint it or apply an oil and wax finish (see pages 121–23).

A SIMPLE THREE-LEGGED STOOL

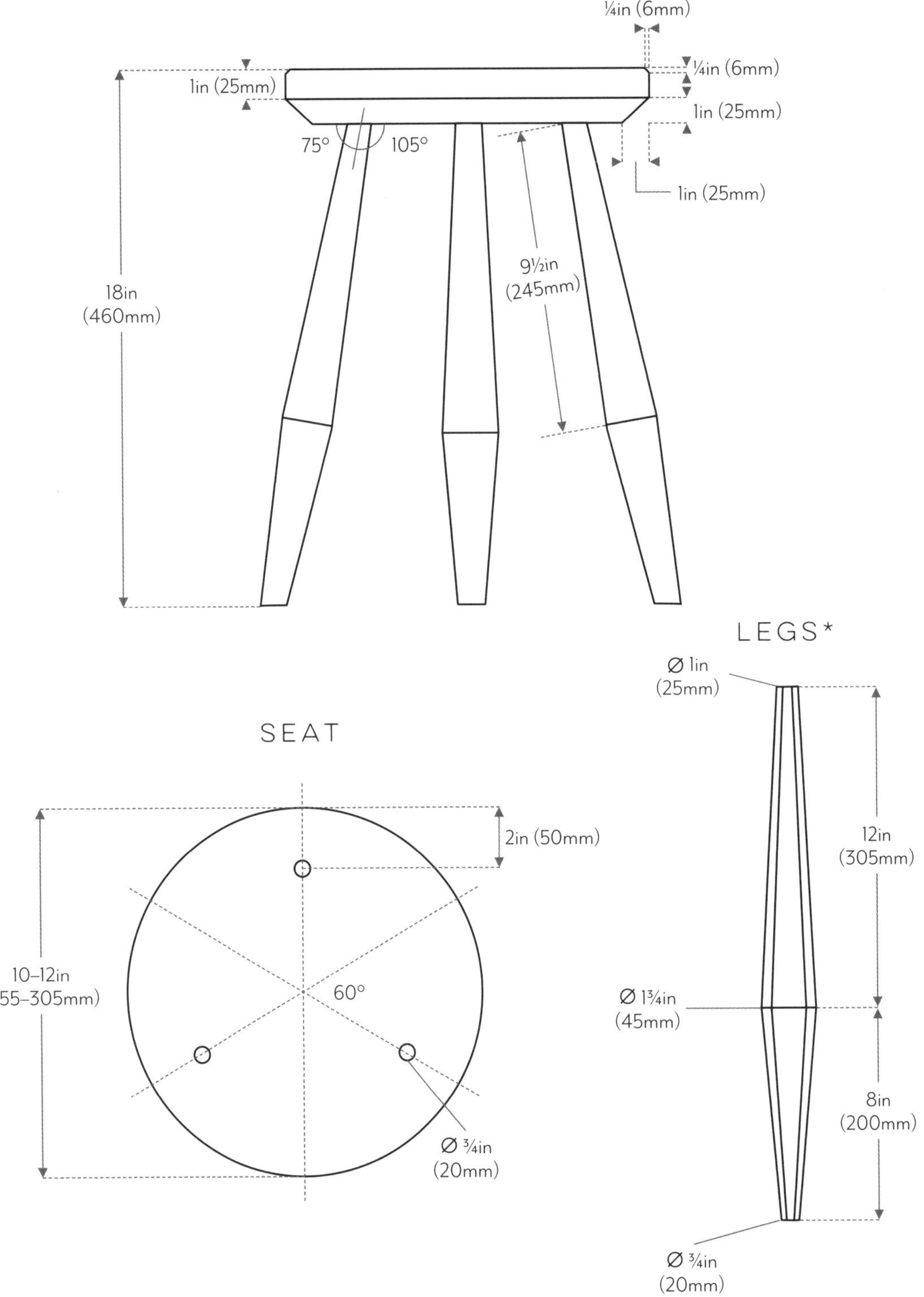

* Lengths are before parts have been cut to size and diameters are before tenons have been cut.

A STURDY SQUARE STOOL OR TABLE

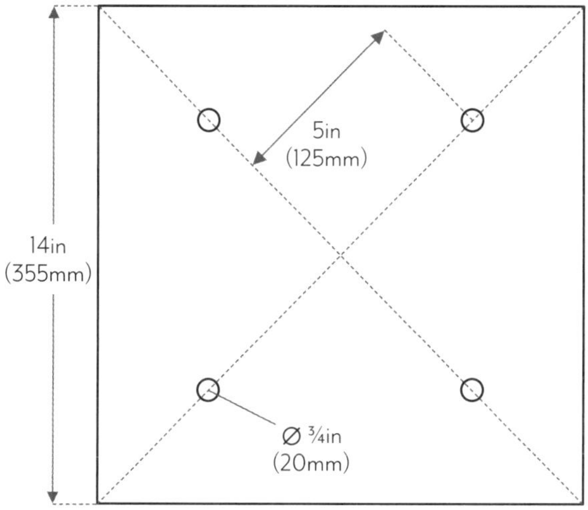

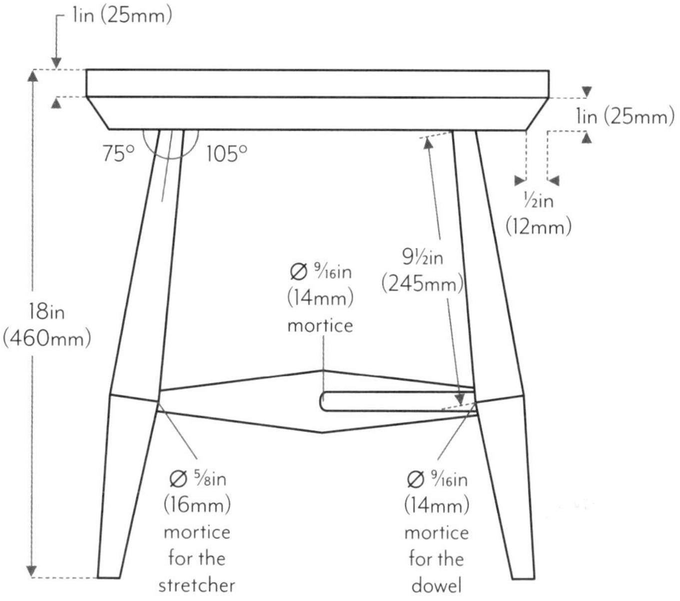

14in (355mm)
5in (125mm)
Ø ¾in (20mm)

1in (25mm)
75°
105°
1in (25mm)
½in (12mm)
18in (460mm)
Ø 9⁄16in (14mm) mortice
9½in (245mm)
Ø ⅝in (16mm) mortice for the stretcher
Ø 9⁄16in (14mm) mortice for the dowel

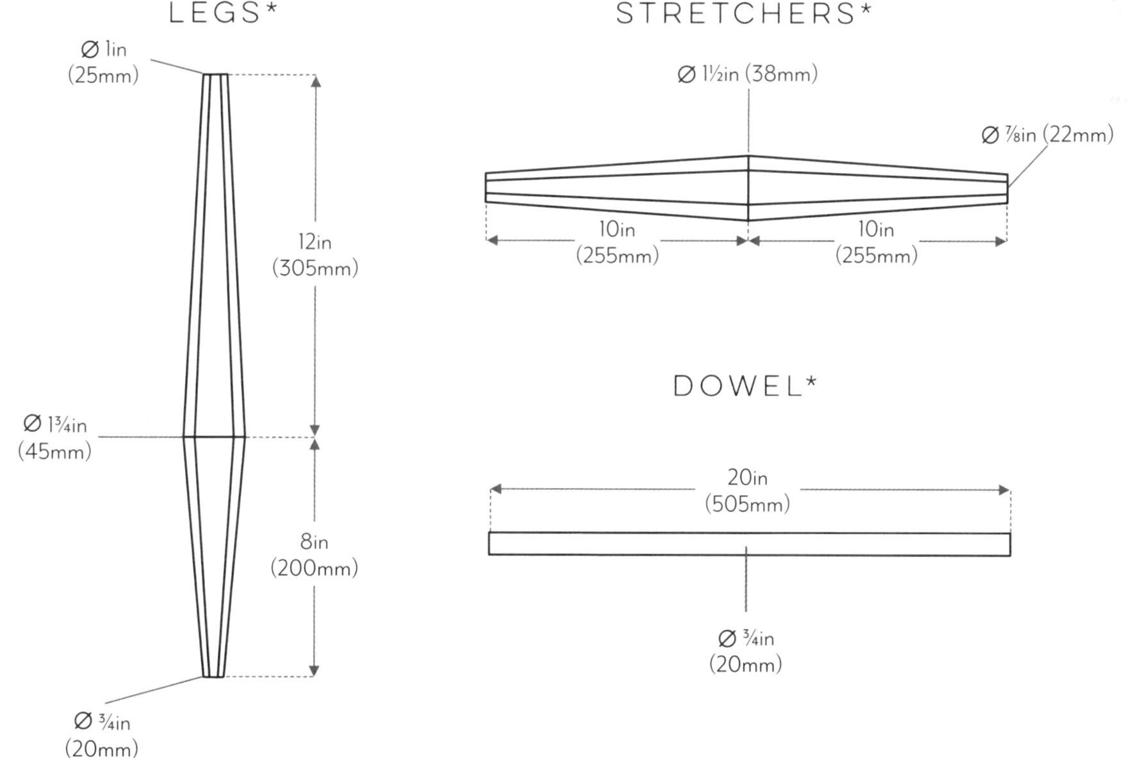

* Lengths are before parts have been cut to size and diameters are before tenons have been cut.

LOW BACK ARMCHAIR

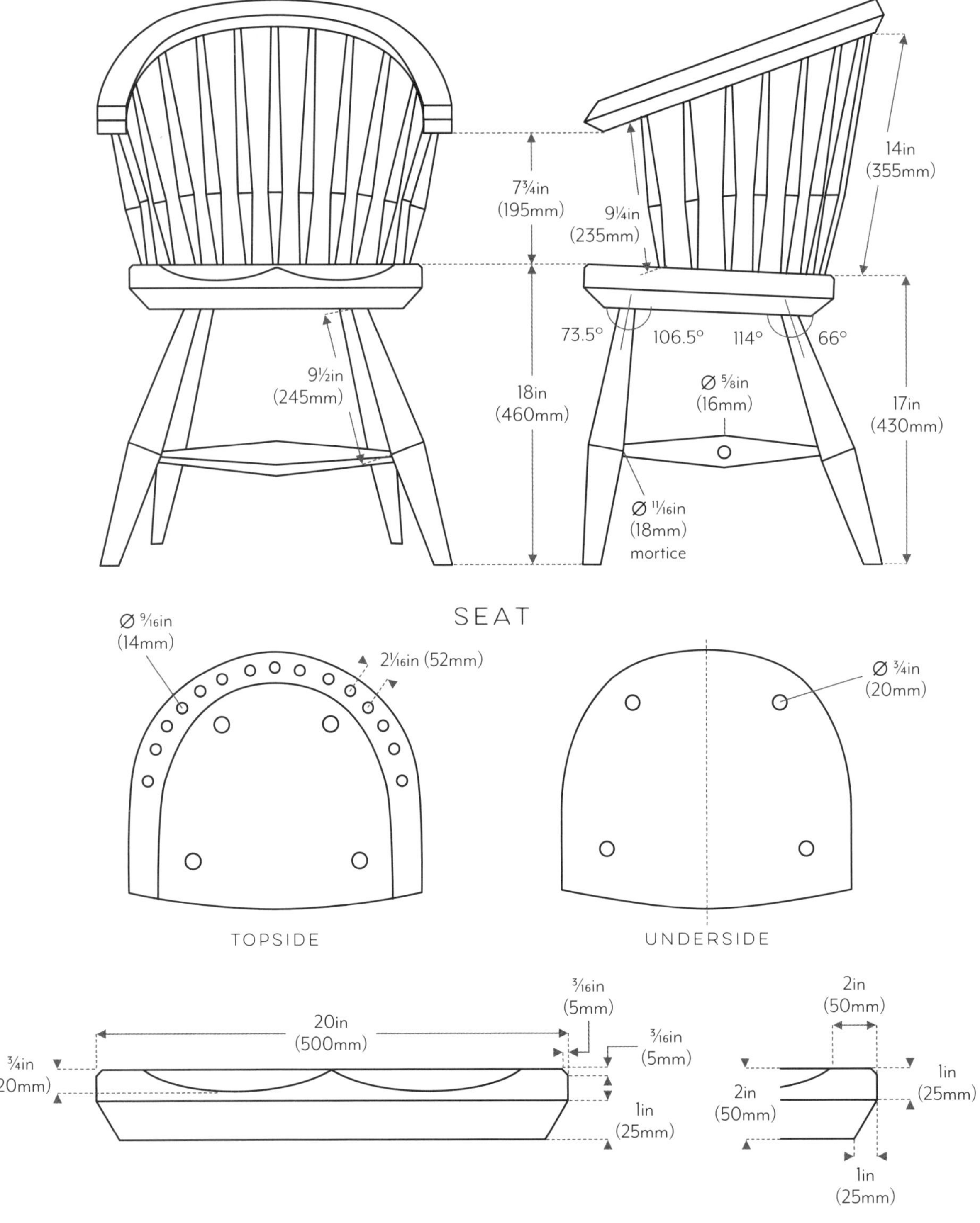

ARM BOW

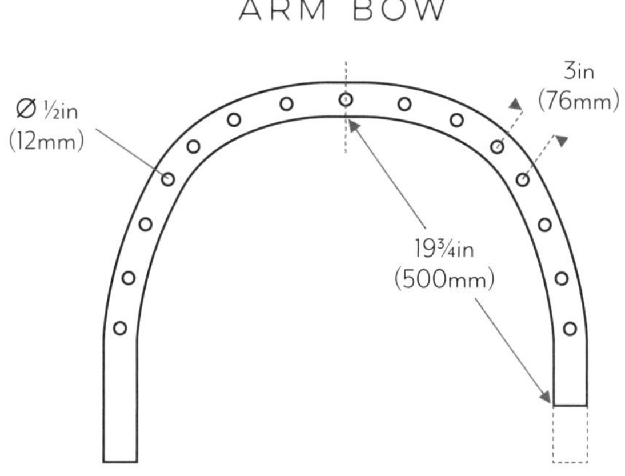

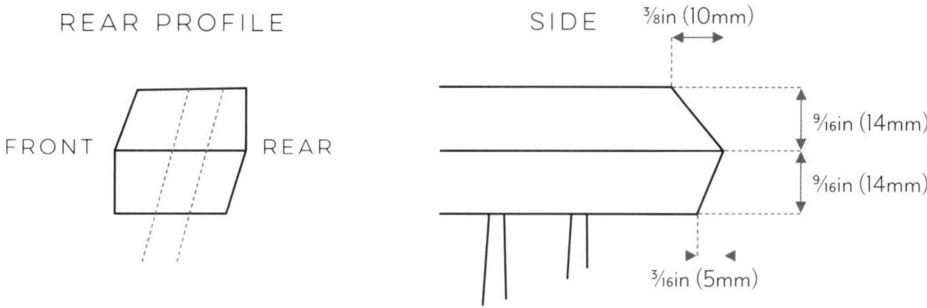

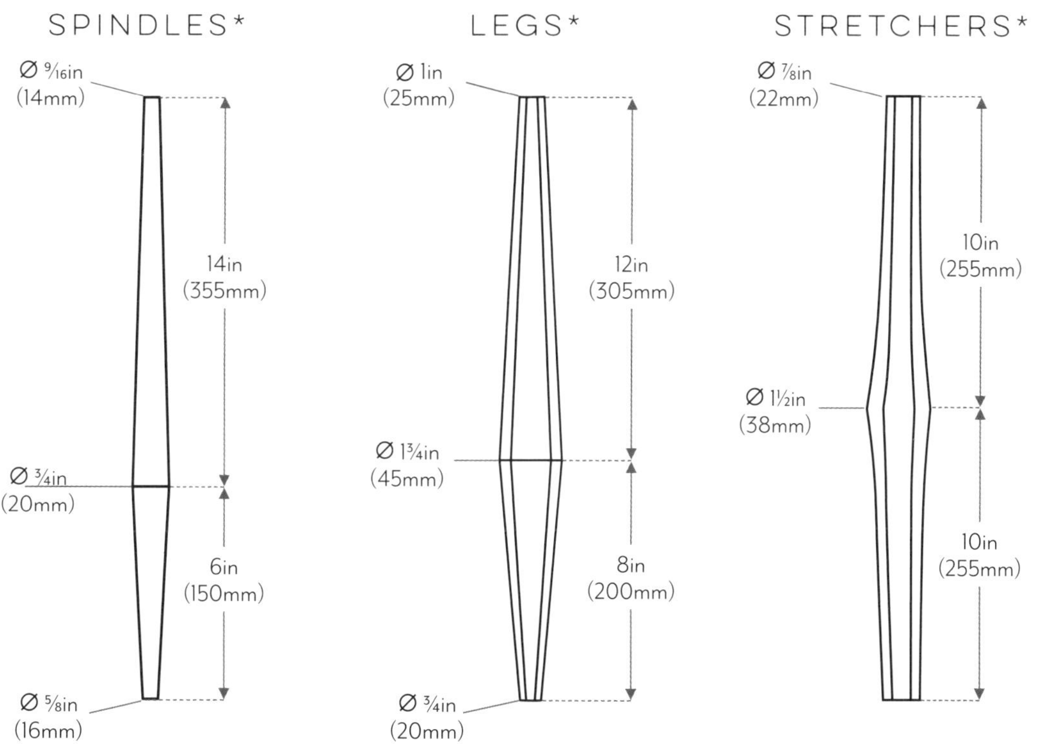

* Lengths are before parts have been cut to size and diameters before tenons have been cut.

SHAKER BENCH

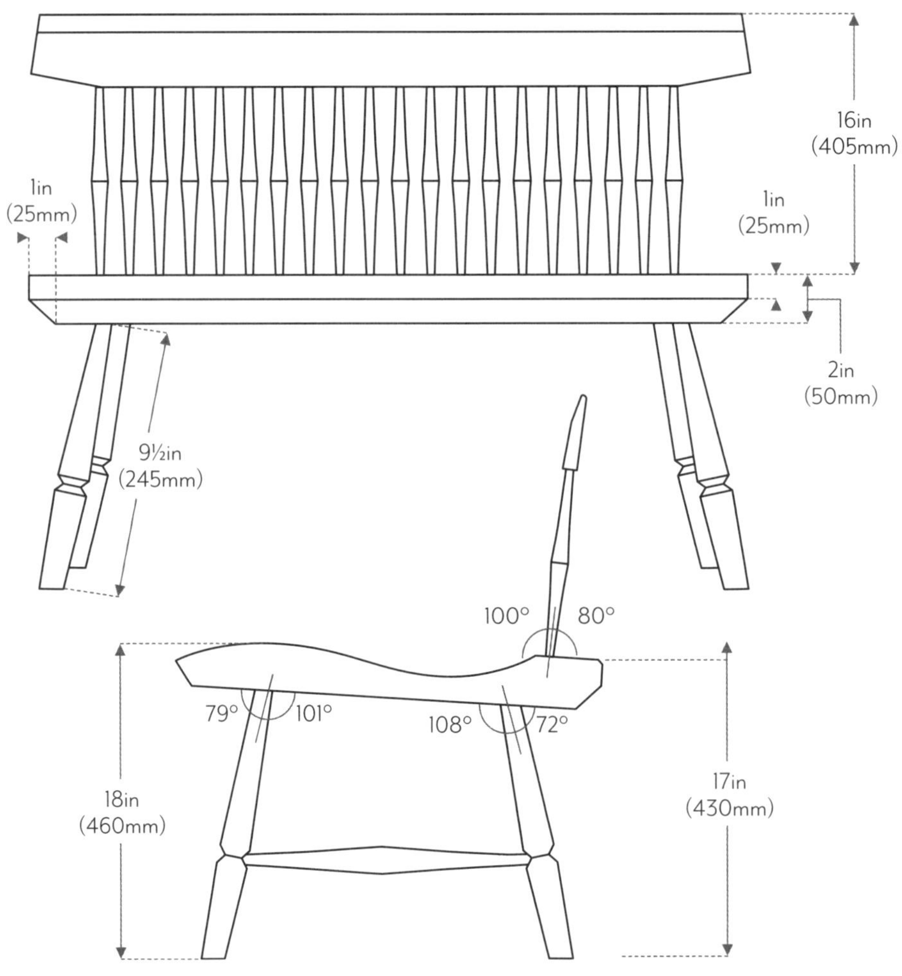

SEAT

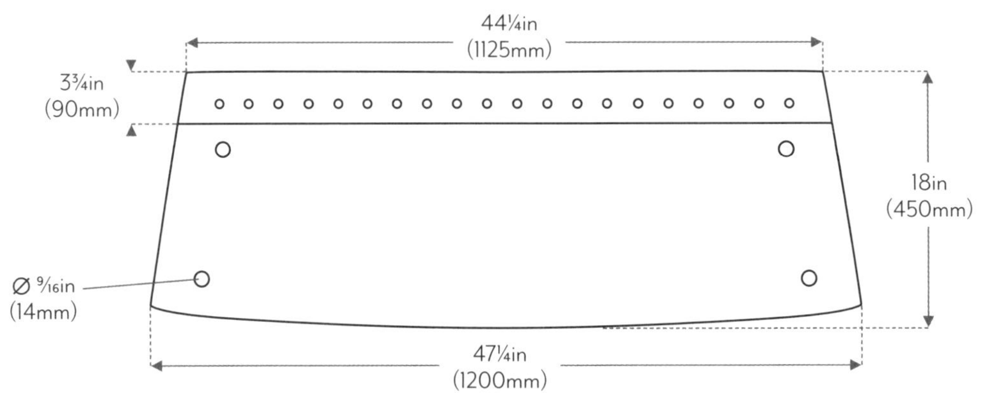

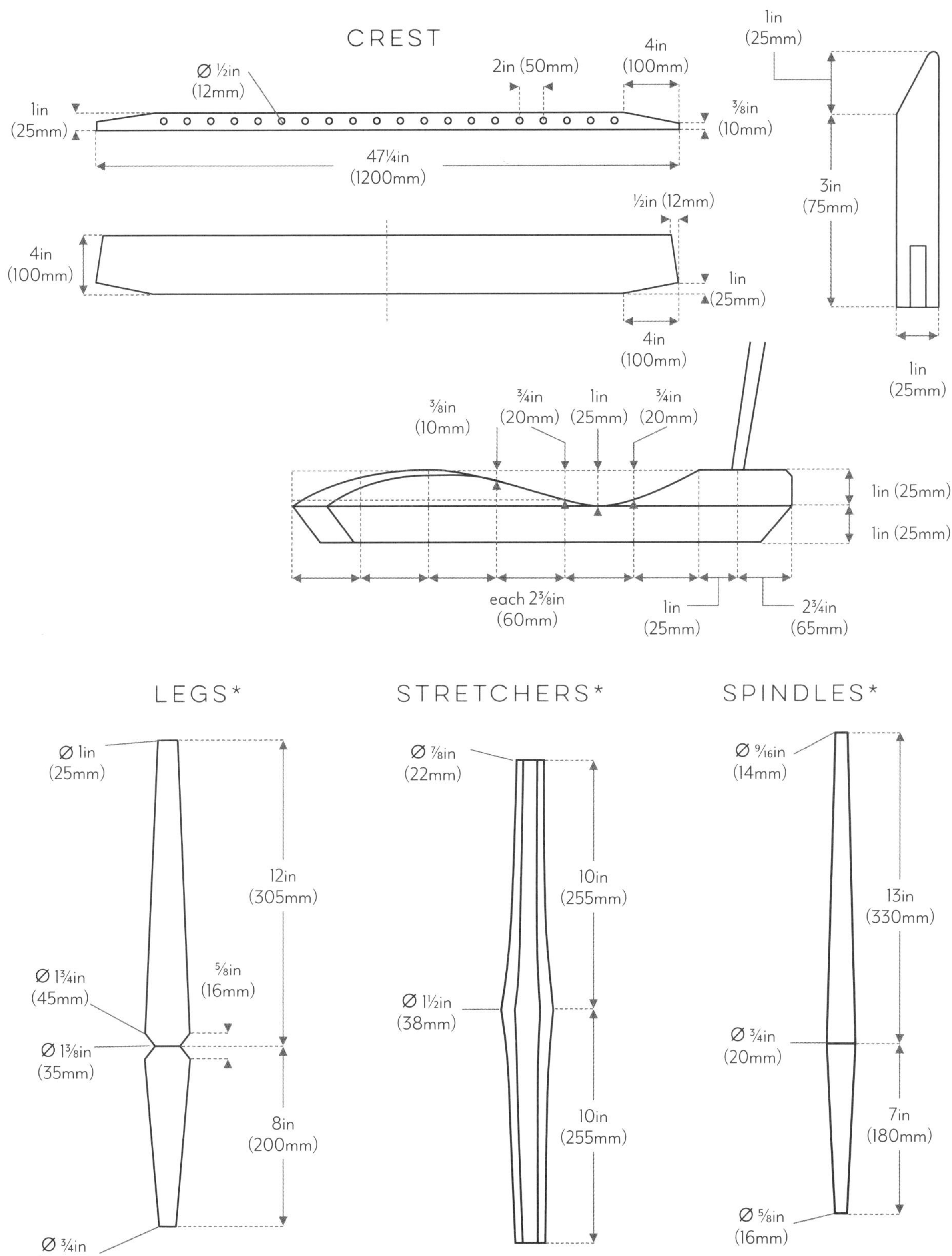

* Lengths are before parts have been cut to size and diameters are before tenons have been cut.

LOBSTER POT ARMCHAIR

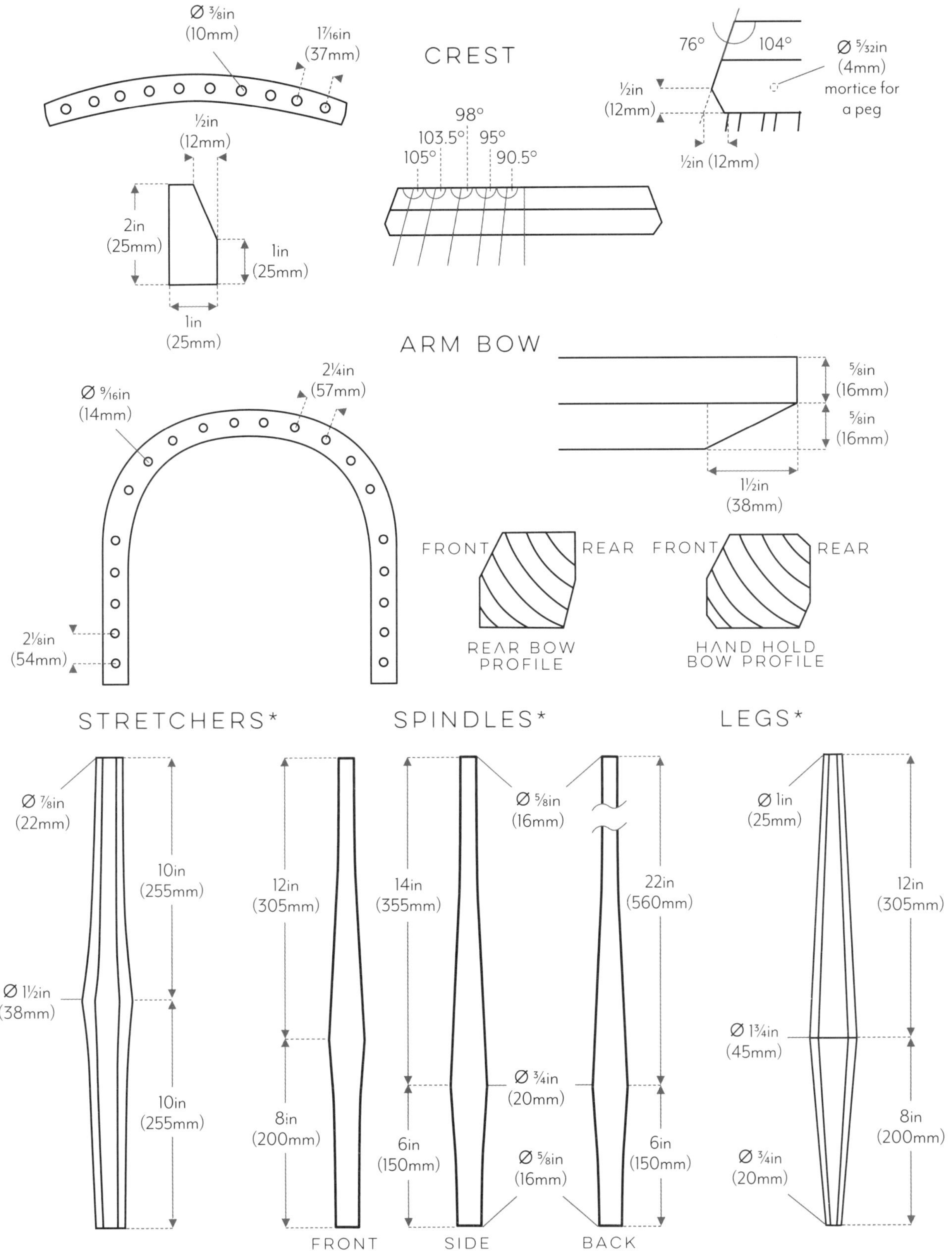

* Lengths are before parts have been cut to size and diameters are before tenons have been cut.

LOW BACK ARMCHAIR

For practical reasons, each square is ½in or 12.5mm. As this isn't an exact conversion, the total lengths are very slightly different depending on whether you are using metric or imperial measurements.

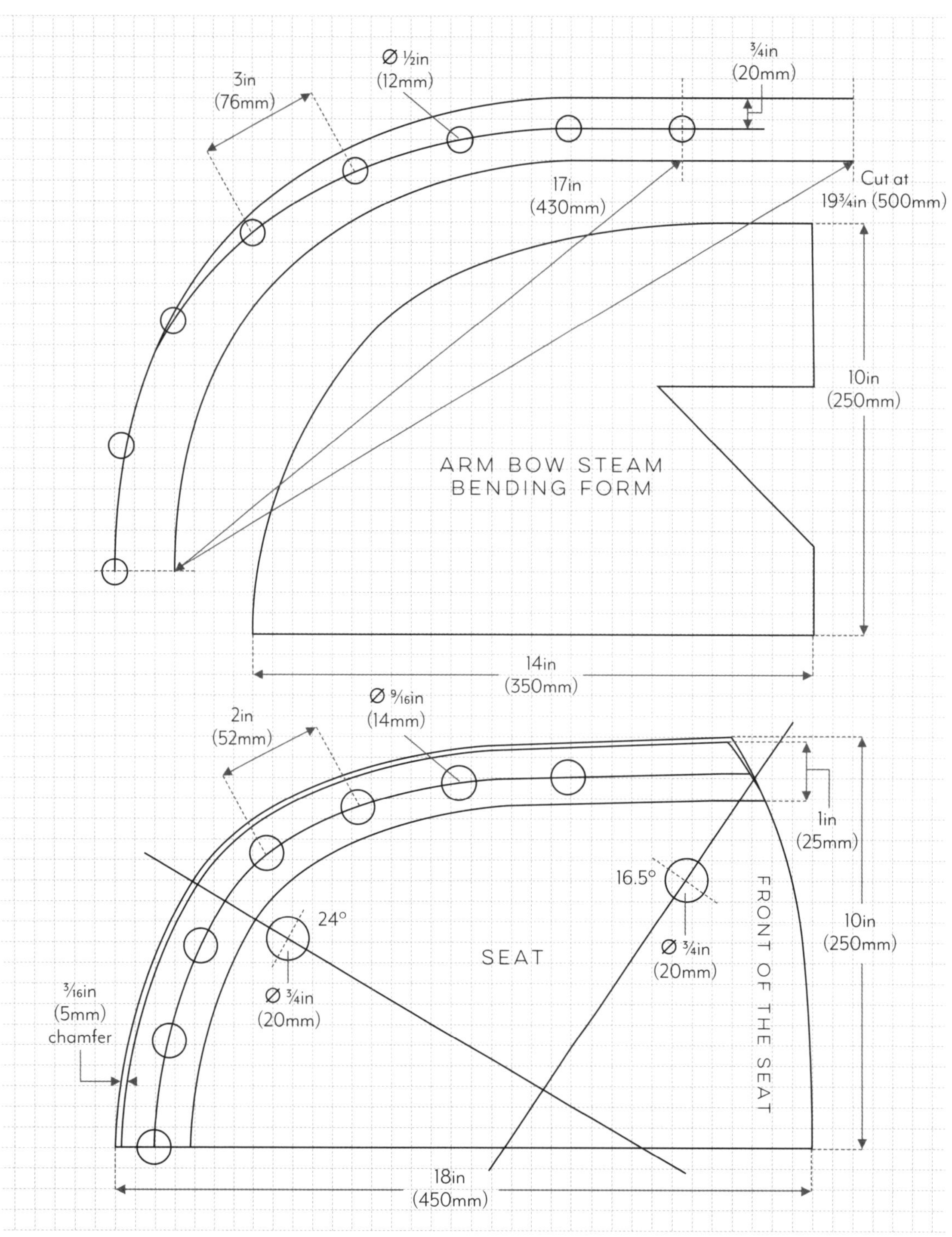

LOBSTER POT ARMCHAIR

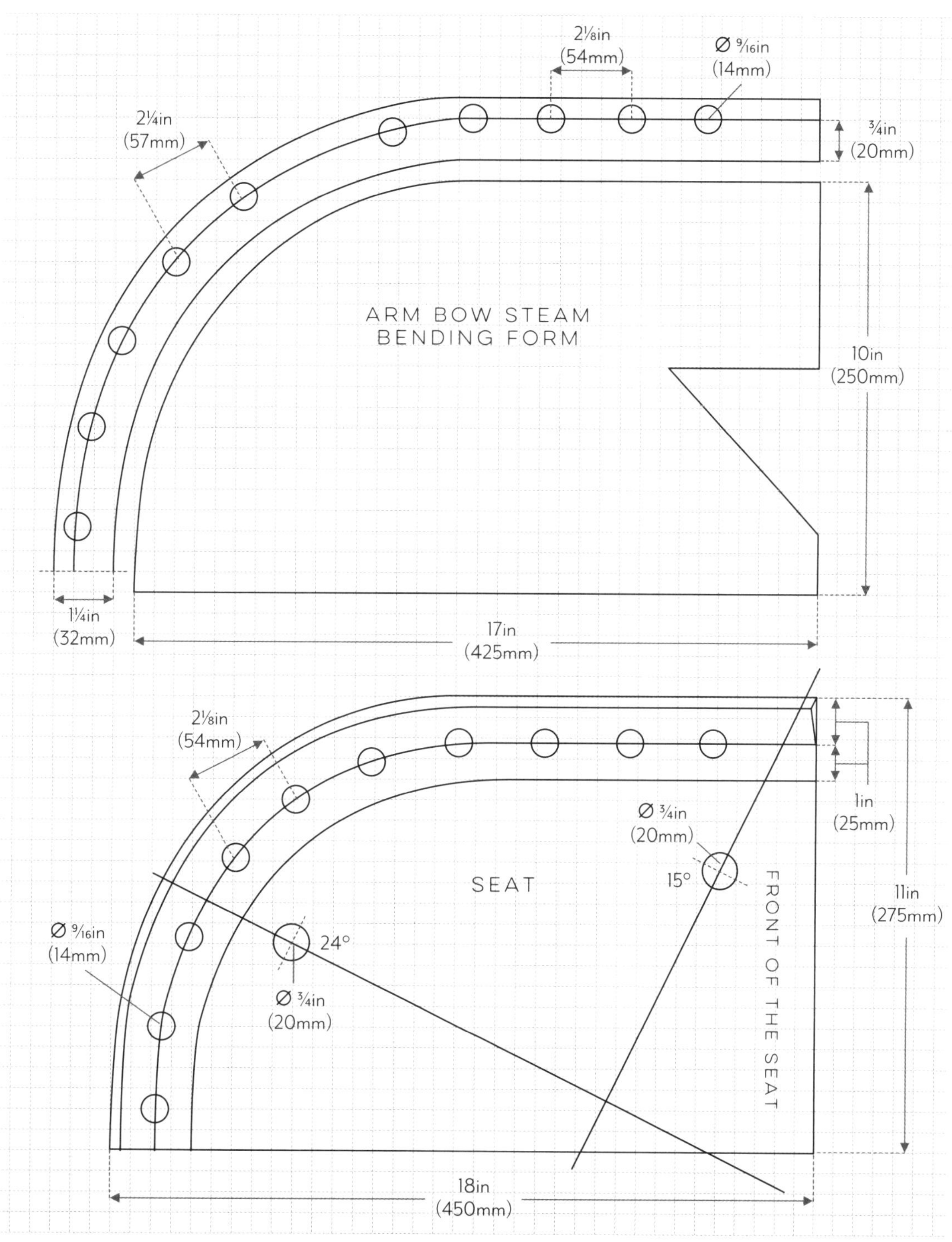

SHAKER BENCH

For practical reasons, each square is ½in or 12.5mm. As this isn't an exact conversion, the total lengths are very slightly different depending on whether you are using metric or imperial measurements.

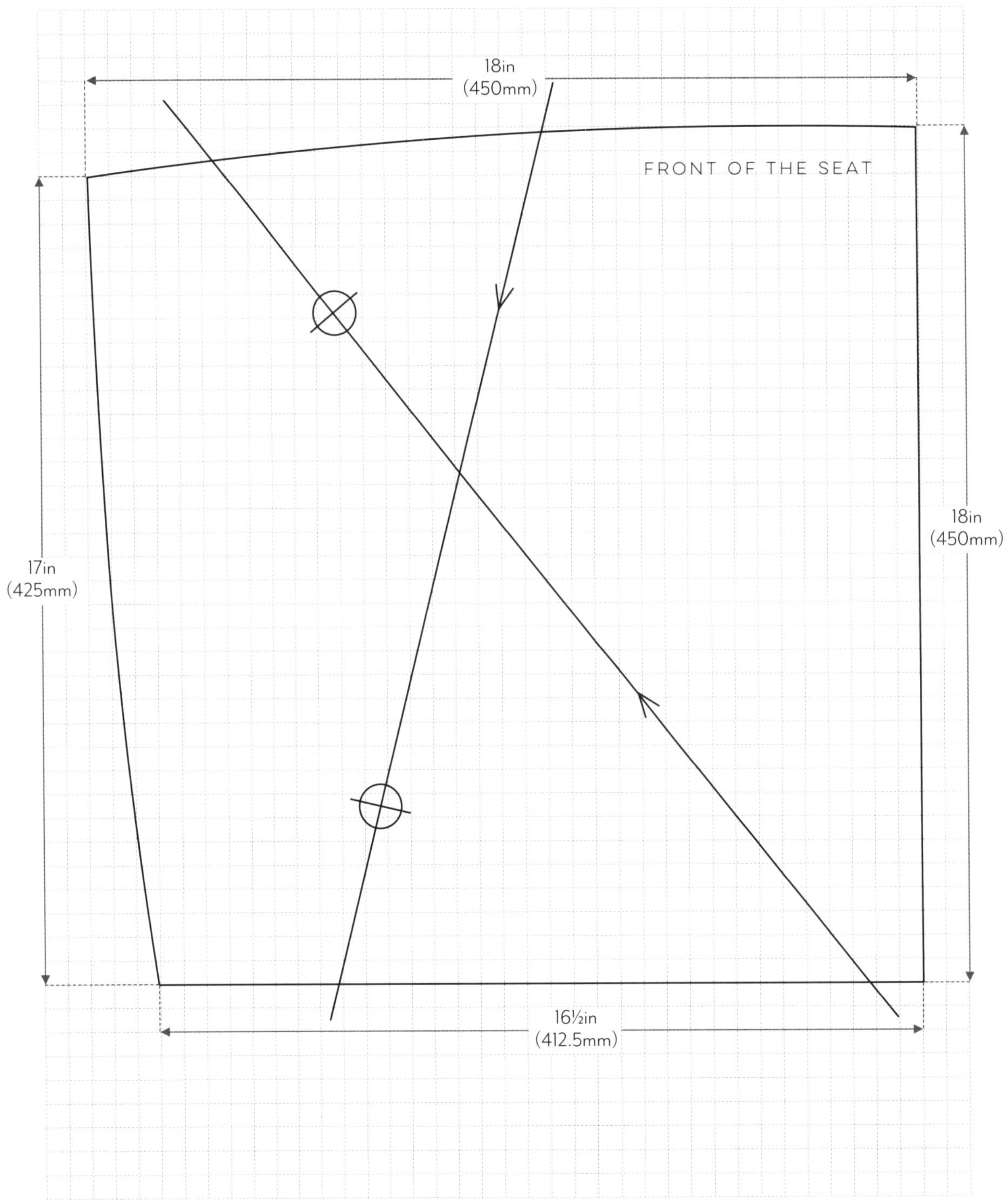

LOBSTER POT ARMCHAIR ARM BOW DRILLING JIG

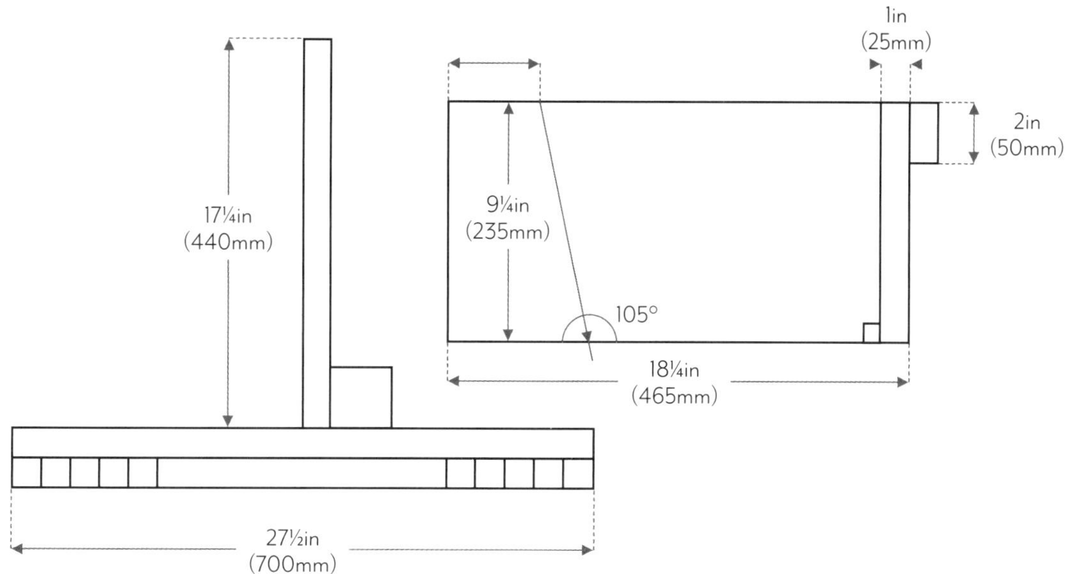

LOW BACK ARMCHAIR ARM BOW DRILLING JIG

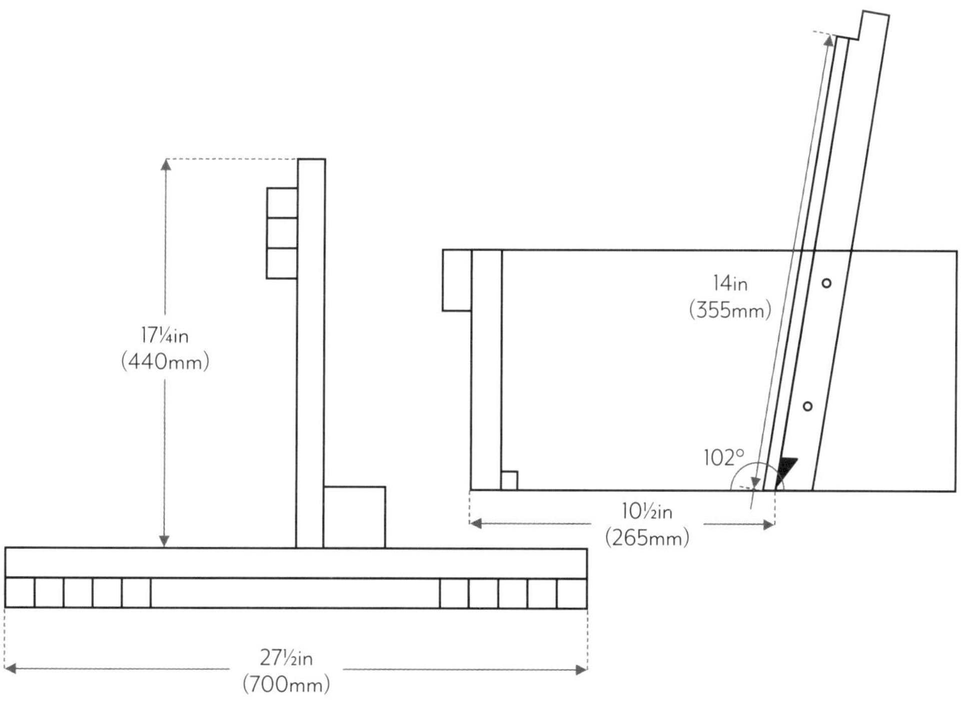

CREST BENDING FORM TEMPLATE

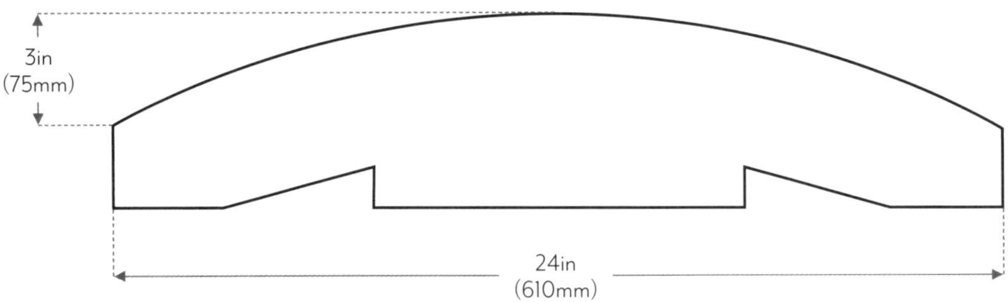

STEAM BOARD BASE FOR ATTACHING FORMS

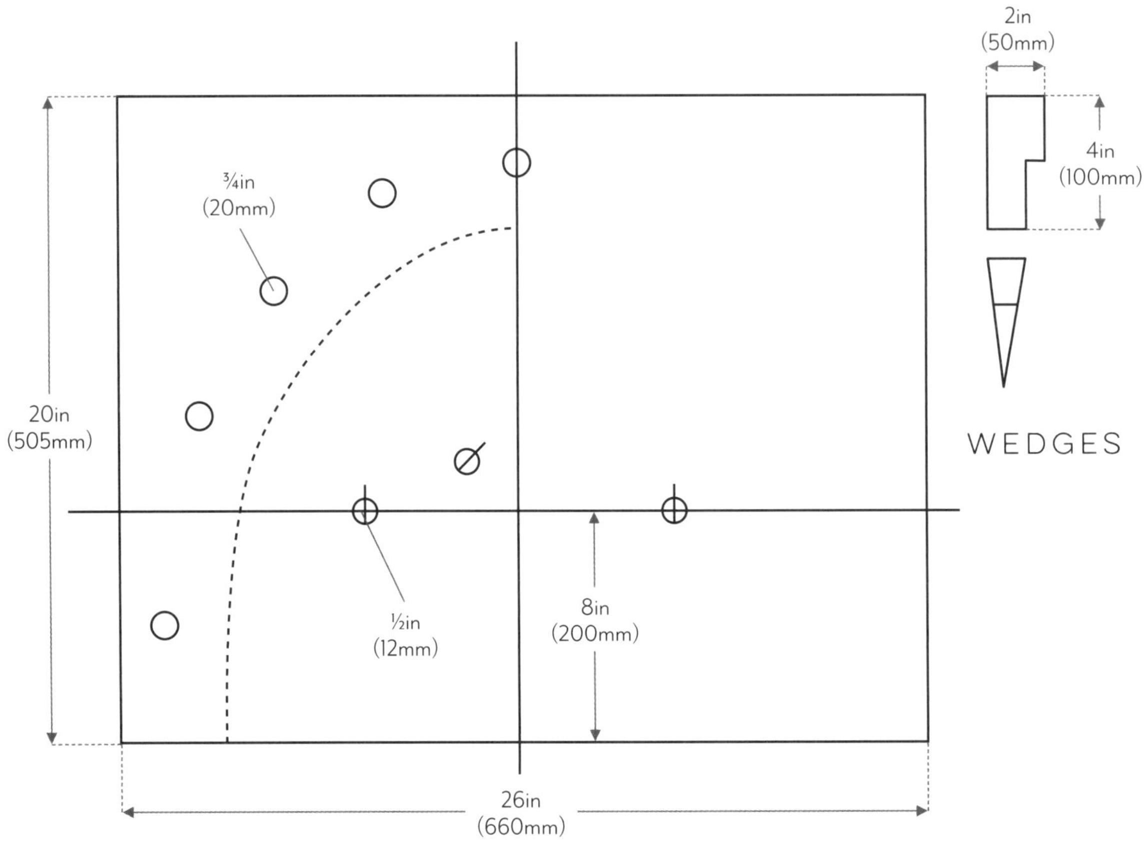

¾in
(20mm)

20in
(505mm)

½in
(12mm)

8in
(200mm)

26in
(660mm)

2in
(50mm)

4in
(100mm)

WEDGES

ACKNOWLEDGEMENTS

Writing this book was a new and challenging experience for me, but I hope I have managed to convey the love that I have for chairmaking. I'd like to thank the team at GMC Publishing for all their encouragement and support; in particular Jonathan, my publisher, and Tom and Robin (who may have inadvertently learnt how to make a chair). I am indebted to the crafts people of the past, and to all my teachers. A special thank you to Paul Hayden and Curtis Buchanan, for setting me out on this path. Thank you my dearest Abby for all your support, and thank you to the spirits of nature.

Jason Mosseri
www.hopespringschairs.com

PICTURE CREDITS

Jonathan Bassett: 169, 189.
Jason Mosseri: 4–5 (illustration), 17, 18, 19, 20, 23 (left), 24 (illustration), 25 (illustration), 53, 56, 57, 60 (illustration), 61, 62, 63, 64, 65, 66, 67, 68, 69, 70, 71, 73 (top left and right), 74, 76, 77, 78, 79, 81, 84, 85, 91, 92, 93, 94, 96, 99, 100 (illustration), 101, 103, 104, 105, 106, 107, 108, 111 (top), 112, 113, 114, 116, 119, 122, 123, 128, 129 (illustration), 131, 136, 138, 139 (illustration), 140, 142, 144, 150, 151 (illustration), 152, 153, 154 (illustration), 155, 156, 159, 160, 162, 165, 170, 172 (middle and right), 173 (illustration), 175, 176 (illustration), 177, 178, 179, 180, 181, 182, 184, 190, 193 (illustration), 195, 196 (illustration), 197, 198, 200, 202, 204, 206.
Andrew Perris: 2, 4, 5, 7, 9, 10, 12, 13, 15, 21, 22, 23 (right), 24–25 (photo), 27, 29, 31, 33, 35, 37, 39, 41, 43, 45, 47, 49, 51, 55, 58, 59, 60 (photo), 73 (bottom), 80, 83, 86, 88, 90, 97, 100 (photo), 109, 111 (bottom), 120, 121, 125, 126, 129 (photo), 132, 133, 135, 139 (photo), 145, 147, 148, 151 (photo), 154 (photo), 166, 167, 172 (left), 173 (photo), 176 (photo), 186, 187, 193 (photo), 196 (photo), 207, 224.
Shutterstock/smereka: 54

INDEX

First published 2025 by
Guild of Master Craftsman Publications Ltd,
Castle Place, 166 High Street, Lewes, East Sussex, BN7 1XU, UK
www.gmcbooks.com

ISBN 978 1 78494 701 9

The EEA authorised representative is Authorised Rep Compliance Ltd.
Ground Floor, 71 Baggot Street Lower, Dublin, DO2 P593, Ireland
www.arccompliance.com

A catalogue record for this book is available from the British Library.

Publisher Jonathan Bailey
Production Director Jim Bulley
Senior Project Editor Tom Kitch
Design Manager Robin Shields
Editor Theresa Bebbington

Colour origination by GMC Reprographics
Printed and bound in China

To order a book, contact:
GMC Publications Ltd
Castle Place, 166 High Street,
Lewes, East Sussex, BN7 1XU,
United Kingdom
Tel: +44 (0)1273 488005
www.gmcbooks.com

ARMCHAIR

FORMS &

PLANS

1200 MM

SPINDLE DECK
BACK EDGE
SIDE VIEW

90 MM

LEG
STRETCHER
SIDE
CREST

2" CENTRES, 14 MM MORTICES

120 CM

CARVING DEPTHS

FINAL SPINDLE LENGTH 14"

ELIJAH CRAIG
WILD TURKEY
RYE

For our cheeky Nonna Lidia – we love you and thank you.